THE STORY OF D. S. BURNET:

UNDESERVED OBSCURITY

The Story of D. S. Burnet:

UNDESERVED OBSCURITY

By

NOEL L. KEITH

Chairman of the Department of Religion
Texas Christian University

WIPF & STOCK · Eugene, Oregon

Wipf and Stock Publishers
199 W 8th Ave, Suite 3
Eugene, OR 97401

The Story of D. S. Burnett
Undeserved Obscurity
By Keith, Noel L
ISBN 13: 978-1-62032-681-7
Publication date 12/15/2012
Previously published by The Bethany Press, 1954

To All
who love the Bible
and who seek cooperative means
for the purpose of propagating
the Christian faith

Preface

Several years ago I began a study of the historical antecedents to the modern cooperative missionary, educational and benevolent organizations of the brotherhood of Disciples of Christ. Many of my early problems centered around the activities of the first general convention (1849) of that body. It was in that manner that I discovered the significance of D. S. Burnet.

Upon learning that the Christian statesmanship of Burnet had brought three cooperative societies into existence before Alexander Campbell assumed a place of active leadership in them, I became intensely interested in the persons who actually constituted the rudimentary organizations for financing programs of education, benevolence, and missions. This interest on my part was accentuated at Iliff School of Theology where I pursued the subject further as a research project for the doctorate.

The constant reappearance of the name D. S. Burnet in the minutes of the anniversary meetings of Disciples of Christ a hundred years ago suggested to me that this man may have been of more importance than most history books gave him credit. Therefore, in the survey of how the Disciples financed their first cooperative work my interest began to center around the question, "Who was D. S. Burnet?" Very early in the research I realized that he was the prime mover of cooperation and financial stewardship, of Bible distribution and book publication, and of missionary endeavor. If Burnet deserved to be given a place of prominence among the founding fathers of Disciples of Christ, I wondered why his name dropped into comparative obscurity.

The contents of this volume are designed to furnish the reader with a partial answer to this problem. The evaluation of Burnet's connection with the work of organizing societies for aiding the causes of the church gives something of a solution to many problems which have confronted historians of the Nineteenth-Century Reformation. Any study of the convention system used by Disciples of Christ which fails properly to take into account the work of D. S. Burnet, results in inadequate understanding.

I do not profess to have written a definitive biography of this man. Neither do I pretend in this study to be adequate in my interpretation. I have aimed herein to present D. S. Burnet as the "all but forgotten" disciple who became primarily responsible for the "engine of cooperation and cohesion" which he believed would bring simple faith in Christ to all the world.

Some of the questions which guided this study were such as the following: What is the significance of the life and work of Burnet in American church history? Who was he? Where did he live and work? What were his ideas and how did he get them? What was his relationship to Alexander Campbell, Walter Scott, Isaac Errett, and other better-known Disciples of Christ? What were some of his outstanding achievements? How was he esteemed by his contemporaries? How should he be evaluated today?

Because some of the facts set forth in this work may seem utterly fantastic to some readers, I have attempted to give a rather full documentation of the sources. Four areas of literature furnished data.

1. Records of the Annual Proceedings of such institutions as the American Christian Missionary Society, American Christian Bible Society, American Christian Publication Society, American Christian Tract Society, Ohio Christian Missionary Society, etc., have been available. Although the original printings of minutes of these meetings are rarely available, I have had full access to them, either through typescript or printed copies of the original or by microfilm copies.

2. The extant works of D. S. Burnet himself, such as his books, pamphlets and journals, have proved very helpful. Some of his works of this kind, such as the *Christian Preacher* and his one-volume edition of *The Christian Baptist* were directly available through the Disciples Room of the Mary Couts Burnett Library of Texas Christian University. His works are widely scattered and it was necessary for me to get photostat and microfilm copies. A search in the Manuscripts Division of the

Library of Congress shows that there is no collection of the papers of Burnet, and none are mentioned in the Guides on Manuscript Collections as being in collections of the papers of other men.

3. Contemporary journals which carried writings and news about him furnished considerable data. Exchange of articles and news in such periodicals as the *Millennial Harbinger, American Christian Review, Christian Standard,* and others, gave considerable aid to the work.

4. Books and histories which directly and indirectly reflected the situation were also used.

Some of the terms I have used may not be clear to the average reader. For example, *Disciples of Christ* is sometimes denoted by the names Christian Church and Church of Christ; *Board of Managers* usually refers to a group of directors or officers elected to act as a body in behalf of a church institution; *centralism* was a term used a century ago to denote the cohesive process of a functioning church organization. The word *cooperation* is taken to mean the voluntary association of persons and churches in carrying on the business of the church; *human creeds* was often taken to mean the historic creeds of Christendom (such as the Westminster Confession, the Philadelphia Confession, the Augsburg Confession, the Tridentine Confession, and others) by Disciples of Christ who held that they should not be made tests of Christian fellowship or required for church membership.

The term *Society System* was used early by Disciples of Christ to describe the organizations which became united by common interests and purposes for fostering programs of education, missions, benevolence and publishing. It was in the early development of the society system that the modern organizations among Disciples of Christ had their roots. The conventions and societies of the brotherhood today had their beginnings in the early advent of these "societies."

Acknowledgments

Since it is acceptable historical and scientific methodology to verify one's findings by some kind of objective test, I set to work to inquire of reputable bibliographers and historians, librarians and folklore lovers, teachers and friends, concerning the life and work of Burnet. Among the first to respond to my inquires were Claude E. Spencer, curator of the Disciples of Christ Historical Society; C. C. Ware, collector of Discipliana in North Carolina; and Henry K. Shaw, historian and pastor in Ohio. Each expressed some interest to see further investigation into the place of Burnet in the history of Disciples of Christ.

In the research which ensued I regard myself as most fortunate to have had the objective viewpoint of Christian scholars and teachers at Iliff School of Theology, Denver. Martin Rist was my major professor for this project, and I believe Disciples of Christ may owe him a debt of gratitude for the direction of the processes of methodology for this dissertation, especially the microfilming of widely scattered sources. If this thesis adds some insights into American church history, gathers together some fragments worthy of preservation, and sets forth a historical figure among Disciples of Christ who most certainly deserved not to be lost to memory, I have found the results worth the effort.

I also am deeply indebted to William H. Bernhardt, acting president of The Iliff School of Theology, Denver, Colorado; W. B. Blakemore, head of Disciples Divinity House, University of Chicago, Chicago, Illinois; Nelson Burr, of the Library of Congress, Washington, D. C.; Lin D. Cartwright, editor of *The Christian-Evangelist,* St. Louis, Mo.; Jack Chitwood, humanities librarian of Drake University, Des Moines, Iowa; Wilbur H. Cramblet, president of the Christian Board of Publication, St. Louis, Mo.; A. T. DeGroot, dean of the graduate school of Texas

Christian University, Fort Worth, Texas; M. W. Fogle, minister of Central Christian Church, Dayton, Ohio; W. E. Garrison, professor of church history at University of Houston, Houston, Texas; Colby D. Hall, dean emeritus of Brite College of the Bible, Texas Christian University, Fort Worth, Texas; Janet Hamer, reference assistant of The Ohio State Archaeological and Historical Society, Ohio State Museum, Columbus, Ohio; Wilfred P. Harmon, general representative of the Disciples of Christ Historical Society, Nashville, Tenn.; Mrs. Alice P. Hook, librarian of the Historical and Philosophical Society of Ohio, Cincinnati, Ohio; Willis R. Jones, director of church relations at Hiram College, Hiram, Ohio; H. E. McCartney, historian of Central Christian Church, Dayton, Ohio; Mrs. Bertie Mothershead, librarian of Mary Couts Burnett Library of Texas Christian University, Fort Worth, Texas; Roscoe M. Pierson, librarian of Bosworth Memorial Library, The College of the Bible, Lexington, Ky.; O. L. Shelton, dean of Butler School of Religion, Indianapolis, Ind.; Howard Elmo Short, professor of church history, The College of the Bible, Lexington, Ky.; Mrs. Stanley B. Smith, Ohio historian, Garrettsville, Ohio; H. Gordon Van Sickle, professor of church history, The Iliff School of Theology, Denver, Colo.; and Mrs. Alene Lowe White, librarian of The Western Reserve Historical Society, Cleveland, Ohio.

Furthermore, this work could never have been done without the assistance of Mrs. L. C. Brite, of Marfa, Texas, and President M. E. Sadler, of Texas Christian University. Nor could it have been done without the actual aid and sympathetic understanding of my wife and son, Beulah Irene and Marvin.

Special acknowledgment is made to First Christian Church, Baltimore, Maryland, for permission to quote from *Across a Century*, by Andrew W. Gottschall, copyright, 1932; and to Ohio Christian Missionary Society for excerpts from *Buckeye Disciples*, by Henry K. Shaw, copyright.

NOEL L. KEITH

Texas Christian University

Contents

PREFACE 7

I. THE BOY PREACHER 17
   1808-1823: Born a Shareholder in Pioneering . . 17
   1825-1827: Consignment of a Boy Preacher to the Baptists 26
   1828-1830: Alienations Among the Baptists 35
   1830: Fortunate Merger of Lives 40

II. MATURITY OF A LEADER 43
   1831-1836: A Tour to Evict Error 43
   1836-1844: College and Journal as the Christian Way to Solvency 54
   1844-1845: Ordeal by Fever 66
   1845-1849: The Bible and Tract Societies as Liens on the Future 71

III. DIPLOMACY ON THE FRONTIER 82
   1849: Opening the Purse of a Brotherhood: First General Convention of Disciples of Christ . . . 82
   1850: Negotiations with A. Campbell 104

IV. DESERVED LEADERSHIP 117
   1851-1854: American Bible Union Project 117
   1851-1856: The Unmarketable Brotherhood Publishing House 121
   1852: Making Capital Out of the Opposition's Designed Contempt 139
   1852: Missions Organized in Ohio 144
   1853-1854: Ohio in Africa 149

V. APPARENT FAILURE 152
   1857-1860: Getting Away for Awhile 152
   1861-1864: Adding Heartbreak to Failure 159

VI. RECOGNIZED SUCCESS AT LAST	165
1863-1864: Baltimore and Resignation	165
1865-1866: President of a Going Concern	171
1867: In the Midst of Success	176
1954: Undeserved Obscurity	191
APPENDIXES	201
I. Chronology	201
II. Notes on Genealogy of D. S. Burnet	208
III. Address to the Churches	220
IV. Memorial Discourse on the Occasion of the Death of Alexander Campbell	226
V. A Synopsis of Divine Revelation	241
VI. Constitution, American Christian Bible Society	242
VII. Notes from Sermons and Addresses of D. S. Burnet	244
VIII. Fourth of July Address by Isaac G. Burnet, Cincinnati, 1808	255
INDEX	261

SOME QUOTATIONS

"He was a giant among the pioneer Disciples, but has all but been forgotten."
—Claude E. Spencer

"Burnet was an outstanding Disciple. In many ways he ranked with Isaac Errett, Walter Scott, and Alexander Campbell."
—Henry K. Shaw

"Somebody ought to have written a definitive biography of him a long time ago. He has been deserving it all these years."
—C. C. Ware

"During the first half of the nineteenth century, Burnet was really looked upon as the normal recipient of the mantle of Alexander Campbell."
—Frederick D. Kershner

CHAPTER I

The Boy Preacher

1808-1823: Born a Shareholder in Pioneering

DAVID STAATS BURNET was born July 6, 1808, in Dayton, Ohio,¹ two days after his father's Fourth of July speech in Cincinnati and five years after that vast province of Louisiana ceded by France for $15,000,000 became the property of the United States. A new epoch of migration and settlement began almost simultaneously with the beginning of the life of David Burnet. Of Scotch forebears, his was the enviable place of the eldest child. His father, Isaac G., and his mother, Kittie Winn,² were prominent Dayton citizens. His mother was the daughter of an eminent Cincinnati physician.³

It was a proud heritage that caused him later in life to claim "lineal descent from Gilbert Burnet, Bishop of Salisbury, so conspicuous during the great English Revolution, under William, Prince of Orange."⁴ Neither is it any wonder that the lad became sensitive to the religious needs abroad in the land. The War of 1812 brought its aftermath to Ohio in the form of crowding population, expansion of trade, industry, agriculture, wildcat banking and feverish speculation.⁵ Lyman

¹William Thomas Moore, *The Living Pulpit of the Christian Church* (Cincinnati: R. W. Carroll Co., 1868), p. 33. Cf. H. Leo Boles, *Biographical Sketches of Gospel Preachers* (Nashville: Gospel Advocate Co., 1932), p. 140.
²Frederick D. Power, *Sketches of Our Pioneer* (Chicago, New York and Toronto: Fleming H. Revell Co., 1898), p. 125.
³*Ohio State Archaeological and Historical Quarterly*, XLVIII, No. 3 (1939), 237.
⁴Moore, *Living Pulpit*, p. 34. See also Appendix II.
⁵"Ohio," *Encyclopedia Americana*, XVI (1951).

Beecher stood in the center of things with his opposition to dueling, drunkenness, and the feverish discussions of the slavery question.[6]

Although his family had heard very little, if anything, of Thomas and Alexander Campbell, David was but four years old when the Campbells were immersed. They had been Presbyterians, like the Burnets, but were determined to accept a scriptural basis for their religious conduct. Hence Thomas Campbell, his son Alexander, and his daughter were baptized by a Baptist preacher, Luce—not into the Baptist church but upon a simple confession of faith. Soon thereafter the Brush Run church joined the Baptists' Red Stone Association which opened the way for the Campbells to have a free itineration as preachers and evangelists among the Baptists of Pennsylvania, Virginia, and Ohio.[7] This action of the Campbells was to serve as an earlier parallel of the actions of the young child born into the home of the Burnets. The Baptists established their General Missionary Convention in 1814, beginning something of a stimulus to later similar movements among Disciples of Christ with whom David Staats Burnet was to become associated.

The hustle and bustle of new forms of transportation put many families of the Western Reserve on the move. Steam navigation began on the Ohio River in 1816, the same year that David's parents moved from Dayton to Cincinnati. His father formed a law partnership with Nicholas Longworth, that odd man of wealth, in the Queen City, and the family moved to Cincinnati when David was eight.[8]

Cincinnati was located in the area of two plateaus or terraces of nature. The lower flat was about sixty feet

---

[6]Williston Walker, *A History of the Christian Church* (New York: Charles Scribner's Sons, 1934), pp. 583, 584.

[7]W. E. Garrison, *Religion Follows the Frontier*, New York: Harper and Bros., 1931, p. 106.

[8]Moore, *Living Pulpit*, p. 34. Cf. Power, *Sketches of Our Pioneers*, p. 125. Cf. Boles, *Biographical Sketches*, pp. 140, 141.

above water and the higher about twice that. Some hills around the young Queen of the West enclosed the area on three sides. When David's family arrived in Cincinnati in 1816, the total area of the city was approximately three square miles. But it was growing. It was chartered as a city in 1819; later, David's father served as mayor for twelve years. Cincinnati was along the advance line of pioneers streaming from Kentucky in a sweeping movement down through Tennessee and western Alabama to Louisiana.

The educational opportunities in Cincinnati were above the average, inasmuch as many of the city fathers were determined to make the place a center of culture, religion, and learning. David Burnet grew up in the traditional Presbyterian beliefs, although among Presbyterians at that time were discussions of the "New Light" and the "Old Light" platforms. This meant that as a child he had perhaps received the rite of baptism by the customary form of sprinkling,[9] and that his parents accepted for him the creedal requirements of that body. But his family had long been reformers and inclined to exercise a free spirit in religious matters.

One of David Staats Burnet's distinguished kinsmen was an uncle, Judge Jacob Burnet, also of Cincinnati.[10] He was born February 22, 1770, in Newark, N. J. In some autobiographical notes prefacing his *History of the Northwestern Territory*, Judge Jacob tells of his own education at Nassau Hall, Princeton, under the presidency of Dr. Witherspoon. He was graduated in September, 1791. "Before he had finished his collegiate course, he determined to settle himself in the Miami country, where his father had made a considerable investment."[11]

Jacob completed his professional studies and was admitted to the bar by the supreme court of the state

---

[9]Moore, *Living Pulpit*, p. 34. Cf. Boles, *Biographical Sketches*, p. 141.
[10]Cf., *Appleton's Cyclopaedia of American Biography*, I, 458.
[11]*Ibid.*

of New Jersey in the spring of 1796. After becoming a full-fledged lawyer, he set out in the same year for Cincinnati, determined to cast his lot with the rise or fall of that growing, sprawling territorial settlement. Three years later, in 1799, his appointment to the legislative council of the territory plunged him into active politics. He was instrumental in the formation of the state government, and in 1812 went to the state legislature. Later he became judge of the supreme court of Ohio (1821-1828), and United States senator (1828-1831).

His statesmanship was recognized by the neighboring state of Kentucky, for which he was chosen by their legislature to be commissioner in the settlement of border disputes with Virginia. His interest in education is reflected in the fact that he was one of the founders of the Lancastrian Academy in Cincinnati as well as one of the leaders in establishing Cincinnati College. Of the latter he became the first president. Also, he took an active hand in reorganizing the Medical College of Ohio. But his greatest leadership was not in the educational field, but in the political. "He was a delegate to the Harrisburg Convention in 1839, and was mainly instrumental in securing the nomination of Harrison to the presidency."[12] People of the Western Reserve were grateful to Judge Burnet for extricating the settlers of that region from the more than twenty million dollars' debt to the federal government for purchases of western lands, which distress was further augmented by the small volume of money in circulation in that area. His publication in 1847 of *Notes on the Early Settlement of the Northwestern Territory* was of extreme importance to the writers of histories of the Western Reserve. He was married January 1, 1800, to Rebecca Wallace. They became parents of seven children: Mary (1802-1834), George Whitfield (1804-1859), William (1806-1892),

---
[12] *Appleton's Cyclopaedia of American Biography*, I, 458.

Robert Wallace (1808-1864), Elizabeth (1817-1889), and twins, Caroline Thew (1820-1856) and Harriet (1820-?), who died young.[13]

Judge and Mrs. Burnet became "first citizens" of Ohio. Those who knew him observed that he later in life walked with a cane, his hair was done up in a queue, and neighbors were impressed with the ruffled shirt he wore.[14] His Scotch dignity was matched by the house in which he lived—a large, square, old-style mansion with a broad hall through the center, at Seventh and Elm Streets in Cincinnati.[15]

So it was that in 1818 David's uncle, Judge Jacob Burnet, aided the movement in Cincinnati to launch the famed "Second Church" of the Presbyterian denomination there. It was a split off the First Presbyterian Church, the body that had both the prestige of priority[16] and the status of one of Cincinnati's most cultured and elite groups.

Another uncle of David Staats Burnet moved on to Texas. David Gouverneur Burnet[17] (April 4, 1788—December 5, 1870) was born also in Newark, N. J., another distinguished scion of Dr. William Burnet, Sr. He married Hannah Este (February 17, 1800—October 30, 1858) and became the first president of the Republic of Texas. He participated in Francisco de Miranda's expedition to Venezuela in 1806.

In 1817 he located a merchandise store in Natchetoches, La., near what was then one of the frontiers of Texas.

---

[13]Isabella Neff Burnet, *Dr. William Burnet and his Sons, Jacob Isaac and David. A Chart of Their Forefathers and Descendants in America 1640-1938.* (Univ. of Va., Mimeograph, 1938), pp. 3, 4.

[14]*Ibid.*, p. 65.

[15]*Ibid.*

[16]Charles Frederic Goss, *Cincinnati, The Queen City* (Chicago and Cincinnati: S. J. Clark, 1912), p. 154.

[17]Wheeler Preston, *American Biographies* (New York: Harper and Bros., 1940), p. 132. Cf. John Henry Brown, *History of Texas from 1685 to 1892* (St. Louis: L. E. Daniell, c. 1892-93). Also, Francis White Johnson and Eugene C. Barker, *A History of Texas and Texans* (Chicago and New York: The American Historical Society, 1914), I.

Later he studied law in Cincinnati, after which he moved on into Texas, settling on the San Jacinto River in 1831. In his rise to leadership as a statesman he became judge of the municipality of San Felipe de Austin, 1834.

The primary item of his fame lies in the fact that he was a member of the Washington Convention which declared Texas' independence in 1836, and became the provisional president of the Republic of Texas. It was D. G. Burnet who handed over the Texas government to Sam Houston, the constitutionally elected president, after the former's retreat to Galveston before the invasion of Santa Anna. David was made vice-president of the Republic in 1838. During Mirabeau B. Lamar's presidency he acted as secretary of state. In 1841 he was a candidate for the presidency, but was defeated; he became again secretary of state, 1846-47.

After the Civil War, Texas elected him to the United States Senate (1866), but Congress refused to seat him. His was a stormy career in a period of struggle and achievement in the Southwest. He was buried in Galveston, Texas, in 1870, the last of his immediate family, inasmuch as his son William Este had been killed at the battle of Mobile, March 31, 1865.[18] His wife was buried at Oakland, Harris County, Texas, but was reinterred in 1936 in Galveston beside her husband.[19]

David's father, Isaac Gouverneur Burnet (1784-1856), was one of the very distinguished sons of Dr. William Burnet, the elder. Married in 1806 to Kittie Winn Gordon, daughter of George Gordon and Sallie Winn Moss Gordon, Isaac and Kittie became parents of eleven children, the eldest of whom was the subject of this biography, David Staats. Other children were Mary Thew, Julia Ann, Nancy, Jacob, Gertrude, Isaac, Staats Gouverneur, Cornelia, Hanna Kinney, and Kittie.[20]

---

[18]Isabella Neff Burnet, *Dr. William Burnet*, p. 3.
[19]*Ibid.*, p. 38.
[20]*Ibid.*, p. 13.

The Fourth of July, 1808, was significant for Isaac G. Burnet, destined to be the mayor of Cincinnati six successive terms after moving to that city in 1816 from Dayton, Ohio.[21] Isaac had planned an anniversary speech of considerable significance to him and his family. Only twenty-four years old, he was regarded by the town of Cincinnati as one of the rising young political leaders. He was under tremendous pressure because of his desire to make a good impression, but more than that, his eighteen-year-old wife was pregnant, expecting any day the arrival of a child. In fact, two days after Isaac delivered the patriotic address in Cincinnati their first child was born in Dayton. By examination of the thoughts expressed in the speech (Appendix VIII) it may be inferred that the child-to-be-born would be tutored on ideas of freedom and liberty.

The Fourth of July address was indicative of Isaac's deep conviction that American constitutional government offered the world a new era in political statesmanship. He showed keen awareness that men are "susceptible of different impressions" and this diversity of viewpoint, he held, could never be restrained by despotic powers.[22] Only by liberal education could the world achieve any means whereby wide diversities could exist within a free land. He would supplant emotional bigotry with intelligence and reason.[23] It is important to an understanding of future events in the life of his son that consideration should be given the fact that Isaac G. Burnet was insisting upon a system of government "where man will be free under restraint." Isaac held that "all necessary restraints [of government] are infringements upon the rights of the People and by being tolerated will imperceptibly induce oppressions."[24]

---
[21]Power, *Sketches of Our Pioneers*, p. 125.
[22]Isabella Neff Burnet, *Dr. William Burnet*, p. 68.
[23]*Ibid.*
[24]*Ibid.*, pp. 71, 72. (Brackets mine.)

A brief table of the genealogy of David Staats Burnet's paternal lineage indicates some remarkable religious leaders, colonial pioneers, governors, physicians, lawyers, judges, and army officers (See Appendix II).

At thirteen David entered his father's office as clerk.[25] This kind of apprenticeship was designed to help him follow in the footsteps of his father and his two uncles. The young mind of the lad was well suited to the legal profession, because of the eagerness with which he sought to become aware of the truth. He watched the procedures of legal trials, how the inquisitive lawyers applied the principles which were designed to get at the truth. He observed the processes of political organization as they took shape in the newly incorporated city. He was keenly aware of the legislative, administrative, and judicial operations of civil government.

It was the impression created in his youthful mind which led him later to apply some of the same principles to his religious studies; caused him to investigate the constitutions of religion; caused him to be judiciously determined to search out the truths of the Christian faith. It can scarcely be minimized that the place of clerk in his father's employment, which afforded opportunities to observe legal proceedings and court actions, was one of the most potent factors in the development of his character. Moore said that while young David was in this employment "under the watchful care of his father," he "acquired those habits of industry and faithfulness which characterized him through life, and which laid the foundation of his future career."[26]

While young David applied himself in the study of law an epoch-making event occurred in the national government—the setting forth of the Monroe Doctrine in 1823. During December of that year President Monroe's mes-

---
[25]Moore, *Living Pulpit*, p. 34. Cf. Boles, *Biographical Sketches*, p. 141.
[26]*Ibid.*, p. 34.

sage to Congress declared that there should be no further colonization in the Western Hemisphere and there would be no tolerance of those who would seek to compel South American republics to return to former Spanish allegiance. With this declaration to the world there was a greater surge of internal expansion and development. This meant that a new political and territorial concentration would be attempted farther west. It meant that pioneers would move into the central territories without fear of opposition by foreign powers. It meant that law and order would be brought to the unsettled West.

If these things seemed of greatest importance to those in the legal profession, there was something of the same concern among religious leaders of the times. It was in this period that the prolific pen of Alexander Campbell began to drive the sharp invectives into the weaknesses of the inherited religions. It is important to the understanding of Burnet's future activities to understand that Campbell's magazine, *The Christian Baptist* (1823-1830), struck out repeatedly against missionary societies, a paid clergy, associations, and church organizations. Although Burnet probably was unfamiliar with the viewpoints and activities of Alexander Campbell as early as 1823, he was later to become a leader of leaders in a movement among Disciples of Christ. He grew up to cross intellectual swords with the outstanding leader of the movement, Campbell. Although Burnet lost the battle, a century's elapse indicates that he was the ultimate victor.

Since the illustrious forefathers of D. S. Burnet were for the most part loyal Church of England leaders or strong guiding lights of the Presbyterian persuasion, it is strange that one like David, who went beyond any of them in the reformation of the church, should have been dropped with disapproval as one who "went off with the Campbellites." Only now, after a century past the time of his most signal achievement, is it possible to see the Cincinnati pastor in a better light. Fortunately his leadership was of such lasting importance that we have many evidences of the quality of his mind and character, as well as records of his overt achievements for the cause of good religion in America. With all his glittering array of forebears, their shining did not obscure the light he set afoot in the national scene of the history of Disciples of Christ.

By evaluating the future of David Staats Burnet from his childhood and youth, therefore, some vital antecedents to his character are apparent. He came of a notable reformation lineage; he grew up in a highly changing cultural situation; he had some of the basic training necessary for a legal career; he developed a highly inquisitive mind; and his youth was spent during the formative ideologies which brought into being the Christian Church movement of the nineteenth century.

1825-1827: Consignment of a Boy Preacher to the Baptists

At sixteen David became intensely interested in the program of religious education. Sunday schools were being opened and promoted among the Presbyterians. The church in Cincinnati where David was a member launched a growing program of this kind. The youth became associated with an official of the local church in conducting one of the outstanding Sunday schools in the city.[27] This was indicative of the important urge within him to become a religious leader and educator.

It was during this period that the Campbells, also Presbyterians, had found themselves assimilated with the Baptists. But young David was not acquainted with the

---

[27]Moore, *Living Pulpit*, p. 34. Cf. Boles, *Biographical Sketches*, p. 141.

teachings of Alexander Campbell.[28] He is said to have been at the time unaware of the plea of that movement for a return to primitive Christianity.[29] His ideas in connection with his own work in the Presbyterian Sunday school must have led him to much the same conclusions reached by the Campbell movement quite independently of direct influence.[30] David's eagerness to express his new-found beliefs could be achieved only by leaving the stricter disciplines of the Presbyterian church. But there was not only a greater freedom of self-expression among the Baptists, there were for David some evidences of truth which needed clarification.

Baptists had long held the view that Christian baptism formally meant an immersion in water in the name of the Father, Son, and Holy Spirit, for the Greek word *baptizo* in the Scriptures meant *to immerse* or its equivalent. They held that the primitive church practiced immersion. They insisted that the Scriptures become meaningful in the discussion of baptism only by the connotation of immersion as the apostolic practice. Young Burnet examined these arguments as a lawyer examines evidence in a case. More and more the mode of baptism expressed by the Baptists became acceptable to him. There were arguments also on the "subjects" of baptism. Who was eligible for baptism? Infants, said the Baptists, logically should not be baptized because the child must first reach an age where he could be held accountable for the qualification to believe. Furthermore, the practice of making members of infants was considered by many as detrimental to the spiritual and intellectual development of the church in that it often failed to create an individual conscience about one's Christian citizenship in the church.

---
[28]*Ibid.*, pp. 34, 35.
[29]*Ibid.*
[30]*Ibid.*

Consequently, the view was widespread that many persons were in the church who were "unconverted." This viewpoint became highly favorable to young Burnet. David was inclined to accept the view that anyone may baptize, since the efficacy for the meaningful action was neither inherently within the administrator nor in the water. The purpose of baptism was considered primarily for the remission of past sins by submergence in and emergence from the spirit of Christ, symbolized in a meaningful action. These views deviated extremely from Presbyterian conceptions of ordinations, creeds, and sacraments of that day.

David Staats Burnet had rejected the authority of creeds.[31] He refused to accept any test of his membership except a biblical one.[32] He examined the New Testament teachings on the matter. Consequently, he applied to the Baptists for his baptism on the basis of Romans 10:6-10.[33] Belief in Christ and the Good Confession were all that was necessary, he thought, to be saved. If a person believed and confessed the Christian faith he had met the requirements and was in a position then to ask for any of the services the church might perform for him including baptism, communion, worship, an opportunity to serve, etc. Baptism was not the ritual of induction into the church as the Baptists had claimed. The scriptures read:

6. But the righteousness which is of faith speaketh on this wise, Say not in thine heart, Who shall ascend into heaven? (that is, to bring Christ down *from above:*)

7. Or, Who shall descend into the deep? (that is, to bring up Christ again from the dead.)

---

[31]Power, *Sketches of Our Pioneers,* p. 126.
[32]*Ibid.*
[33]Moore, *Living Pulpit,* pp. 34, 35.

8. But what saith it? The word is nigh thee, *even* in thy mouth, and in thy heart: that is, the word of faith, which we preach;

9. That if thou shalt confess with thy mouth the Lord Jesus, and shalt believe in thine heart that God hath raised him from the dead, thou shalt be saved.

10. For with the heart man believeth unto righteousness; and with the mouth confession is made unto salvation.[34]

This was to become the central biblical theme of his total reform efforts. He saw in the simple confession of faith the only test of Christian fellowship. Those who made the Good Confession should ask for the privilege of baptism, or immersion as he came to believe, on this simple but sublime teaching. The legalism of creeds among his own Presbyterian contemporaries, accented by the emphasis which his family (particularly his father and uncles, Jacob and David) gave to the importance of law, had much to do with his acceptance of a nonlegalistic criterion for his citizenship in the Christian kingdom. Neither the lengthy creeds nor the authoritative ordinations were reconcilable with this simple statement concerning the Good Confession. Both by prayer and by strong personal courage he changed his religious connections. His views and his eager ambitions were radically opposed to his previous affiliations.

Alexander Campbell had visited Kentucky in the fall of 1824.[35] At Louisville in November he called at the residence of P. S. Fall, and after supper attended a Presbyterian church service. Mr. Campbell was asked to preach. Consequently Fall became a convert to the ideas of the Reformation. Soon after Fall's meeting with Campbell the former visited the Enon Baptist Church in Cincinnati where he delivered a series of sermons

---

[34]Rom. 10:6-10. King James Version.
[35]Robert Richardson, *Memoirs of Alexander Campbell* (Cincinnati: Standard Publishing Co., 1897), II, 120-122.

upon the themes which were popular at the time. Robert Richardson in his *Memoirs of Alexander Campbell* describes Mr. Fall's visit in the Burnet home, and gave an impression of D. S. Burnet:

> During this visit, Mr. Fall was invited to dine with Jacob[36] Burnet, Esq., the mayor of the city, and witnessed the baptism of his son David S. Burnet, who soon after, entering the ministry at the age of sixteen, became known as the "boy-preacher." We was quite low in stature, but erect in carriage. His head was large and finely formed; his eyes prominent, full and sparkling, his features regular with a mouth somewhat large, but firmly set, while in his bearing he was remarkably self-possessed, dignified and courteous. Giving himself wholly to the cause of the Reformation, after a few years he became one of its most distinguished and successful advocates, delighting large audiences by his elegant and copious diction, and his able presentations of the principles of the gospel, which he widely disseminated, not only in Cincinnati, but through many of the States, from Maryland and Virginia to Kansas.[37]

In this indirect process, through the preaching of Fall, young Burnet became acquainted with the Reformation tenets which stemmed from the teachings of Campbell. But the probable first meeting of Burnet and Campbell was in 1826. Thirty-two years later Burnet said:

> Well do I remember his remark to me as we were being ferried across the Ohio, at Cincinnati, in a skiff, in 1826—"I have but one object in this world, and that is to know and enjoy the meaning of that book," pointing to a Testament. The writer or writers of Ps. cxix, could not have possessed a more superlative love for the Word of God.[38]

The fact that Burnet applied to a Baptist preacher (John Boyd) for immersion on the basis of Rom. 10:6-10,

---

[36]Richardson, *Memoirs of Alexander Campbell*, p. 122, Note: Richardson is in error about the name; Jacob was David's uncle; Isaac was David's father, the mayor.

[37]*Ibid.*, II, 120-122.

[38]"In Memoriam, President Alexander Campbell," *Millennial Harbinger*, 1866, p. 304.

was somewhat irregular also with the Baptists because to them baptism was the rite of initiation into the church. But Boyd immersed the sixteen-year-old youth, Dec. 26, 1824, and he was received into the Enon Baptist Church.[39] It has been said that the Baptists received him with some reluctance because of the specific grounds upon which he sought membership with them.[40] If the Baptists in order to receive him were giving up some of their demands for immersion to stand as the rite of induction, he was giving up something also to become a part of their denomination. The aristocratic family reaction was perhaps at first only a mild censure, but it was soon to become a furious condemnation. The move he had taken further attracted him because he could start preaching at once. Shortly after he was baptized he began to be known as the "Boy Preacher" among the Baptists.[41] From the first he was regarded as an orator of great power.

His emerging popularity was soon recognized by his family. Uncle Jacob, Uncle William, Jr., Uncle David, and his father, Isaac, all became concerned. They conceived the idea of gaining an appointment to West Point for the youth. Judge Jacob Burnet was in a position to obtain the appointment and offered this honor to his nephew in order to keep him from continuing as a Baptist preacher. The scholarship in West Point Military Academy was refused by young David. Although the records do not indicate exactly the reasons for his decision, his contemporaries inferred that the young man desired to be a preacher rather than a military officer.

Available records also are not very clear on how the family reacted to David's refusal of the West Point scholarship. There has been much speculation, however, and a little more speculation is not amiss. One of the

[39]Moore, *Living Pulpit*, p. 34. Cf. Boles, *Biographical Sketches*, p. 141.
[40]*Ibid.*, p. 35. Cf. Boles, *op. cit.*
[41]Power, *Sketches of Our Pioneers*, p. 126. Moore, *op. cit.* Boles, *op. cit.*

best commentaries on this period of David's life is that of W. T. Moore, when he says:

> His life at this time becomes an interesting study, and the moral sublimity of his character challenges our unaffected admiration. Surrounded by a large circle of influential relatives and friends, who, if religious at all, had little or no sympathy with his views of Christianity; with wealth and worldly honors offered him without stint, he turned his back upon them all, and, like the great Lawgiver of Israel, chose rather to suffer affliction with the people of God, than to enjoy the pleasures of sin for a season; esteeming the reproach of Christ greater riches than all the treasures and honors of the world. It is only now and then that a young man, under such circumstances, deliberately selects the profession of an humble preacher of the Gospel. And when one does have the moral courage, by the help of God, to do it, his name should be held in everlasting remembrance among those who "contend for the faith once delivered to the saints."[42]

Moore's view is too laudatory. It was not a completely selfless act that plunged young David Burnet into the ranks of the Baptist preachers. This was his great opportunity to be free of the strong Calvinistic restraints which had been imposed upon him. David wanted to preach. He found ready access to eager audiences among the Baptists, while the Presbyterians had conferred upon him the place of an understudy, a novice. On top of it all, he had an intelligent basis for his action which would be acceptable to the principles of the sternest court in the land. The evidences in behalf of his action were adequate to his own mind, and he had discovered the basic Scripture upon which he believed all the Christian world could unite. Although he had some divergence with the Baptists, he found coalescence with them. He wanted, above everything else, to preach.

Fortunately he realized that he was not as well prepared to be a preacher as would be helpful. Consequent

---
[42]Moore, *Living Pulpit*, p. 35.

to this realization, he set himself to study earnestly and devotedly the various aspects of his chosen work. The four years following his baptism were important years of discovery. He was described as an earnest, faithful, and eloquent preacher.⁴³ He applied himself to religious studies with more zeal than he had had in working as an apprentice in the law office. He discovered in those years the importance of a pastorate, where the settled minister grew with his congregation. Success came quickly in his ministry.

In 1827, at the age of twenty, Burnet became pastor of a Baptist church in Dayton, Ohio, his native town.⁴⁴ Later that church became Central Church of Christ (still later it was called Central Christian Church). For awhile he preached at the courthouse and continued until quarters were obtained in a room on St. Clair Street.⁴⁵ During his first year as pastor the membership increased to forty, then to eighty-four the next year. Under his leadership the congregation built a $2,000 house of worship on the west side of Main Street between Water (now known as Monument Avenue) and First Streets.⁴⁶

On March 21, 1829, the church passed a resolution (with only eight dissenting votes) to reject all written Articles of Faith. They then withdrew from the Miami Baptist Association. The eight members who had dissented "attempted to hold the Main street property; however, in 1832 a decision by the State Supreme Court gave the property to the followers of Mr. Burnet" on the fact that the church was congregational in government, and that the majority of the members favored the

---

⁴³*Ibid.*, pp. 35, 36.

⁴⁴*Ibid.* Cf. Power, *Sketches of Our Pioneers*, p. 126.

⁴⁵*History of the Four Christian-Disciple Churches, Dayton, Ohio, 1829-1947* (Dayton; Dayton Disciples Union, 1947), p. 7. Cf. Power, *op. cit.*, p. 126. And, Boles, *Biographical Sketches*, pp. 141, 142.

⁴⁶*Ibid.*

new relationship with Disciples of Christ.[47] Burnet remained with the Dayton church until 1832, and was known as "a man of unusual powers of mind, cultured, refined, and a foremost factor in the early days of the movement to which he dedicated his life."[48]

The experience in Dayton further convinced the young preacher that sufficient pastoral care would aid in keeping a growing, united local church from all kinds of apostasy. Although this pastorate was of short duration it had its lessons on the care and oversight which ministers should exercise when once a congregation was established.

However, young David was restless, ambitious, and homesick in spirit. He returned to Cincinnati. Sometime in the autumn or winter of 1827 he had started the work of organizing a new Baptist church on Sycamore Street. Elder William Montague, of Kentucky, was his companion in this enterprise. It was the first church he had aided in organization. This church numbered about eighty members at the time of its organization. Evidently the liberal and progressive principles of church polity introduced by the young preacher were much in advance of what many of the local Baptists held to be "orthodox."

It was at this time that the views of both Alexander Campbell and Walter Scott began to penetrate deeply the Baptist churches of Ohio. Walter Scott had just entered on the work of evangelism for the Baptist Mahoning Association. He began to appeal to the people that the salvation of men is not in the Bible or in a creedal formulation but it is in Christ as a person. This viewpoint so nearly approximated the position which David Burnet had taken when he applied for baptism, that he was intensely attracted by it. He urged the Sycamore

---

[47]*History of the Four Christian-Disciple Churches, Dayton, Ohio,* 1829-1947 (Dayton: Dayton Disciples Union, 1947), p. 7.
[48]*Ibid.,* p. 8.

Street Baptist Church to have nothing to do with human creeds and to make only the Good Confession the test of fellowship. He urged that they accept the Scriptures as their only rule of faith and practice.

On being accused of being a "Campbellite," Burnet defended his position as that of "only a Christian." This put the Sycamore Street church on the threshold of issuing its ultimatum to Burnet. But what did David Burnet care for ultimatums? He had faced frustrations worse than congregational ultimatums. He would not be coerced into acceptance of a narrow, sectarian denominationalism at a time when it seemed the whole world so desperately needed what he called a restoration of primitive Christianity.

1828-1830: ALIENATIONS AMONG THE BAPTISTS

In the Enon Baptist Church, David Burnet was influenced by James Challen. Although small in stature, Challen was of a sinewy and energetic build, able to withstand great physical activity and endurance. He was six years older than Burnet. His small, sharp, penetrating eyes were but part of his total animation. His speaking voice was of wide range, pleasing, and used to good advantage in instructive preaching. As a Junior in Transylvania College, Challen had been called to the Enon Baptist Church about 1826 where he remained until the formation of the Sycamore Street Baptist Church in the autumn or winter of 1827. Although his father was a Methodist and his mother a Baptist, he saw in the movement of Disciples of Christ the hopes of a union of the bodies represented by his parents. He thought that a church ought to be formed on the basis of "the Bible and the Bible alone." It was his like-mindedness to young Burnet that led them together to be among the first to withdraw from the Baptists and to form the congregation that has often been cited as the first church of Disciples of Christ.

Burnet and Challen led in the creation of the Christian Church at the corner of Eighth and Walnut Streets early in 1828, leaving the Ninth Street Baptist Church to continue in the more conservative Baptist tradition. This marked the beginning of David Burnet's identity with the reform movement. From this time until his death he was thoroughly and actively identified with Disciples of Christ,[49] defending their principles, evangelizing in their behalf, as an educator and teacher, as a publisher and organizer. Advocating the principles and practices fostered by the movement he was destined to become the active herald of a new order of things.

The debate which Alexander Campbell had in Cincinnati with Robert Owen, April 13-23, 1829, was one which Mr. Owen expected to give great publicity to communism and "to attract tens of thousands to his common stock Paradise."[50] Owen was engaged in developing a Utopia at New Harmony, Indiana, upon communistic lines and without religion. The debate with Campbell was held in the old Cincinnati Methodist Church and the President of Moderators for the debate was D. S. Burnet's Uncle Jacob, Judge of the Supreme Court of Ohio. Burnet said of his uncle that "his sympathies divorced him from Mr. Campbell religiously," but that the Judge made this emphatic remark: "I have been listening to a man who seems as one who had lived in all ages."[51]

Burnet's admiration for Campbell continued to increase, as reflected in the letter written later that summer:

Dayton, August 25, 1829

Dear Brother Campbell:

I hasten to inform you of the result of our meeting in this place, on Saturday and Sunday last. There were ten or twelve preachers here, all of whom were either partially or altogether

---

[49]Moore, *Living Pulpit*, p. 36.
[50]*Millennial Harbinger*, 1866, p. 311.
[51]*Ibid.*, pp. 311, 312.

reformed, as far as reformation now goes. The congregation was very large, and on Sunday looked extremely interesting, assembled in one of the finest groves our country affords. After three sermons on Saturday, in the evening, in the presence of many hundreds, in the meetinghouse, our public teachers rehearsed, one by one, accounts of the congregations with which they were respectively connected, informing us of their order, duties, relations and prospects; and all concurred in acknowledging but one law book, from whose decision they never attempt to appeal. This was one of the most interesting exercises in which I ever participated or ever witnessed. Its influence was visible upon all the brethren. With each other they were immediately acquainted, and mutual confidence and a reciprocation of Christian feeling were the consequences. At ten the next morning, I immersed William R. Cole, Esq., of Wilmington, with whom you are acquainted, and three others. After some of the brethren had labored in word and doctrine, two or three hundred feasted at the King's table upon bread and wine; all of them having previously had their hearts sprinkled from an evil conscience, and their bodies washed with pure water. I believe we had no sectarianism among us. Not a discordant note was heard in the house or among the trees. Brother Rains was with us. Our exercises were resumed and terminated pleasantly in the evening. Upon the whole, I believe, such a meeting is rarely held.

Week before last, I attended Todd's Fork Association, where I received encouraging news from Indiana. We had a very interesting meeting. It was resolved with but one dissentient vote, that the association request the churches to consider this question, *"Shall we dissolve our association, and as a substitute, hold an annual meeting for worship and acquaintance?"* and disclose the result of their deliberations at their next session.

By a letter from your father, which I have seen, I learn that the gospel is very successful with you. Remember me to him.

Yours in Christ,

D. S. Burnet[52]

It is impossible to cite any specific date in the history of the movement of Disciples of Christ as the time of

---

[52]*Christian Baptist*, p. 587.

actual separation from the Baptists. Historians have often turned to the year 1830 as the most evident time of full separation. Garrison and DeGroot have a splendid chapter on the first decade of independence of Disciples of Christ from the Baptists, showing how the process cannot be dated arbitrarily by any single event.[53] The reason for noting the year 1830 as the time of separation is that a strong feeling of separation came into existence when Mr. Campbell ceased to classify himself as a Baptist. Three events have marked the final break of Campbell with the Baptists: (1) the dissolution of the Mahoning Association in August, 1830; (2) the beginning of publication of *The Millennial Harbinger,* January 4, 1830; (3) and the last issue of *The Christian Baptist,* July 5, 1830, by which action the name "Baptist" was dropped from the usage that had indicated affiliation with that denomination.

Therefore, when Burnet and Challen withdrew from Baptist affiliation in 1828 they began to accomplish what Campbell had advocated but what he did not act upon until two years later. Burnet's was the business of a religious trail-blazer on the western frontier of Ohio and in the large cities of the East. The year 1828 marks a stage in the separation of Disciples of Christ from the Baptists in Ohio. There were already existing the "Christian" or New Light congregations; there were Baptist churches that had developed principles of Disciples of Christ until they were Baptists in name only; and there were new churches being founded by evangelists in accord with the new movement. Not only did the church at Eighth and Walnut Streets, in Cinncinati, accept the new order of things (which they called the "ancient order of things"), the Dayton Baptist Church which young Burnet had served a few years earlier soon followed the example in 1829.

---

[53] W. E. Garrison and A. T. DeGroot, *The Disciples of Christ, A History* (St. Louis: Christian Board of Publication, 1948), pp. 201ff.

It is equally impossible to cite any local church and say with historical accuracy that this was the first church established among Disciples of Christ in America, or in Ohio. The framework of the movement was too much in the process of change to be so easily identified. However, as one sees the creative work done by Burnet, one begins to wonder if he ought not be listed among the founding fathers. Instead of regarding only four men as rightly being regarded the founders of Disciples of Christ, is it possible that here is the fifth? Instead of Walter Scott being the youngest of the founders, is not this youth (ten years younger than Scott and twenty years younger than Campbell) worthy of closer observation?[54]

We find him yielding to honest convictions, opposing the abuses and worldly interests of his contemporaries. His moral courage is doubly evident in his separation from "wealth, position, fame, friends, relatives, and last, though not least, religious associations,"[55] and his further adherence to a movement which was scorned and ridiculed by the more solidly organized religious bodies of his day. Either he was mentally unstable and socially a misfit, or he was a man of deep and earnest convictions, willing to tackle a high adventure in religious leadership. Moore says:

> The people with whom he associated himself religiously were, at that time, held in very low esteem by the different religious parties into which the Protestant world was divided. Nor could it be expected otherwise. The plea which they made struck at the very foundation of all the existing religious sects; hence it is reasonable enough to suppose the sects would bitterly denounce a movement which had for its object their complete destruction. This very attitude of the Reformation arrayed all the hosts of sectarianism against it. The contest was a fearful one, and the odds against the little Spartan band who pled for a return to apostolic Christianity were truly appalling.[56]

---
[54]*Ibid.*, p. 180.
[55]Moore, *Living Pulpit*, p. 37.
[56]*Ibid.*

Obviously Burnet knew what he was doing. He was no martyr. Even though he had suffered many frustrations in his efforts at leadership and in gaining a place for himself in the New World, he challenged every opposition with cool Scotch calculation. If the denominations held in low esteem the Campbell, Stone, and Scott movement, Disciples of Christ arose to their dignity and held in similar disapproval the sectarian world. This mutual exploitation was highly suitable to Burnet's purposes. He went to work taking advantage of the alienations within the Baptist ranks.

1830: Fortunate Merger of Lives

In Ohio the new Reformation movement particularly aroused the Baptist denomination into considerable controversy. The westward surge of peoples increased to another level with the completion in 1830 of the Miami Canal. The influx of new peoples and the admixture of widely various religious viewpoints set the stage for religious debate and discussion among all major Protestant groups. In 1829 the Second Presbyterian Church, of Cincinnati, had erected a large building between Vine and Race Streets. Lyman Beecher began in 1830 thundering forth with "sermons that echoed all over America."[57] This was Uncle Jacob's church, a Presbyterian congregation which was to go through the Reformation with the New- and Old-Light controversy.

David Burnet was almost twenty-two years old, when on March 30, 1830, he was married to Mary G. Gano, youngest daughter of Major General John S. Gano and Mrs. Mary (Goforth) Gano.[58] Her father, General Gano, was a native of New York City; born there in 1766. He had died nine years before Mary's marriage to David Burnet. General Gano was one of the founders of the

---
[57]Goss, *Cincinnati, The Queeen City*, p. 154.
[58]From an old newspaper clipping (source unknown).

city of Covington, Kentucky, and was for a long while Clerk of the Court and Major General of Militia.

Mary Gano's mother was the daughter of William and Catherine Goforth, also of New York City. She was born there November 21, 1768. She was married to John S. Gano, January 31, 1787. They came west (to Ohio) soon after their marriage and were among the first party of twenty-six men, women and children, which landed near the mouth of the Little Miami and took possession of an Indian clearing near Columbia in November, 1788. They built a home, noted for pioneer hospitality. Mrs. Gano lived to be the oldest pioneer remaining in Cincinnati in 1856. She died in New York City in 1857, after having lived sixty-eight years in Cincinnati, to which place she had come with her husband shortly after their marriage. "From the time the Indian and the wolf prowled through the forest and the ponds where now the city stands," said the newspaper eulogy, "to this day of its beautiful and magnificent growth, she was here, part and parcel of that growth itself. She saw the whole of that great, rapid, and unequalled development of this Western metropolis." She returned to New York City near the place of her birth in the autumn of 1856 and died there the following year. Her obituary emphasized also that she was "intelligent, sociable and pleasant and her mind and spirit kept active to the last."[59]

Her daughter, also named Mary, and David Burnet were married in the spring of 1830. Mary had been immersed in 1827 by Jeremiah Vardeman.[60] She entered faithfully into cooperation with David in the preaching and teaching to which he had already committed his life.[61]

---
[59]Taken from a newspaper clipping found attached to the end papers of Jacob Burnet's *History of the North-Western Territory,* in the Denver Public Library, May, 1952. Clipping probably was from a Cincinnati Newspaper of 1857.
[60]Moore, *Living Pulpit,* pp. 37, 38.
[61]*Ibid.*

One of their first ventures together was a history-making periodical, *The Evangelical Enquirer*. This paper was conducted at Dayton, Ohio, 1830-31, and is regarded as the earliest Disciple publication. When Burnet's journal came off the press, it represented the distinct emergence of a new order of things. Campbell soon took the name *Millennial Harbinger* for his paper and abandoned the name of *Christian Baptist*. Although Campbell was still regarded as a Baptist, it was not a satisfactory classification for either himself or the Baptists. In the publication of papers distinctly devoted to Disciples of Christ the place of the trail-blazer ought to be given to D. S. Burnet, who entered upon this venture the year he was married. A copy of this earliest journal of Disciples of Christ is to be found preserved in the Coe Collection, in the Yale University Library, New Haven, Connecticut.

CHAPTER II

Maturity of a Leader

1831-1836: A TOUR TO EVICT ERROR

THE FAR WEST WAS A NATURAL setting for the work of an aggressive controversialist in 1832. Chicago was the "Far West"¹ and Ohio was simply "The West." The first railroad to operate in Ohio, the Erie and Kalamazoo, was completed from Toledo to Adrian, Michigan, in 1836. It was the pioneer railroad of the West.² On February 12, 1834, the two-million-dollar Ohio Life Insurance and Trust Co., with 35 incorporators, was established with Judge Jacob Burnet among the prominent founders.³ Bustling with quick growth, the city of Cincinnati was an easy victim of fire, flood, and fights. Fire devastated a large portion of the business district of the city between Third and Fourth Streets in 1832. Shortly after that, the first of the great floods burst in upon the terrified people. Prior to 1834 there were thirteen months of horrible disease when cholera broke out and 813 citizens died in a single year. What has been described as "the darkest period in our city's history"⁴—the period from 1819 to 1839—was also the era when the population doubled.

The most violent controversies of the time were those centering around the slavery issue. James G. Birney established his anti-slavery journal in Cincinnati about the same time that Burnet began publishing *The Chris-*

---
[1] "United States," *Ency. Amer.* XXII (1951), 379.
[2] "Ohio," *Ency. Amer.* XVI (1951), 618.
[3] *Ohio State Archaeological and Historical Quarterly*, LVII, No. 3, 247.
[4] Goss, *Cincinnati, The Queen City*, pp. 143, 144.

tian Preacher. A mob destroyed the presses of Birney's *The Philanthropist* partly because some citizens of Cincinnati did not want agitation that would deprive the city of southern trade. Harriet Beecher Stowe lived in Cincinnati from 1832 to 1850, where she busied herself gathering material which finally emerged as *Uncle Tom's Cabin.* Founded in 1829, Lane Seminary (Presbyterian) had become an important factor in the city's life as early as 1834. In August of that year the trustees took advantage of the temporary absence of Professors Beecher and Stowe and voted to suppress discussion of slavery, because the controversy threatened to destroy the very existence of the seminary. Fifty-one students left the school in a body.[5]

Probably the first use of the designations, Old and New School Presbyterians, arose from an article published by Dr. Ashbel Green's Presbyterian magazine, the *Christian Advocate,* in 1824. The article referred to a certain theological author as "a staunch Calvanist, of the old school."[6] Dr. Green was ridiculed by Old School teachers in some later doggerel designed to shame his New School views:

> In Adam's fall, We sinned all,
> In Abel's murder, We sinned furder,
> In Tubal Cain, We sinned again.
> In Doctor Green, Our sin is seen.[7]

The debate was expressed in doctrinal terms which the orthodox cited as a renewal of the old Pelagian Controversy. It ultimately divided the Presbyterians in 1838. But if it was doctrinal it was also practical. If God required men to make within themselves a new heart

---

[5]Goss, *Cincinnati, The Queen City,* p. 169.

[6]Samuel J. Baird, *A History of the New School, and of the Questions Involved in the Disruption of the Presbyterian Church in 1838,* (Philadelphia: Claxton, Remsen and Haffelfinger, 1868), preface, p. xi.

[7]*Ibid.,* p. 488.

(which was not in accord with the Westminster Confession) there was need for a "breakdown" of the sinner's hardened will and a preachment that would induce him to "submit to God."[8] The church under the New School theology was obligated to bring about reformations. This meant that there were some things God could not do without the will of man. "God cannot sustain this free and blessed country, which we love and pray for, unless the Church will take right ground in regard to politics."[9] The Old School preachers, loyal to the Calvinistic creed, found these new views of freedom very obnoxious. But Judge Jacob Burnet's close association with the political scene, and his connection with the Beechers and with Lane Seminary, led him to identify himself with the New School division. These controversial jolts were typical of the times. Thoughtful persons were forced to consider the issues which were so much alive.

In the religious controversies David Burnet had thrown down the gauntlet by his rejection of creeds, by his insistence on being regarded a member of the church on a simple confession of faith without being required to relate an "experience," by insisting that a simple believer could administer both Baptism and the Lord's Supper, and by refusal to admit that authority could be legislated upon the local congregations by any power from above.

Burnet did not deny the need for organization. Living in a family as conscious of political activities as Burnet's, he must have been aware of the first Democratic national convention which met in May, 1832. It was called by New Hampshire politicians and was composed of delegates from all the states except Missouri.[10] The

[8] *Ibid.*, p. 223.
[9] Baird, *Hist. of the New School*, p. 488.
[10] "United States," *Ency. Amer.*, XXII, 350.

arguments for and against States' Rights were similar to those for the rights of local church congregations, in much of the discussion between Disciples of Christ and Baptists of the time.

Alexander Campbell's views were penetrating deep into Ohio in 1831.[11] The Lexington meeting of the followers of Barton W. Stone and Alexander Campbell had brought forth on January 1, 1832, the union of the major portion of their forces.[12] There was a rising sense of solidarity among Disciples of Christ both because of their new sense of power and because of the ridicule and attack upon the movement by existing denominations. This sense of solidarity grew quickly under the stimulus of a strong polemic evangelism, vigorous journals, and the periodic holding of general meetings for mutual exchange of ideas. In these means, or "appliances," Burnet took an active leadership. The common ideas of the movement were at the point of crystallization, which Campbell ably expressed in his volume, *The Christian System* (1836). He was accused of setting forth a creed, but certainly none of his more vigorous contemporaries felt themselves bound to subscribe to it. It became, however, the target for much controversy.

In 1833, Burnet left Cincinnati and went out upon the full-time work of an evangelist.[13] Preaching what he called the Primitive Gospel in company with Alexander Campbell, he toured the eastern states, through Virginia and farther north to the seaboard cities.[14]

This tour with Campbell was a memorable one. They traveled through the hills of Virginia on both sides of the river. Cholera was striking cities and towns from Virginia westward into Ohio. Wheeling suffered great

---
[11] Garrison, *Religion Follows the Frontier*, p. 204.
[12] Cf. *Ibid.*, pp. 153, 154.
[13] Moore, *Living Pulpit*, p. 38.
[14] *Ibid.*, Cf. Boles, *Biographical Sketches*, p. 142.

losses and Burnet never forgot the self-possession exhibited by Campbell during the weeks of peril. The night of November 12, 1833, they shared the same bed in Richmond. Toward midnight the head of city police called the citizens of Richmond out of bed to see "the heavens falling." When Burnet and Campbell went outside they found crowds of Negroes and whites as excited as the city official. Burnet described what they saw that night as "the grandest sight recorded since the deluge—the great storm of meteors—the snow storm of fire. He [Campbell] alone stood tranquil, and dealt out in encouraging strains his philosophy of the phenomenon. Long after the day broke, these flakes of fire seemed to touch the earth."[15]

Burnet found himself more at home in the cities than in the rural areas. W. T. Moore says that it was the result of his 1833 tour of the eastern cities that ultimately established many of the churches in those localities. His instructions on local church organization aided the development of a more democratic process of congregational polity.

David Burnet attended in the fall of 1833 the Dover Association, the largest Baptist assembly in the East at the time. The meeting was held in Williamsburg, Virginia, and produced on Burnet a profound impression of Baptist "tyrannical exercises." Mr. Burnet had been making his headquarters in Richmond and spent about two months in a tour through a dozen or so counties between Richmond and the Bay Coast.[16] He visited churches, villages, cities, neighborhoods, and preached an average of more than once each day. Many confessions of faith were witnessed. After one sermon there were eighteen confessions. He spent two or three days in Norfolk and lodged at the hotel, then preached in the

[15] *Millennial Harbinger*, 1866, pp. 320, 321.
[16] *Ibid.*, 1833, pp. 390, 391.

courthouse to all who could get in. A pastor of a Norfolk Baptist church brought in a series of resolutions and submitted them in meeting, but they were voted out and down. It was Burnet's continued conflict with Baptist lack of liberty. But the climax of it came at the meeting of the Dover Association.[17]

The first speaker at the Association meeting set out by taking Mark 14:41, as his text for an open verbal warfare against Unitarians, Universalists, and "a Nameless party," whose sin was "undefined and undefinable error." Luther Rice, the introductory speaker, was followed by Andrew Broaddus, as moderator. Burnet saw the Association as a vast ecclesiastical body "with no sympathetic feeling." It was one thing to have huge machinery, and another to have huge machinery with "no bowels of mercy."[18]

A caucus had convened before the morning service to determine who should speak and who should not. Consequently the sessions became uproarious. Burnet's later report of the meeting, October 16, 1833, discloses his feeling about Baptist polity:

Mr. B.[roaddus] is not fitted for controlling or correcting unruly bodies, and in this instance the *Moderator had to be executive of the will of the caucus.* Never did I so fully apprehend, or deprecate the miseries of perverted Baptist Associations. Not a civil or ecclesiastic body exists that more loudly disclaims or more tyrannically exercises the supreme power. The preacher, minister, or ambassador system has so far usurped the government of the church and Association, that personal consideration, *alias* the judgment of the flesh, determines the point in every case of litigation; and in such bodies there is no want of business. In some other sects the higher courts, synods, assemblies, conferences, &c. afford some prospect of justice in the end by a change of tribunal and the place of trial. But among our

---
[17] *Millennial Harbinger*, 1833, pp. 591, ff.
[18] *Ibid.*, p. 592.

quondam associates a man for teaching the words of Jesus Christ, the burden of salvation, is condemned and punished without the liberty of speech or right of appeal, by a body of which he may, or may not be a member, and which, by its constitution and its avowal annually renewed, disclaims all, any, and every kind of authority over individuals or churches, further than the decorum of the session requires. Here liberty and right exist only in name; and, as the long shadow that does at noon, disappears at the moment of anxious search.[19]

Several letters which criticized the operations of the Dover Association were on a table as the business session began. Some of them were still unopened but were thought to contain criticism of the unconstitutional actions of the Association. Burnet was amused at the attitude toward the letters, wondering if the brethren thought the letters ought to be burned or their authors decapitated! Someone raised the question whether the letters should be read before business of the Association could be carried on. Reporting on the incident, Burnet said: "Moderator and moderated were much perplexed; and the by-standers were amused at the perplexity caused by so rational suggestion."

Burnet's boyhood experiences in the courts of law and his familiarity with orderly proceedings caused him to realize that the minority of the Association had thought it necessary even to the "perpetuation of outrage" to carry their point. This kind of failure at impartiality irked Burnet's sense of justice in meeting any error that invited scrutiny.

He had an appointment to preach at evening candle-lighting in the Williamsburg courthouse. The house filled at an early hour and before time announced for the address Burnet began an exposition and history of the reformation as he understood it. He preached for

[19] *Ibid.*, 1833, p. 592. (Brackets mine.)

two or three hours and adjourned until morning. The audience made a request that such meetings should continue twice a day. Burnet preached about five hours daily as long as the session lasted. It was such a popularly attended meeting that all the ladies could not find comfortable seats in the courtroom, and all the men could not gain entrance into the building because of the crowds.[20]

It was during this tour that he saw the vital need for more trained preachers. Upon returning to Cincinnati in 1834 he began to edit what was the second[21] of his many publications, *The Christian Preacher*. It was a monthly journal, containing sermons and essays.[22] In the next chapter some evaluation of its significance is set forth.

During the same year (1834) he set to work upon an editorial project of tremendous scope. He had been an enthusiastic reader of the highly polemic magazine, *The Christian Baptist*, published by Campbell until the summer of 1830. The idea of having the main features of *The Christian Baptist* in a single volume for distribution appealed to Burnet. He began the process of making a digest of that journal to be issued in book form. It was in the work of editing the one-volume edition of Campbell's magazine that Burnet most completely clarified his own sense of mission. He had already faced the reality of the separateness between his own views and those of the Baptists. Now he was further activated by a restudy of the pages of that "vigorous and vitriolic magazine."[23] On his tour of the eastern states he had found the need for such a volume, as well as the need

---

[20] *Millennial Harbinger*, 1833, pp. 593, 594.

[21] Moore, *Living Pulpit*, p. 38. Cf. Boles, *Biographical Sketches*, p. 143. Also, Garrison and DeGroot, *The Disciples of Christ*, p. 300 (1836, *erratum*). Also Power, *Sketches of Our Pioneers*, p. 126.

[22] *Ibid.*, "Commenced his career as editor and publisher" is incorrect; he earlier edited and published *The Christian Enquirer*.

[23] Garrison, *Religion Follows the Frontier*, p. 130.

to supply preachers with pulpit ammunition. *The Christian Preacher* and *The Christian Baptist* would be satisfactory answers to all the antagonistic controversy with which Christian preachers would come in contact in their evangelistic itineraries. Garrison has said, *"The Christian Baptist,* rather than any local church, was the nucleus around which the new movement developed its sense of mission, which soon led to a sense of separateness."[24] If it was the nucleus of this sense of mission, it was more clearly understood by Burnet than by any other person after he had finished his editorial work. Even Campbell himself, who edited and published the journal, probably did not have as objective a view of the contents of *The Christian Baptist* as Burnet must have had as the result of his selective approach to the contents in preparing the edition which appeared in 1835.

In the hope of attaining greater accuracy for its contents and to replenish the available book stock for public distribution, Burnet set forth on the editorial project. Some of the "ephemeral matter" (*e.g.*, notices, correspondence of local interest, personalities, etc.) was omitted. The style was modernized, with Mr. Campbell's approval.

The book contained a large variety of articles on Man, The Ancient Gospel, The Christian Religion, The Ancient Order of Things, Bible, Church, Faith, Immersion, Missionaries, Religious News, Skepticism, Catholicism, and other articles of like nature. Most of the work was vitriolic and polemic in attitude. Even with its overdrawn criticisms, Burnet regarded it as the best of all of Campbell's published works throughout his life.

At the end of the eastern tour Burnet held a meeting in Baltimore, Maryland, which raised the question of the youngest age at which one could become a member of the church. January 28, 1834, he visited Baltimore on

[24] *Ibid.*

his way home to Cincinnati. Fortunately, Andrew W. Gottschall in his *Across a Century, being the History of the First Christian Church, Baltimore, Md.*, has preserved a transcript of the discussions[25] which prevailed and something of a record of that meeting. The *Millennial Harbinger* printed in March, 1834, a letter by Wm. Carmen,[26] member of the North Street Church, setting forth his confidence in the belief that Burnet had done well in receiving very small children into the church upon their simple confession of faith. Some of the older members of the congregation raised questions of the propriety of baptizing little children as "believers." The letter also reveals something of the procedures and effectiveness of Burnet's evangelistic activities.

Baltimore, Md., February 11, 1834.

On the 28th ult. our brother D. S. Burnett came to this city on his way home to Cincinnati. We again rented Scotti's Hall, in South Street, that the Citizens might have an opportunity to hear the gospel, (I don't use the word *ancient* more than *modern*, for I think neither is in the Scriptures, only the Gospel of God). He commenced on Friday evening, January 31. Saturday evening was very stormy, yet we had a meeting. On Lord's day afternoon and evening the hall was full. When our brother gave an invitation to those whose minds were made up to obey the gospel, one came forward. On Monday, the 3rd, at seven o'clock, the good news was again proclaimed. At the close an invitation was given, and the first that accepted was the dear little daughter of our friend, G—A—; seven others followed, all of whom were immersed next morning at Spring Gardens. On Tuesday evening again eight obeyed the Lord. On Wednesday morning they were immersed. On Wednesday evening seven came forward, and were immersed on Thursday morning. On Thursday evening five came to show their submission to their Lord, and were immersed on Friday morning. On Lord's day morning four were immersed, one of whom came forward at

---

[25] Andrew W. Gottschall, *Across a Century* (Baltimore: Hess Printing Co., 1932), pp. 26-29.
[26] *Millennial Harbinger*, 1834, pp. 126-128.

the river. At our next meeting five more confessed the Lord and were immersed. Besides the 38 which came out from the world, twelve baptized persons from the other churches joined us; so that in about ten days we have received fifty new members. We are now about one hundred. Some of the new converts are little boys and girls, say from 10 to 14. They are, however, as intelligent as any of their years which can be found. You know many of them. Among them are the daughter of our friend G. Austin, the daughter of our brother and sister Sands, the daughter of our brother Thomas, and the adopted daughter of brother and sister Bell. I question if many persons of five times their age can give a better reason for the hope which is in them. Ask them for their Christian experience, they have none to tell—no, not one word. But ask any of them, "My dear, do you expect to rise from the dead?" "Yes, that is my joy, that when my Lord Jesus shall appear I shall be like Him, for I shall see Him as He is; and for this end and purpose I purify myself even as He is pure."

After these children came forward there was chattering all around—"What do these people mean?" "These children are not fit members of a church." "Can they eat the Lord's Supper understandingly?" And many like sayings. We could hear comments on every side.

A day or two after, a little daughter of respectable parents, under ten years, died, and from the account given of her in the newspapers of that day, all were satisfied this little girl died a sincere Christian. Hence our practice was got over, and no more is said of our receiving children. The reason why many more children are not following the Lord, is because of the neglect of those under whose care they are placed, whether parents or guardians. The Scriptures are neglected—that which is given to make men wise unto salvation is thrown out of use in the family and school. A very religious man (now dead) said to me that he would not have the Scriptures put into the hands of children until they were of mature age. What a mistake! Had it been so when I was a boy, not 9 years of age, what would have been the consequence? I could read. The 139th Psalm filled me with fear. . . .

This was present with me wherever I went, and I was fully persuaded of its truth, as if it was written for me alone; and from that day to this it is seldom out of my mind. I am now an old man, 65 years of age, and the fear of God in my youthful days has kept me marvelously free from every vice calculated to destroy my constitution; so that I enjoy as good health now as many not half my years. Hence I lament the neglect of the Scriptures in families and schools.

Among the number immersed last week were several boys, none less than 14 years of age. Several of the brethren were concerned for them, and wished to know from themselves why they believed that Jesus was the Son of God. That question was asked by one of the brethren in the presence of several. "Why," replied the lad, "the Apostles have said Jesus raised the dead, gave sight to the blind, and healed the sick." All present were fully convinced the lad was a fit subject for immersion.

WM. CARMEN.

1836-1844: COLLEGE AND JOURNAL AS THE CHRISTIAN WAY TO SOLVENCY

Beginning in 1836, Burnet edited *The Christian Preacher* through five annual volumes. When Burnet issued his magazine, Alexander Campbell thought he might cease publishing a periodical and devote his attention to writing more permanent volumes on important topics. He continued publishing the *Harbinger*, however, until his death, realizing later the need for periodical literature and a central organ.[27] It was during this same period that Burnet ventured forth as college president of the first actual college among Disciples of Christ. The relationship between his activities as editor and publisher, on the one hand, and educator on the other, indicates something of his versatility.

His journal strongly set forth the Messiahship of Jesus, the Incarnation and the Resurrection. The pa-

---
[27]*Millennial Harbinger*, 1866, p. 312.

per presented strong intimations that the Second Advent of Christ was imminent. The Jewish attitude toward Jesus seemed to be changing favorably toward possible acceptance of him as their Messiah. Curiously enough, a Zionist movement was anticipated. The magazine referred to the Jews as "exalted once above all other people, they are now the fallen nobility of the world; but they will be raised again, and placed, we may believe, at the head of all the redeemed. . . ."[28] The stage was being set for a timely mission to Jerusalem if Christians were to avail themselves of the glorious circumstances which seemed surely but a short time until full accomplishment. Accentuating the idea of Jerusalem as being the future center of God's activity was the whole doctrine of Restoration.

Burnet's incisive mind had the habit of categorizing his thought. He pointed out that

there are three kingdoms, into which it may be the destiny, and into which we may have the privilege, upon hearing the gospel, of being naturalized. Of the first, we all now compose a part; and the three may be styled Nature, Grace, and Glory: or, in more familiar terms, the world, the church, and heaven.[29]

He further developed a scheme which he called "A Synopsis of Divine Revelation" which he published both in his introduction to the one-volume edition of the *Christian Baptist* and in an article on "Christian Baptism" published in the *Christian Preacher* in 1838 (See Appendix V). This scheme was the briefest kind of outline of the gospel as Burnet then understood it. By examination of the "Synopsis" one is impressed with Burnet's analytical disposition.

---

[28] "The Jews," *Christian Preacher*, IV, 160-161. Article from the *Missionary Chronicle*.

[29] "Additional Remarks by the Editor," *Christian Preacher*, I, 43. Cited by Frederic John Forney, "An Analytical Evaluation of the *Christian Preacher*" (B. D. Thesis, Butler University, 1945), p. 30.

In his journal Burnet did not miss an opportunity to call attention to the matter of Christian stewardship, giving and spending money in behalf of the church. When the question came up among some churches whether the practice should be to meet each Lord's Day for worship the editor reminded his readers that Paul in 1 Corinthians had said, "Upon the first day of the week let every one of you lay by him in store, as God hath prospered him that there be no gatherings when I come." Burnet queries "what treasury could this be but the church treasury?"[30]

Extremely liberal views seem to have broken into the pages of the *Christian Preacher* in 1838 concerning who may participate in the Communion. Burnet said, "an evangelist may, under some circumstances, be justified, perhaps, in exemplifying a Christian ordinance, and some points of order in connection with preaching the Gospel, by eating the Lord's Supper with some brethren who might be among the unconverted."[31] Whether he held that those in other denominations were the "unconverted" is difficult to determine. At any rate, this view was very far removed from his earlier Baptist practice of closed communion. In this gesture toward neither open nor closed communion, Burnet was quick to qualify his statement by words that may have eased the shock of what he already had put in print. He said, "I say the wisdom of a discreet evangelist might deem some circumstances authority for such procedure, but it appears to me most expedient, generally to confine the ordinances of worship to the church."[32]

Burnet used the printed page as a call to action as well as a training ground for preachers. He was fully

---

[30] "Reply," *Christian Preacher*, IV (1839), 242. Cf. Forney, thesis, p. 48.

[31] "Queries," *Christian Preacher*, III (1838), 140. Cf. Forney, thesis, p. 58.

[32] *Ibid.*, p. 58.

conscious of the need for workers in the growing new movement. Typical of his many calls for evangelistic effort is the following:

> Now is the accepted time, brethren. Be up! the fields are white! The reaper who is not now in the field will not gather many sheaves for years to come. The church that does not fill its granary now, must be expected to endure a seven years' famine, or live by scanty gleanings.
>
> The spirit of the people is moved! and all parties see it, or will see it; the whole country will be swept by some religious influence pure or corrupt; and shall we sheath the sword of the spirit when half a nation is to be gained to God? This is our Father's land, and these are his creatures. Let us, brethren, assert his claims. Let the hosts of Israel arm for the conflict from Dan to Beersheba.[33]

He urged that faithful men be kept in the field of labor, teaching and evangelizing the world.[34] The movement was in a period of rapid growth. While preaching in southwestern Ohio Burnet estimated that at least 100,000 persons had entered the fellowship in fifteen years. Henry K. Shaw, Ohio Disciple historian, thinks this may have been accurate although there is no cited authority for Burnet's estimates.[35]

As editor of the *Christian Preacher* Burnet was called to the presidency of Bacon College, Georgetown, Kentucky, where he remained for two years. Then naturally the magazine reflected his interest in higher education. He knew of the widespread need for training leaders to foster the movement and to prevent losses which already were beginning to be evident.

---

[33]"The Times—The Crisis," *Christian Preacher*, III (1838), 40. Cf. Forney, thesis, p. 90.

[34]"Progress of the Present Reformation," *Christian Preacher*, I (1836), 69. Cf. Forney, thesis, p. 91.

[35]Henry K. Shaw, *Buckeye Disciples* (Cleveland: Ohio Christian Missionary Society, 1952), p. 98. Cf. *Millennial Harbinger*, 1836, pp. 143, 144.

Although Bacon College was the first actual college of the brotherhood, there had been other previous actions in that direction which had been frustrated.[36] Walter Scott was Bacon's first president, but he remained there less than a year before being succeeded by Burnet.[37] He and Burnet became warm friends when Scott in 1832 moved to Carthage, Ohio, near Cincinnati.[38] Scott was publishing *The Evangelist* and preaching in the area. He preached sometimes in Cincinnati where James Challen was the leader. After 1832 Scott and Burnet had many common interests including the enlistment and training of ministers, the editing of Christian journals, and the fostering of the causes of the colleges. They eventually joined forces in the publishing business. Both of them saw the need of higher education and both were college presidents four years before Mr. Campbell opened Bethany College.

Bacon College was founded in 1836 as the aftermath of a split with the Baptist college at Georgetown. Named in memory of Francis Bacon, the college aimed to carry on the "empirical philosophy and scientific method"[39] in its approach to education. The school came into existence to train in technical fields, such as that of Civil Engineering,[40] but it was committed also to liberal education from the Baconian viewpoint. It offered also the opportunity to find and to train young men for the ministry.[41] Although it was called a college, it would compare today with our secondary schools.

---

[36]Winfred Ernest Garrison, *An American Religious Movement* (St. Louis: Christian Board of Publication, 1945), pp. 106, 107. Also, Garrison, *Religion Follows the Frontier*, pp. 168, 169. Cf. Garrison and DeGroot, *Disciples of Christ*, p. 224.

[37]*Ibid.*, pp. 106, 107.

[38]Shaw, *Buckeye Disciples*, p. 91.

[39]Garrison and DeGroot, *Disciples of Christ*, p. 224.

[40]Garrison, *Religion Follows the Frontier*, pp. 168, 169.

[41]J. T. Johnson, "Bacon College," *Christian Preacher*, II (1837), 285. (From the *Christian*.)

The presidency of the college was at first refused by Burnet. He said he did so "not merely because the acceptance necessarily sundered some of the dearest ties, domestic, ecclesiastic, and civil, but because the duties of the situation would so little resemble the active engagements which have engrossed my attention since I was seventeen years of age."[42] Apparently, however, Burnet was easily persuaded to accept the task.[43] It was plain that he need not relinquish totally his evangelistic labor but could join that effort with the intellectual and moral training of youth.[44] Probably the greatest appeal to him was in the agreement he held with J. T. Johnson that "education is a matter of supreme regard" and worthy of great sacrifice.[45] Bacon College afforded the opportunity in an institution of higher learning "to set forth Christianity, unfettered by any party bias."[46] This was an emphatic purpose both of Burnet's journal and of the college to which he gave leadership. The idea that a school and a church should be free from denominationalism was an enchanting dream for those severely stricken with party strife and highly emotional sectarian exclusiveness. Johnson proclaimed with great confidence that the friends of truth "have now an opportunity of sending their sons to an institution untrammelled by sectarianism, and sustained emphatically by Christians and the friends of Christianity."[47]

Soon after Burnet went to the presidency of Bacon College, Alexander Campbell for the first time announced his approval of the aims and purposes as well as the

[42] *Ibid.*, p. 286.
[43] Forney, thesis, p. 63.
[44] *Christian Preacher*, II, p. 286.
[45] Forney, *loc. cit.* Cf. John Rogers, *The Biography of Elder J. T. Johnson* (Cincinnati: Standard Publishing Co., 1861), p. 126.
[46] J. T. Johnson, "Bacon College," *Christian Preacher*. II (1837), 285. (From the *Christian*.)
[47] *Ibid.*

leaders of the school. Campbell's Bethany College had not yet been established when he wrote in the *Millennial Harbinger* a statement about Bacon College:

> Its learned and talented Faculty, its freedom from sectarian influence, and its plan of adopting its course of instruction to the genius of the age, have given it even at this early day a very high standing with the community.
>
> I have been backward hitherto to say much about the institution, until I could ascertain from a personal interview with its principal managers and conductors, their views and designs, their prospects and means, &c. but especially with reference to the discipline and moral culture under which the youth are to be placed who attend this College; for this, with me, now is above all other sorts of eminence. I give my vote for learning and science and for high attainments in all branches of useful knowledge, but I would not give morality for them all; and therefore I have resolved never to speak in favor of any literary institution, from a common school to a University, however superior their literary eminence, guardianship over the morals of its students and wards, and endeavor to make good rather than great men. Colleges without this are no blessing to any country. So I think.
>
> I was happy to learn that such is the firm determination of each of the Trustees and Faculty with whom I conversed. They have, indeed, given their pledge that the morals and moral culture of the youth shall be their paramount concern. Believing, then, that parents may safely send their sons to Georgetown as respects their moral safety; and as for literary and scientific advantages, it is already known that there is everything which the students need. Therefore we can now say, that we hope that all who wish their sons well educated in all that is valuable in literature and science, without any hazard to their morals, will send them to Georgetown; and that our Christian brethren especially will patronize and build up an institution of inestimable value to themselves and their posterity.[48]

When he moved to Georgetown the publication of the *Christian Preacher* was also moved from Cincinnati.

---

[48]Alexander Campbell, "Bacon College," *Millennial Harbinger*, December, 1837. Cf. Forney, thesis, p. 65.

The editorship of the journal was shared with J. T. Johnson. The *Christian*, a periodical formerly published by Johnson and Walter Scott, was absorbed by Burnet's publication. The journal aimed to be helpful in bringing to public attention the need for funds if Bacon College was to do its work well. Subsequently, Burnet and the Trustees sent Brother Wm. Hatch, of Georgetown, as a solicitor to visit the churches and individuals in the quest for funds. The *Christian Preacher* announced his coming and described him as "an acceptable teacher of religion, and will frequently deliver lectures upon education, and such public statements and illustrations of the claims of this object upon public munificence, as cannot fail to prove interesting to his hearers, and a permanent advantage to the Institution."[49] The method of financing the program of Bacon College foreshadows the combination of publicity and traveling agents later devised in the organizations of Bible, Tract, and Missionary societies.

It was shortly before Burnet's first year of presidency at Bacon that the school gained a charter from the legislature of Kentucky, February 1837. Efforts had not been made to secure permanent funds or endowments. The school almost immediately incurred a debt of approximately seven thousand dollars as a result of purchase of buildings. Contributions of churches and friends soon dropped off because of rumors that Bacon was financially secure.

Burnet then made a startling announcement in the pages of his periodical. He said that the Trustees had resolved to constitute a permanent fund for the college and that if 100 individuals would subscribe $500 each the majority of them should have the privilege of locating the college at any place in Kentucky they might choose.[50]

---

[49] *Christian Preacher*, III (1838), 142.

[50] "To the Public," *Christian Preacher*, IV (1839), 134. Cf. Forney, thesis, p. 67.

The announcement indicated also that such action was necessary if Bacon College was to survive. A meeting of subscribers was held at Georgetown, May 1, 1839, and they oversubscribed the amount by $10,000. The majority of financial support was from Harrodsburg, Kentucky, and the Trustees were under obligation to move there.[51] President Burnet then declined the invitation of the Trustees to move along with the college to the resort town of Harrodsburg. His reasons for resigning are not clear. He may have questioned the moral situation in Harrodsburg, there may have been personality clashes, he may have felt his usefulness with the college was at an end, and he may have wished to be nearer Cincinnati. It was not due to a break with J. T. Johnson, however, because their intimate friendship lasted until Johnson's death of pneumonia on Christmas Eve, 1856.

After the two years with Bacon College, Burnet became "Principal and Proprietor of Hygeia Female Atheneum, situated on the heights, seven miles back of Cincinnati."[52] This school for girls was nearer home and Mr. and Mrs. Burnet could drive into Cincinnati more often to visit relatives. During his stay with both these institutions he continued to edit the magazine, *The Christian Preacher.* Alexander Campbell established Bethany College in 1840, about a year after Burnet terminated his relationship with Bacon College.[53]

Cincinnati was the scene of great political happenings in 1840. W. H. Harrison, native son, was elected to the presidency of the United States. The campaign had been one which featured the "Log Cabin," "Coonskin Caps," and "Hard Cider." He was in office only a short while before he died of pneumonia. Uncle Jacob Burnet,

---

[51]*Christian Preacher*, 1839, p. 134. Cf. Forney, thesis, p. 67.
[52]Moore, *Living Pulpit*, p. 38. Cf., Boles, *Biographical Sketches*, p. 143.
[53]Garrison, *Religion Follows the Frontier*, p. 169. Cf. Garrison and DeGroot, *Disciples of Christ*, p. 224.

who was a leader in the campaign, was on the committee to bring the President's body back home for burial.[54]

While he was proprietor of the Hygeia Female Atheneum, David Burnet found opportunities to visit the churches and yearly meetings in some parts of Ohio. A. S. Hayden, in his history of the Disciples in the Western Reserve, Ohio, said that "several times in the great yearly meetings [at Stowe, Ohio] Bro. D. S. Burnett, of Cincinnati, has pled here, with his great abilities, the claims of the Lord Jesus."[55] Hayden's book is highly autobiographical and minimizes the work of others in Ohio. However, he recognized the great ability of Burnet (and he, like many others, spelled Burnet with two t's).

A series of race riots began in Cincinnati in June and September of 1841.[56] A riot in 1842 occurred when the Bank of Cincinnati closed its doors.[57] Almost as great excitement was created by the visit that same year of the English novelist, Charles Dickens.[58] Burnet found excitement in the discovery that Alexander Campbell was holding a new attitude toward some form of organization among Disciples of Christ.

Extracts from the *Millennial Harbinger* during 1842[59] indicate that the new views of Campbell on organization were taking shape:

1. That the elders, or bishops, as he liked to call them, constituted the teaching portion of the Christian ministry, and were teachers, preachers, and pastors.

2. That when called to service, they had a two-fold task, local and general. He is concerned especially with the general task

---

[54] Goss, *Cincinnati: Queen City*, pp. 195, 196.
[55] Amos Sutton Hayden, *Early History of the Disciples in the Western Reserve, Ohio* (Cincinnati: Chase and Hill, 1875), pp. 384, 385.
[56] Goss, *Cincinnati: Queen City*, pp. 179-181.
[57] *Ibid.*
[58] *Ibid.*, p. 195.
[59] *Millennial Harbinger*, 1842, pp. 59-64; 183-185.

and maintains that it is the duty, backed by the churches, to undertake all of the interests of the kingdom beyond the sphere of the local congregation.

3. He suggests no form of organization for doing this general work, leaving that to the needs as they may arise. But that some form of organization is, in his judgment, essential, is manifest from his constant reference to the need of church organization.[60]

Campbell said there was great need of a "more rational and scriptural" organization and listed five arguments in the *Millennial Harbinger* for such an organization:[61]

1. We can do comparatively nothing in distributing the Bible abroad without co-operation.

2. We can do comparatively but little in the great missionary field of the world either at home or abroad without co-operation.

3. We can do little or nothing to improve and elevate the Christian ministry without co-operation.

4. We can do but little to check, restrain, and remove the flood of imposture and fraud committed upon the benevolence of the brethren by irresponsible, plausible, and deceptive persons, without co-operation.

5. We can not concentrate the action of the tens of thousands of Israel, in any great Christian effort, but by co-operation.

6. We can have no thorough co-operation without a more ample, extensive, and thorough church organization.

Such a blueprint for action was exactly what the practical Mr. Burnet and his associates had been awaiting. An organized society would be the "engine" of the movement. Through it could be applied power. Power was regarded highly in every field—new power like that used on the recently completed Little Miami Railway, or the engines on rivers and canals, except it would be spiritual and organizational power. The organization of a Bible

---

[60] Allen R. Moore, *Alexander Campbell and the General Convention* (St. Louis: Christian Board of Publication, 1914), p. 36.

[61] *Millennial Harbinger*, 1842, p. 523. Quoted by A. R. Moore, *Alexander Campbell and the General Convention*, p. 42.

Society, for example, would meet the needs of Mr. Campbell's first item. Burnet turned these ideas over in his own practical mind and began to evolve a great dream of circulating the Bible in all parts of the world, probably with headquarters at Jerusalem, where he thought the Chosen People would one day accept Jesus as the Messiah and where the Restoration would center.

While Burnet was laying plans for establishing a Bible Society, Campbell went forth with other matters—particularly the debate in 1843 with N. L. Rice. In that famous sixteen-day debate, Henry Clay served as moderator while Campbell discussed six propositions. Four of the propositions pertained to the subject, action, design, and administrator of baptism. One proposition was on the operation of the Holy Spirit. The final proposition was one in which Campbell affirmed that human creeds, as bonds of union and communion, are necessarily heretical and schismatical. By the end of the debate Disciples of Christ then had clearly defined for them their own "homogeneous ... body of doctrine."[62] If they had developed by this time no creed, they had at least a body of beliefs which set the pattern of denominational expectancy. A thoroughgoing organization was all that was lacking to make the movement into an institution, holding and administering property in a community of churches relationship. The question before Disciples of Christ then seemed to be: Is it possible to have cooperation and financial stewardship in a brotherhood without resorting to the ancient practices of canon law?

The answer to that question appealed to the young preacher who had been reared in a family of legally illustrious statesmen. Could there be a democratic organization of the churches without the dangers of historical ecclesiasticism? Burnet believed there could be such.

[62]Garrison, *Religion Follows the Frontier*, p. 176.

1844-1845: ORDEAL BY FEVER

As a college president Burnet proved to be an able executive and scholar.[63] But it was not the kind of work he most desired. At the close of the term at Hygeia in 1844 he returned to Cincinnati and took up the pastoral care of the church on Sycamore Street. This church was later moved to the corner of Eighth and Walnut Streets. Burnet was the first settled pastor among Disciples of Christ, serving this one church for sixteen years.[64] Other preachers had been itinerant evangelists among the churches and most of them looked with disfavor upon the idea of a man being limited in his work to the pastoral charge of one congregation. Here, as a Cincinnati pastor, is where he discovered the importance of pastoral oversight. It was "a department of labor not very well understood at that time by preachers of the Christian Church."[65] Few churches could afford the luxury of a resident minister. Shaw says that "many of the brethren objected to the settled ministry on what they considered scriptural grounds."[66] Alanson Wilcox, in his history of Ohio Disciples, claims that Isaac Errett was the first settled minister among Disciples of Christ, having taken the pastorate at New Lisbon in 1844.[67] Burnet's Cincinnati and Dayton pastorates were very much earlier, as has been noted previously.

A comparatively small number of traveling evangelists, or elders, were attempting to serve the needs of a large number of churches. Training men for the ministry was a long process and was one of the major reasons Mr.

---

[63]Moore, *Living Pulpit*, pp. 38, 39.
[64]Power, *Sketches of Our Pioneers*, p. 127.
[65]Moore, *op. cit.*, pp. 39, 40.
[66]Shaw, *Buckeye Disciples*, p. 32.
[67]*Ibid.*, p. 32. Cf. Alanson Wilcox, *A History of the Disciples of Christ in Ohio* (Cincinnati: Standard Publishing Co., 1918), p. 43.

Campbell had established Bethany College. The churches could not hope for full-time ministers until they could be trained. The people in the cities were desperately in need of pastoral oversight, as Burnet saw it. W. T. Moore interprets the action of his predecessor in the pastorate at Eighth and Walnut Streets as follows:

> The preachers had to do chiefly evangelical work, and, consequently, had little or no experience in developing the resources of a single church. Brother Burnet saw that pastoral labor must be done in the churches, and especially the city churches, before they could ever reach that spiritual growth which would enable them to exert a proper influence on the world. Holding these views, he labored not only for an increase of the ministry, but for such a ministry as would be able to build up the *churches* as well as convert the world. He did not measure power by *many*, but by *much*. Numbers in a church are well enough, but strength is not always in numbers. Discipline, long and patient discipline, is necessary to develop *real power*, and this can not be had without a thorough organization, and some one to take the oversight, who feels the responsibility of watching for the souls of the people. He did not argue that the pastoral office is a distinct office from the eldership, but that it is a part of the work of the eldership. But as the elders selected by the churches are generally not competent, or else will not perform this work, such men should be provided as conscientiously feel it to be their duty to "feed the flock of God." This course would alone give such prosperity to the churches as would make them the "pillar and support of the truth."[68]

The work of the pastorate in Cincinnati had other advantages for Burnet besides giving him opportunity to concentrate his efforts in building up a strong congregation. It was his home town, with all the advantages of the intimate relations of kinsmen; and he was in the cultural center of what was then the West, where he could devote himself to study and writing. He was an

---

[68]Moore, *Living Pulpit*, pp. 39, 40.

avid student of ancient and modern history, and the libraries and bookstores of Cincinnati satisfied his thirst for such knowledge.

With the view of satisfying the needs of the home and family life of the churches, he began publishing the *Christian Family Magazine* in 1845. There was something in his analytical mind which insisted that a journal should have a specific purpose and that it was impossible to print an all-purpose magazine which would meet all the needs of the growing fellowship. Now that Bethany College was in operation training preachers, there was no longer need for *The Christian Preacher* and the last issue had appeared at the opening of Bethany (1840).

The development of the Cincinnati pastorate was steady and permanent but was never attended with any great upsurge of unusual activity. Burnet himself seems never to have made any very marked impression upon the city, entering into no very obvious rivalry with the existing denominational *status quo*. The church kept growing. Burnet was honored with the confidence and trust of his brethren in the church. He seems to have had the respect and esteem of all who knew him. But his very great abilities as a preacher, executive, and editor were somewhat overlooked by his home city. Only those who came from all over the growing, youthful America seemed to appreciate his genius. He was a prophet damned with faint praise in his home town.

There was an increasing sense of the importance of the pastorate among Disciples of Christ and by 1856 the discussions were widespread. This meant that if Burnet's ideas were followed it would be necessary to have "educated pastors" to take the oversight of local churches. An opponent of the plan of the pastorate ridiculed the idea as an ecclesiastical way of "developing the resources of the churches."[69] In the long run the opponents of

---

[69] John R. Rowe and G. W. Rice, *Biographical Sketch and Writings of Elder Benjamin Franklin* (Cincinnati: G. W. Rice, 1881), p. 34.

the pastorate viewed with alarm the possibility of curtailing the work of the itinerant evangelist. It must be credited to Burnet that he was the leader among Disciples with the cry for an "educated ministry" and "settled pastors."[70] The position which he assumed regarding the function of the pastor in a local church has been fully vindicated during the century. Burnet published a sermon in which he strongly set forth his views relative to the importance and function of the pastorate.[71] (See Appendix VII.)

Much of Burnet's activity for more than 30 years had been the result of frustrating experiences. His actions seemed like a series of movements to satisfy the disequilibrium which surged to extremes within him. All kinds of annoyances kept pushing at him to arouse the aggressive spirit. Deprived of the social set and circle in which his father and illustrious uncles moved freely, given small consideration and attention by his family and their Presbyterian friends, probably robbed by them of some of the affection due even a stranger, he felt the thwartings of his purposes. As a thirteen-year-old lad he had experienced the domination and bullying of the law office. At sixteen, as a boy preacher, he knew the aversion, repugnance, and loathing of the sophisticated and calm Calvinists who folded their arms in disapproval, scorn, and derision at his actions while they waited for the election and predestination of God to come especially to them. At twenty when he cast his lot with the Campbell movement he suffered further social mistreatment by open dislike, enmity, and hate.

There was a certain amount of compensation in Burnet's activities among Disciples of Christ. In his youth he had had remarkable inducements to become a lawyer,

---

[70]*Ibid.*

[71]D. S. Burnet, *The Pastorate, a Discourse* (Cincinnati: American Christian Publication Society, 1856).

statesman, public official, army officer. Turning from these proffered courses of action he had adopted a life of work which offered some substitution for his original impulses of expression. He now began to realize that he was associated with a group of intelligent leaders, very much like himself, to whom he was socially acceptable.

It was in this situation where he reached the most frustrating experience of all—disease, extreme illness, fever. The threat to his life took hold of him like a new outburst of the Black Death. As he lay ill his mind kept alive to the needs of the new movement which he called the Reformation. He said to himself, "Opportunities and appliances for the propagation of Christianity are to be accounted for, as is the gospel itself. It is our duty to organize Societies for the purpose of concentrating our means, and applying them to the conversion of the outcasts of Israel, and the sinners of the Gentiles. It is our duty to organize. We must circulate the Bible and other religious writings, for the support of preaching in destitute parts of our own and foreign lands."[72]

He had heard the criticism that the Power of God is not in "Societies" but in the "Gospel." He admitted that a society or organization would not be a generator of power in the movement. However, such organization would be the "distributors" and "appliers" of power to the resistance. He reasoned that the Power— the Primitive Gospel (more specifically written in the New Testament)—must be first supplied and kept supplied. The societies would be like a requisite force of engineers and tenders "always present to ensure efficiency and success."[73]

He was so enamored of the conviction that Disciples of Christ could use the power at their disposal

---

[72]Adapted from *Annual Proceedings*, American Christian Bible Society, 1851, p. 6.
[73]*Ibid.*

with greater efficiency and success if they were organized that he came out of his prolonged illness into the period of his most active aggressiveness. Long years of anxiety in reaction to the frustrating distress of his life had demanded many an adjustment. He looked upon the status of things among Disciples of Christ from the sickbed and vowed to fight as he had never done before to bring some kind of unifying experience to those who preached unity so fervently.

The struggle of aggressive action, even against some of his closest companions in the movement if need be, would be necessary for survival of the new reform movement. It would be a normal, premeditated aggression, not pathological. He would have to repress many an impulse; he would plan how to escape the conditions which would be most disagreeable; he would disguise the significance of his ultimate aims by attacking the less obnoxious problems first; he would test the reality and seriousness of the claims of his fellow preachers in their published and preached tenets of unity and brotherly love. If it was God's will that he should rise from his illness, he would enter the conflict for Christ's cause with all the power of his talents. Burnet had now found the cause on which he could lavish his utmost affection.

1845-1849: The Bible and Tract Societies as Liens on the Future

The early ideas of organized cooperation were frowned upon by Disciples of Christ. Campbell was against missionary societies in his earlier career, apparently because a return to the strict "ancient order of things" seemed to forbid modern conceptions of organization. Restoring the ancient things meant the restoring of primitive customs and practices in religious matters. This they thought would be getting back to the purest state in which the church had ever been.

Opposition to associations was a protest against the ecclesiastical polity as then known by those who came into the American frontier with their background experiences as members of groups governed by highly authoritarian religious polity. The Mahoning Association had been dissolved into a simple annual meeting and finally put out of existence altogether because preachers of the brotherhood were of the opinion that any cooperative meeting should be only for simple fellowship and evangelistic preaching.

In fifteen years of separation from the Baptists the new frontier movement had taken on all the characteristics of a denomination except that of a unifying central organization. There were many areas of the country where churches were agreeable to some kind of interchurch assembly for the promotion of worship and evangelism, but the idea of setting up a permanent interchurch organization for stewardship aims smacked of ecclesiasticism.

Garrison says,

> It was a natural development for a company of people, assembled from a considerable area for worship and evangelistic services, to bethink them that it would be a good idea to take up a collection and send out preachers to evangelize among those who had not come to the meeting, and then to meet the next year to hear reports of the work done and to raise more money to carry it on. And there is the seed of a missionary society with an annual convention backing it.[74]

But while the seed of the society system was growing in various areas, with a strong rootage in Indiana, Ohio, Kentucky, Virginia, and elsewhere, Burnet sensed keenly the first item which Mr. Campbell had listed in the *Millennial Harbinger* of 1842: "We can do compara-

---

[74]Garrison, *Religion Follows the Frontier*, p. 181.

tively nothing in distributing the Bible abroad without co-operation."[75] He realized that some practical move had to be made; and he had vowed to make that move. There were sermons everywhere among Disciples of Christ at that time that the Word of God (by which was usually meant the Bible) must be restored to its proper authority. Burnet, like his contemporaries, realized that the Lutheran Reformation had made an appeal to the Bible as an authority in religious matters, saying that it ought to be held superior to popes and councils. But Luther's primary work was believed to have been in restoring the place of conscience in the Christian religion —men were justified by faith, which was a matter of conscience. Calvin's was a restoration of the conceptions of divine sovereignty. Wesley had emphasized human responsibility and personal Christian action. Although Disciples of Christ did not accept all the ideas of Luther, Calvin and Wesley, they held themselves to be in the main stream of the Reformation.

In the opinion of Disciples of Christ there yet remained the need for proper application of the authority of Scriptures. Regardless of previous emphasis on the place of the Bible in the Reformation, Disciples of Christ thought of themselves as having a special responsibility for circulating the Word of God. It was natural that the first cooperative society in the brotherhood should be one for the dissemination of the Bible. Burnet's motive for going ahead with the organization of the Bible Society was the urgency that this need should be translated into action.

An "Address," signed by Burnet, James Challen, and J. J. Moss, appeared in the *Millennial Harbinger* prior to the organization of the American Christian Bible Society

---
[75]*Millennial Harbinger*, 1842, p. 523.

which indicates the thought of the Cincinnati brethren in their aim to go ahead with the organization. The "Address" argues:

1. That appeals on behalf of the American and Foreign Bible Society have brought no adequate response;
2. That we can do more in a year through our own society than in a century by cooperation with another; and
3. That we ought to exhibit our attachment to the Bible by having our own society for its circulation.[76]

Campbell was favorable to continuing support to the Baptist Missionary Society. The difficulties which he faced in keeping Bethany College and the *Millennial Harbinger* solvent had indicated that the brethren across the country were not exceptionally generous in their stewardship. Support of a Bible Society would endanger perhaps the support of his own enterprises.

A modest beginning for Burnet was better than no beginning. So, on January 27, 1845, the representatives of four Cincinnati churches of Disciples of Christ organized a Bible Society.[77] D. S. Burnet was the leader, supported by James Challen and J. J. Moss.[78] They intended from the first to ask for the total concurrence and support of the churches. A glance at the brief constitution of that body indicates something of the same pattern by which other societies and institutions were organized later (See Appendix VI). The simple constitution set the standard for further connectional developments among Disciples of Christ.

Upon the basis of this constitution Burnet was chosen president. The vice-presidents elected were: J. J. Moss, Dr. B. S. Lawson, Walter Scott, Alexander Campbell,

---

[76] Quoted in Garrison, *Religion Follows the Frontier*, p. 184. See also Mr. Campbell's objections, *Millennial Harbinger*, 1845, p. 272.

[77] *Annual Proceedings*, A. C. B. S., 1849, p. 49. Cf. Garrison and DeGroot, *Disciples of Christ*, pp. 242, 243.

[78] Shaw, *Buckeye Disciples*, pp. 137-139.

John T. Johnson, John O'Kane, H. P. Gatchell, Ephraim A. Smith, and Dr. Eleazer Parmly. James Challen was corresponding secretary; George R. Hand, recording secretary; and Thurston Crane, treasurer.[79]

Opposition to the Bible Society came first from Aylett Raines, then from Alexander Campbell. It is difficult to get at the real basis of opposition, although both Raines and Campbell questioned the propriety of the Society on the grounds that there were other organizations existing for the purpose of publishing and circulating the Bible.[80] Although four Cincinnati churches founded the Bible Society, it aimed to seek support and assistance from other cities and states, but Campbell and Burnet were thrust into open conflict over the matter.

Immediately, as soon as the Bible Society was an organized body declaring that it sought support of all the churches, Campbell and his son-in-law, Prof. Pendleton, adversely criticized through the *Harbinger* the actions of Burnet and the Cincinnati churches. Since Burnet was the impulse and initiator of the Bible Society, he felt the sting of Campbell's disapproval.

Campbell held to the view that there was no need for a Bible Society since one was available by operating through the Baptist organization; Burnet believed that funds could not be obtained to do an effective Bible distribution by that means. Campbell held that the infant colleges needed support before the introduction of a business concern for biblical publication and distribution; Burnet thought that both should be sustained. Campbell held that the action of organizing a Bible Society was "premature, that it was not sufficiently representative of the whole brotherhood";[81] and at this objection Burnet

---

[79]*Ibid.*
[80]*Ibid.*
[81]Garrison, *An American Religious Movement*, pp. 108, 109.

wrote Campbell a letter to which the great debater had no very effective rebuttal. Campbell, however, published Burnet's rebuke which said:

> Was there a convention of the churches to establish Bethany College, the claims of which must now be heard, and until they are heard the (Bible) Society must die in despair? The Society, composed of some hundreds, cannot ask aid of their brethren; but Bethany College, called into being by one brother, may.[82]

Campbell's great concern was that the young colleges were inadequately supported because Disciples of Christ were as yet not as liberal with their money as Baptists, Methodists, or Presbyterians.[83] At that time the brotherhood had three colleges: Bacon, Bethany, and Franklin. Having been president of Bacon, Burnet was mindful of the need for stewardship and cooperation among Disciples of Christ. In his view of things, none of the colleges could survive without some means of harnessing the benevolent spirits of the scattered peoples and churches.

Instead of becoming less scattered, the mobile population was even more on the move than earlier, thus creating a very extensive problem. On March 3, 1845, the annexation of Texas was complete in so far as the United States was concerned and Texas ratified the treaty the next June. A whole new empire had entered the political union and was open for missionary efforts. Burnet had no fear that the organization of societies would damage the colleges; his fear was that failure to act would cause the reformation to spend its energies for nothing but disintegration unless it should have a nucleus of polity by which to apply its power.

Shortly after the organization of the Bible Society, the Cincinnati brethren followed the lead of Burnet.

---

[82]*Millennial Harbinger*, 1845, p. 453. Cf. Garrison and DeGroot, *Disciples of Christ*, p. 243.

[83]Garrison, *Religion Follows the Frontier*, p. 185. Noted from *Millennial Harbinger*, 1845, p. 272.

They organized a Sunday School and Tract Society. This was a second agency to appear in the field asking for the benevolent support of the churches. Both agencies met in Cincinnati "on contiguous dates, and these meetings came to be called the 'Anniversaries.' "[84]

Cincinnati was a strategic center for Disciples of Christ to meet. It was a cultural and religious center, a city of churches. There were seventy-six congregations in the city in 1847.[85] The denominations and the number of churches representing each are as follows:

Presbyterian
    Old School, 4
    New School, 3
Congregational, 2
Methodist
    Episcopal, 12
    Protestant, 2
    Wesleyan, 2
    Episcopal South, 1
Bethel, 1
Associate Reformed, 1
Reformed Presbyterian, 1
Baptist, 6
Disciples of Christ, 5
Universalist, 1
Restorationist, 1
Christian, 1
German Lutheran and Reformed, 8
English Lutheran and Reformed, 2
United Brethren, 1
Welsh Calvinist, 1
Welsh Congregational, 1
Unitarian, 1
Friends, 2
New Jerusalem, 1
Catholic, 8 (2 of which were for German-speaking groups)

---

[84]Garrison and DeGroot, *Disciples of Christ*, p. 245.

[85]Henry Howe, *Historical Collection of Ohio* (Cincinnati: State of Ohio, 1888), Vol. I.

Jewish Synagogues, 2
Episcopal, 5
Second Advent, 1

Among all these churches there seemed to be none so aggressive on the slavery question as the Friends. Levi Coffin,[86] a Quaker, came to Cincinnati on April 22, 1847, and was a bitter opponent of slavery. The abolitionist views which were abroad in the country did not create as wide schisms in the churches of Disciples of Christ as they did among some of the more centrally organized congregations and national religious bodies. The ferment of agitation was severely affecting the whole social situation North and South. Burnet was alarmed because if the feeling reached a higher pitch even those who boasted a rational approach to religion might succumb to the ravages of war. Burnet's dream of cooperation and union was threatened. In alarm over the situation he decided not to accompany Mr. Campbell to England. Both had been invited to visit the churches in England. Burnet accompanied Campbell to New York (1847)[87] but did not think it wise to take the ship abroad.

Two situations developed in 1848 which indicated something of the teeming rivalry which began to exist between Alexander Campbell and D. S. Burnet. The first had to do with Campbell's opposition to "moral societies" and the probability that Burnet was a Mason; the second was related to the W. F. M. Arny case, wherein Arny was caught unintentionally in the middle of an argument between the Bethany and the Ohio brethren.

The dispute over participation in "moral societies" arose as the result of a cornerstone laying for a new Masonic Hall at Mount Pleasant, Hamilton County, Ohio. The program for the ceremonies was printed in full and

---
[86]Goss, *Cincinnati: Queen City*, pp. 192, 193.
[87]Robert Richardson, *Memoirs of Alexander Campbell* (Philadelphia: J. B. Lippincott, 1868-70), p. 543.

circulated widely. Someone must have sent a copy to A. Campbell with a note calling attention to item five, *Address by brother Burnet*. Campbell published the complete program in the *Millennial Harbinger*, evidently to challenge Burnet for participating in the function of lodges with their religious rites and ceremonies.[88] Campbell thought that all such ceremonies should be reserved as the function of the church alone. There is something almost to the point of intimidation in Campbell's published criticism:

> It is known to many that few of our brethren have been more esteemed and fraternally regarded by myself, or more beloved than Elder D. S. Burnet; and, in the ratio of that esteem and affection, my indignation burned at the appearance of his name in such a connexion as that noted in a former number [of the *Millennial Harbinger*]. I could neither understand nor believe it to be a proper representation of his position, but resolved to exonerate him from the charge, if false; and if true, to call for his defence—the matter being, as I presume, forwarded to me with that intent.[89]

There is no way of knowing all that Burnet must have written to Campbell, since Campbell published only the single statement, "My name was inserted in that programme contrary to my request and without my knowledge, and consequently the address was not delivered."[90] Apparently Burnet had yielded in deference to Campbell's vow to "call for his defence." Whether Burnet realized that his own growing popularity as a speaker in Ohio had something to do with Campbell's position, we cannot tell. It is not altogether amiss to surmise that Burnet's determined passion to enlist Campbell in behalf of the Societies had something to do with his appeasement of the Bethany leader.

---
[88]Shaw, *Buckeye Disciples*, p. 147. Cf. *Millennial Harbinger* (1848), 646.
[89]*Millennial Harbinger*, 1848, p. 646. (Brackets mine.)
[90]Shaw, *loc. cit.* Cf. *Millennial Harbinger*, 1848, p. 646.

In the same year (1848) a member of the Ohio Disciples of Christ published a statistical *Register* of Christian Churches. Alexander Hall listed the churches by states and counties and estimated the membership of each church. Mr. Campbell attempted in the *Millennial Harbinger* to discredit Hall's "Year Book." He criticized Hall for having "too much on hands to do anything well" and said that there was "too much of this uncalled-for and irresponsible editorship."[91] Campbell's criticism of Hall struck like a boomerang at one of his own staff, W. F. M. Arny, a solicitor for Bethany College and the *Harbinger,* because Arny had apparently examined the statistics and announced them accurate before publication.[92] Arny published an open letter accusing Hall of withholding some of the truth. Hall defended himself in a series of blasts in the columns of the *Gospel Proclamation.* The real issue is reflected in Henry K. Shaw's *Buckeye Disciples* (1952) where the Ohio historian says:

. . . Hall charged that Arny had told him the "Bishop's" opposition to the American Christian Bible Society arose from the fear that Cincinnati would become the Jerusalem of the Reformation instead of Bethany . . . W. K. Pendleton, representing the Bethany church, wrote to both Moss and Mitchell [two Ohio ministers of Disciples of Christ who claimed to be witnesses to Arny's statement], asking for the facts. Each replied Arny actually had made the statement concerning Campbell's opposition to the American Christian Bible Society, as Hall had claimed.[93]

In August, 1850, Hall visited Bethany and after a talk with Campbell seems to have stepped back into the good graces of his rival publisher. But the real clash was

[91]Shaw, *Buckeye Disciples,* p. 147. Cf. *Millennial Harbinger,* XIX (1848), 599, 600.
[92]*Ibid.,* pp. 155-160. See *Millennial Harbinger,* 1848, pp. 385-403, for complete correspondence and trial.
[93]*Ibid.,* pp. 155-160. (Brackets mine.)

between two growing centers of strength of the brotherhood, Bethany and Cincinnati. Campbell was the leader of the one and Burnet the leader of the other. Although they were friends, they were rivals. Many of the minor clashes grew out of the sensitivity abroad that they were rivals. Smaller figures among Disciples of Christ fell into disputes and sought to enlist the aid of the stronger persons in each center of growing strength.

Campbell expected to retain the Ohio constituency in support of Bethany College and the *Millennial Harbinger*. Burnet expected to enlist Campbell in support of the cooperative society system by which congregations would work together in programs of evangelization.

CHAPTER III

Diplomacy on the Frontier

1849: OPENING THE PURSE OF A BROTHERHOOD;
FIRST GENERAL CONVENTION OF DISCIPLES OF CHRIST

ON AND ON THE PULSING STREAM of population moving generally westward found Cincinnati the hub of East-West and North-South where travel and communication grew with the rapid improvement of the agricultural and transportational Ohio Valley. Trading posts in the frontier towns farther west sought their supplies in the Queen City. Trade with the South kept Cincinnati businessmen eager to keep down the slavery question. Cincinnati boasted its growing cultural and religious attainments, its libraries, churches, publishing houses, schools, medical and legal facilities. Not only favorable to the numerical growth of Disciples of Christ, the city was also favorable to the making of a center for religious organization. With the strange new adventures in settlement it was the rare person who knew the meaning of making and sustaining colleges,[1] missions, religious publications, benevolent institutions, and churches.

This new movement of Disciples of Christ for reformation of the church by emphasis upon the place of the "Word of God" demanded attention to the ways and means of circulating the Bible. A Bible Society alone was not enough; a Tract Society was inadequate. What the movement needed was a cooperative center from which persons could be sent to accomplish specific tasks in behalf of those who shared similar religious views and goals.

[1]Garrison, *Religion Follows the Frontier*, p. 218.

Unfortunately, the disjoined brethren had only a growing legalism as their primary bond of fellowship.[2] It was a legalism in which the "plan of salvation" was interpreted by terms of the "law" of the "Word of God." Many did not understand the distinction Mr. Campbell had made between Law and Gospel. Those who found themselves most closely bound by the ties of religious kinship were those who could recite most accurately what the Bible said—usually the King James Version. And since there was no express financial plan, with constitution and bylaws, to be found in the New Testament, there was no apparent need for applying modern organization methods to such an enterprise. It must be said for Campbell[3] and Burnet that they viewed practical righteousness and the spirit of Christian service as more important than exact "conformity to law." Legalism posed a problem to those who would call a general convention, because it had the aim of being both efficient *and* scriptural.[4] Modern ideas of efficiency are sometimes difficult to combine with ancient scriptural views, and both Campbell and Burnet favored what was "expedient."

Burnet favored a general meeting of representatives of Disciples of Christ because of his desire to implement further the functions of the Bible Society. Campbell favored the idea of a convention, also, with some reservations. He thought such a meeting important to the cause of the reformation, that it ought to be in Cincinnati, that it ought to be a delegate convention, that it ought to aim at efficient cooperation in the Bible cause, the missionary cause, and the education cause.[5] He did not think that

---
[2] *Ibid.*, pp. 195, 196.
[3] *Ibid.*
[4] Cf. *Millennial Harbinger*, 1849, pp. 475, 476. Quoted by A. R. Moore, *Alexander Campbell and the General Convention*, p. 40.
[5] *Ibid.*

the representation at such a meeting should be composed primarily of self-appointed messengers, editors and book publishers.⁶

Allen R. Moore says that Campbell wanted a more efficient and scriptural general church organization; and that

> It was not a Publication Society that he advocated, nor a Missionary Society, nor an Educational Society, nor a Benevolent Society; but a convention in which all these interests should be cared for, and every other interest that might arise to claim the attention and meet the approval of the churches.⁷

It is very doubtful if Campbell would have closed up his *Millennial Harbinger* or turned the direction of Bethany College over bodily to even a vastly representative general convention. In this he was not different from the other publishers and educators of the time. Burnet also had some private enterprise he hoped to build by the solicitation of members of the churches.

Both Campbell⁸ and Burnet desired a delegated general convention. Campbell preferred the name "messenger"⁹ for those representing the churches; Burnet simply wished to avoid the unrepresentative character of a self-appointed mass-meeting type of convention which would be overly representative of the nearest or most partisan churches.

At this point it is not possible to see clearly much difference in the viewpoints of Campbell and of Burnet. The historians have observed about Campbell that it "was his habit of mind to generalize rather than specialize."¹⁰ He was agreeable to the idea of a cooperative general convention; but he was unsettled in his accept-

---

⁶*Millennial Harbinger*, 1849, pp. 475, 476.
⁷A. R. Moore, *Alexander Campbell and the General Convention*, p. 41.
⁸*Ibid.*, pp. 40, 41.
⁹*Ibid.*
¹⁰*Ibid.*, p. 38.

ance of such societies as the Tract Society of Cincinnati which four local churches of Disciples of Christ had sponsored, or the Bible Society which had grown up from the same city and now claimed the support of the total brotherhood. It was significant, then, from the viewpoint of both Campbell and Burnet, that "The General Convention of the Christian Churches of the United States of America" was to begin its functions October 23, following the meetings of both the Tract Society and the Bible Society.

B. S. Lawson was president of the Cincinnati Tract Society at its second annual meeting which opened Monday evening, October 21, 1849. In his presidential address he showed himself to be deeply impressed that there were those abroad in the brotherhood who were saying that societies were sinful.[11] He said that when tracts were published by individuals they were designed to foster the "love of gain" rather than "love to God and man." The aim of the Tract Society, he said, was to give, not to gain.[12] The society owned nine tracts[13] with the following titles: (1) The Hundred Witnesses, (2) Manifestations of the Son of God, (3) On Faith, (4) On Baptism, (5) Conversion of the Eunuch, (6) Positive Divine Institutions, (7) On Repentance, (8) Duty of Repentance, and (9) On Dancing.

Burnet was present at the meeting of the Tract Society. The meeting was held in the church where he served as pastor. He seconded the motion adopting the report of the year's activities. Although he was not an officer of this society he was closely associated with James Challen, the corresponding secretary of that

[11] *Annual Proceedings*, 1849, p. 76, from *Proceedings of the General Convention of the Christian Churches (Disciples of Christ) and Other Societies Reporting to the Convention, 1849-1896* (1852 and 1855 excepted), microfilm (Indianapolis, Ind.: United Christian Missionary Society, n.d.).
[12] *Ibid.*, p. 81.
[13] *Ibid.*, p. 81.

body,[14] and was destined to play an active part in its history. Without understanding Burnet's very great concern for cooperatively disseminating educational materials through the printed word, it would be difficult to understand some important later events.

However, the society nearest to the heart of Burnet was the American Christian Bible Society which began its third annual meeting—before the opening of the general convention—in Christian Chapel, Eighth and Walnut Streets, Cincinnati. Burnet was the president of the Bible Society. It was meeting, as did the Tract Society, in the church where he spent his sixteen-year pastorate. The men who had most urged the missionary society as an auxiliary to the work of Disciples of Christ were those who comprised the board of the Bible Society. James Challen was recording secretary; John T. Johnson, John O'Kane, and Walter Scott were among the nine vice-presidents of the society and then later that evening became vice-presidents of the General Convention. Campbell was not present.

President Burnet went to the pulpit to give his annual presidential address to the Bible Society meeting shortly before noon on Tuesday. He was not a tall man, but firmly built and carefully dressed. Those who knew him were impressed with his dignified and commanding pulpit appearance. Well organized physically, he was similarly organized mentally.[15] He gave the impression of one having the capacity for great activity because of his highly centralized energy. Some thought his manners were generally a little formal and stiff. He had that aristocratic bearing which was a part of the illustrious clan of Burnets. Although very sociable and agreeable with his friends, he did not often break down that barrier of reserve he maintained as a gentleman and a

---
[14] *Annual Proceedings*, 1849, p. 83.
[15] Boles, *Biographical Sketches*, pp. 143, 144.

scholar. Not a few of his fellow preachers held him to be "the most eloquent preacher of the brotherhood during his generation."[16] Others said his oratory was of uneven merit and that he did better under certain circumstances and on suitable occasions.[17] At any rate, the annual meeting of his beloved Bible Society was a suitable occasion.

He began his address to an audience of approximately 150 assembled dignitaries of the Disciples' reformation movement. Beginning with a generalized and mystical introduction,[18] he expressed the great happiness at being together.[19] He saw the function of the Bible Society as that of sending forth the Word, the Bible which he regarded as "the exponent of divine will."[20] Burnet recognized the unprecedented growth of the movement of Disciples of Christ,[21] but he regarded it as only a beginning. With keenest insight, he proclaimed it easy to begin, but difficult to sustain, a great cause.[22] At this point in his speech he pulled forth his sharpest rapier and thrust it directly into the heart of the matter. He said that their responsibility was not a matter of believing more, but of doing more than others. The idea of quibbling over doctrinal matters was to Burnet the height of folly. One wonders whether this rapier thrust was at Alexander Campbell, for his constant views on doctrinal matters, or at these independent brethren who loved to speak of doctrine but avoided the subject of financial obligation.

Whatever the answer, Burnet was a practical Scotsman. He was aware of the Baptist missionary organiza-

---
[16]*Ibid.*, pp. 143, 144.
[17]*Ibid.*
[18]*Annual Proceedings*, 1849, p. 52.
[19]*Ibid.*, p. 53.
[20]*Ibid.*, p. 54.
[21]*Ibid.*
[22]*Ibid.*

tion[23] and saw in it the system for accomplishing great and good ends. He drove home the point that Disciples of Christ needed organization—"some permanent, common moral heritage, involving our duty to the world and to each other, which shall call us together, cement and warm our hearts."[24] After explaining why the Bible Society came into being (in order to spread the Word of God),[25] he reported on the year's activities[26] and congratulated the brethren from Indiana[27] on their progressive organizational moves. He expressed his own great dream in the following words:[28]

> Take another view of this matter. "Our Fathers, where are they; the Prophets, do they live forever?" Some are already gone, and we must soon be deprived of the pioneers of the cause, whose learning, zeal, sacrifices, and effective services have served so signally, to animate the whole body as one man. Before any one can say to the array of the faithful, "to your tents, O Israel," we wish to have some monument of their devotion and of our gratitude reared in our midst—some permanent, common moral heritage, involving our duty to the world and to each other, which shall call us together, cement and warm our hearts, and as the chosen engine of our power, apply effectively our Christian benevolence to the actual localities of frightful disease in all the valley of the shadow of moral death. So compacted, dismemberment need not be feared; but flourishing churches all over our land, sustained by a ministry competent to the exigencies of the times, would be electrified by intelligence from abroad of tribes and nations throwing their idols to the moles and the bats.

He saw, therefore, in a national society or convention a living monument, something permanent, the center of

---
[23] *Annual Proceedings*, 1849, p. 55.
[24] *Ibid.*
[25] *Ibid.*
[26] *Ibid.*, pp. 56, 57.
[27] *Ibid.*, p. 57.
[28] *Ibid.*, pp. 55, 56.

a common moral duty of fellowship and missions, a cohesive power, and the "engine" of common stewardship and benevolence. If such a dream could be realized there would not follow the "compaction and dismemberment" of scattered and independent churches. Only in such a cooperation could the brotherhood be freed from the incompetent minister working his way into the local churches and spoiling them.

As a means of raising money for the work of the Bible Society D. S. Burnet proposed that he be one of twenty persons to become Life Members of the Bible Society by paying into the treasury $25.00. His brother, Jacob Burnet, Jr., was one of the many who joined him in this pooling of resources. Some of those present were not happy with the existing translation of the Scriptures and offered to become Life Members in case a new translation could be assured.[29] Mr. Campbell's new translation of the New Testament, *The Living Oracles,* was at first a reprint of Geo. Campbell, Doddridge and McKnight with only minor changes. It was generally thought to need considerable revision.

Whether those present believed they could or would not afford the money to become life members or directors and used the plea for a new translation as an escape from the real issue is not easily determined. At any rate, the American Christian Bible Society meeting was conducted and its work of the third annual session finished before introduction of the "General Convention." The daytime sessions of the Bible Society ended and the evening of Tuesday, October 23, was devoted to the called "General Convention."

There were present 156 self- and church-appointed delegates from 100 churches in eleven states.[30] Most of them were there on their own individual initiative. In enroll-

[29]*Ibid.,* 1849, p. 68.
[30]Garrison, *Religion Follows the Frontier,* p. 186.

ment of delegates, Burnet enrolled with three others from First Church, Cincinnati. The Clinton Street Church was represented by five delegates and Second Church had three, making an even dozen from Cincinnati of the total 156.[31] They continued to meet in the church where Burnet was pastor. The first act of business when the general meeting opened was to name permanent officers of the convention. A. Campbell was strategically made president. Campbell's leadership was readily recognized. Even though he was absent, his cooperation earnestly was sought.

However, since the Sage of Bethany was not present, the function of presiding fell to Burnet.[32] The practical establishment of a means of cooperation was thrust once again upon the executive talents of the man who proved to possess perhaps the greatest practical organizing genius among them. He proceeded to name a committee on business for the following sessions with Elijah Goodwin, of Indiana,[33] as chairman. The Indiana brethren had sent a report to the Bible Society meeting, saying that they favored these societies for the implementation of the world program of the church.

In the meeting, but not named to the committee on business, was one of the most straightforward leaders of Disciples of Christ, John T. Johnson, of Kentucky. He had been associated with Burnet in the development of Bacon College and in publishing *The Christian Preacher.* He was concerned about stewardship and wanted Disciples of Christ to learn to give proportionately to their estate and wealth. So enthusiastic was he for missions that he thought A. Campbell ought to be sent to England as a missionary, and that Burnet ought to be sent to the Old World.[34]

---

[31]*Annual Proceedings*, 1849, p. 7.
[32]*Ibid.*, p. 5.
[33]*Ibid.*
[34]Power, *Sketches of Our Pioneers*, pp. 68, 69.

Johnson ordinarily wore a black broadcloth suit and when out of doors a black fur cap.[35] Remarkably direct in what he said, he usually came to the point without circumlocution or any subtle maneuvering prior to the attack.[36] It was this kind of head-on action which kept him always in the thick of the fight. No ornamentation, no poetry, no emotional appeals, he simply came to the point. In the Wednesday morning session of the convention, he asked if the object of their being there was not to inquire into the expediency of forming a missionary society. Because some were delaying the action and avoiding the difficult topic of discussion—since societies were widely frowned upon by certain independent brethren—Johnson wanted to know if they did not have all the right of expression on the subject. He urged that the matter be brought immediately upon the floor for a full opportunity for discussion.[37]

President Burnet explained that it was not generally understood that they had come there specifically to organize a missionary society.[38] This was a called convention of delegates and their names should be enrolled before others were admitted or the floor fully thrown open for debate and discussion. But Johnson wanted to get at the matter directly. During the noon hour he prepared a resolution:[39]

Resolved, That a missionary society, as a means to concentrate and dispense the wealth and benevolence of the brethren of this reformation, in an effort to convert the world, is both scriptural and expedient.

Resolved, That a committee of seven be appointed, to prepare a constitution for said society.

---

[35] W. C. Rogers, *Recollections of Men of Faith, Containing Conversations with Pioneers of the Current Reformation* (St. Louis: Christian Publishing Co., 1889), p. 53.
[36] *Ibid.*, p. 77.
[37] *Annual Proceedings,* 1849, p. 6.
[38] *Ibid.*
[39] *Ibid.*, p. 12.

The first resolution he believed met the general views of Campbell; the second met the practical requirements of Burnet. The adoption of Johnson's resolution was a turn of events not exactly favorable to the desires of either Campbell or Burnet. Campbell seemed to favor more a general national convention which had no departments or societies. Burnet was hoping that a missionary society would become a department, or "engine," of the greater cooperative structure.[40] Of all the societies, he saw the Bible Society as the one most basic to the restoration of biblical Christianity. A Publication Society would primarily publish the Bible; a Missionary Society would primarily circulate the Bible. The turn of events in the Convention which seemed most to accord with the views of Burnet was the presentation of resolutions which would have enlarged the American Christian Bible Society and created within it a "missionary department."[41]

The business committee under Goodwin's leadership saw to it that the Bible Society was given a clear bill of health and recommended to the brethren "throughout the United States and territories" and that the church ought to support and enlarge that society. This was equivalent to approval of the society system into which Burnet and his associates had brought them.[42]

But by the close of the afternoon session on Wednesday, October 24, Burnet as presiding officer recognized that there was a widespread belief that the Missionary Society ought to be a separate society and not an auxiliary of the Bible Society."[43] He therefore appointed the Committee of Seven, delegated to draft a constitution for the new Missionary Society. He appointed for

---

[40] Cf. *Annual Proceedings*, 1849; Speech to American Christian Bible Society, A. M., Oct. 23, 1849, pp. 52-58.
[41] *Ibid.*, 1849, p. 11.
[42] *Ibid.*, p. 14.
[43] *Ibid.*, p. 15.

this work the men closely associated with him as officers of the Bible Society, of which he was president: John O'Kane, John T. Johnson, H. D. Palmer, W. Scott, John T. Powell, and L. L. Pinkerton.[44] Of these men, it was L. L. Pinkerton who expressed at the Wednesday evening session the basic conception of Disciples of Christ that separate societies, like separate churches, must learn to cooperate. "Our existence as a people is involved in some general cooperation for the conversion of the world," he said.[45] He went further and said that institutions of the brotherhood should also learn to cooperate with the Protestant denominations, and inferred that the Bible Society meant to withdraw its cooperative relation with the American and Foreign Bible Society, a Baptist society. Burnet was quick to respond to this insinuation, showing that cooperation with that Baptist society had been the aim from the very inception of the American Christian Bible Society. Burnet said not only that Disciples of Christ aimed to cooperate with the Baptists in fostering the Bible societies, but that the American and Foreign Bible Society had approved the position taken by the Christians.[46]

By the end of the session on Wednesday night it was fairly clear to Burnet and the others what direction the general convention had taken. It was very much in accord with the views of the Indiana brethren who had sent the letter by their delegates, which had been read both to the Bible Society and to the general meeting by John O'Kane. The letter commended the American Christian Bible Society and noted that Indiana churches were requested to support it; it commended the work of the Cincinnati Christian Tract Society and recommended it to the support of the brotherhood; and the letter con-

[44] *Ibid.*
[45] *Ibid.*, p. 16.
[46] *Ibid.*, p. 16.

cluded by saying "we ought to form a regularly organized missionary society."[47] The general view was to support many societies in one cooperative convention, each finding its commendation in a representative body and each finding its support from a cooperative stewardship of money given for various causes on the part of the growing brotherhood. Professor Pendleton at the close of the Wednesday evening session announced that A. Campbell, of Virginia, was absent due to illness.

The convention had hardly agreed to form the new society before the question arose: Which society is the more important and the chief object of importance among cooperating enterprises of Disciples of Christ? The answer to that question disclosed a touch of genius on the part of President Burnet. When the question came before the convention, James Challen moved that the question could be settled by a select committee which included the presiding officer. Business was promptly suspended and the seven held a meeting. They were: Pendleton, Challen, O'Kane, Burnet, Scott, Kendrick and Johnson. They came back to the general assembly with a compromise suitable for adoption with only one dissenting vote. (At least one dissenting vote has been characteristic of congregational polity!) The final resolution was:

Resolved, That the missionary society which this convention may organize in accordance with the resolution already passed, be and is hereby recommended to the cordial support of the brethren, and that the Managers of the American Christian Bible Society be requested to furnish said missionary society with such Bibles as they may need in their missionary efforts.[48]

This was a most satisfactory solution to a difficult problem because T. J. Melish,[49] of the Second Church, Cin-

---
[47]*Annual Proceedings*, 1849, p. 13.
[48]*Ibid.*, p. 21.
[49]Melish was related by marriage to D. S. Burnet.

cinnati, had proposed to resolve the Bible Society into an Evangelical Society, for the promotion of both Bible and Missionary objects.[50] The debate over names and relationships[51] had been settled by the recognition that two or more societies could be mutually helpful, even as two churches, or two individuals. It was this practical working out of cooperative stewardship in which Burnet showed his greatest leadership.

His was an ecumenical spirit as further revealed by the invitation given through him to the convention delegates from the pastors of Baptist churches in Cincinnati. They would have delegates of Disciples of Christ preach at the Sunday services on October 28, in the local Baptist churches. The convention left the appointment of such persons to the discretion of Burnet.[52]

The constitution adopted for the Missionary Society was a reasonable facsimile of that already in effect for the Bible Society, with minor changes in details. Membership was to be on a money basis. A delegate could be a life member for $20.00 or a life director for $100.00.

There was so much enthusiasm at the time for taking memberships that, although Burnet was one of the first to subscribe $20, he was 26th down the line. The $100 amounts did not come in so quickly. Burnet was the first to be made a Life Director by the process of joint subscriptions.[53] Only three persons had subscribed the $100 to be made life directors before the following persons pooled their funds and made up an amount to constitute Burnet a Life Director: Dr. Marshall, C. H. Gould, Alexander Hall, Walter Scott, Dr. Ramsey, Mrs. S. W. Leonard, J. J. Moss and R. Bishop.[54] Probably because he was absent, Alexander Campbell was the last

[50] *Annual Proceedings*, 1849, p. 19.
[51] *Ibid.*, p. 20.
[52] *Ibid.*, p. 23.
[53] *Ibid.*, p. 26.
[54] *Ibid.*, p. 27.

person named to the office of Life Director. B. B. Howels, of Cincinnati, took it upon himself to subscribe the necessary $100.00.[55]

How often the details of the convention required the personal leadership of Burnet is revealed in some of the following incidents. On Friday morning, October 26, a resolution, to recommend that the churches hold quarterly meetings in every county and annual meetings in every district, came before the convention. This seemed like a directive from headquarters and drew immediate criticism. If one of the first acts of the new society was to tell churches what they must do, there were many present to oppose such action. The committee delegated to meet during the noon hour and solve this knotty problem of cooperation was headed by Burnet. Others were J. Young, S. Ayers, Palmer, Johnson, C. Kendrick, Pendleton, Scott, Barclay, and O'Kane.[56] Burnet's committee, recognizing that Disciples of Christ would not approve strong directives from a national society, softened the resolution to a respectful recommendation to the churches: "the propriety of forming among themselves State and District meetings, to be held annually and quarterly, in such a way as may seem to them most expedient."[57]

Another select committee became necessary for solution of the problem of developing a Sunday School Library. Burnet named nine persons for the committee, according to the convention's motion: Goodwin, Scott, Palmer, Challen, Morton, Young, Pendleton, Geo. Campbell, and Davenport. Then the convention insisted that Burnet himself become a part of that committee because of his previous crusade for such a Library.[58]

---
[55] *Annual Proceedings*, 1849, p. 27.
[56] *Ibid.*, p. 32.
[57] *Ibid.*
[58] *Ibid.*, p. 35.

The Ohio brethren had collected funds for a Sunday School Library. The Cincinnati Tract Society was already in existence. The convention proposed the union of these two resources and the making of the Tract Society a brotherhood society.[59] This connection of Burnet with the educational resources of the young brotherhood was to have future successes and failures in which Burnet figured prominently.

A committee of revision, to cooperate with the Publication Committee of the Tract Society,[60] was headed by Burnet, with others in the group designated as J. W. McCammon, G. R. Hand, W. P. Stratton, and Dr. Wm. Irwin.[61] The final act of the Saturday morning session, October 27, was to name a committee to prepare a catalogue of books already published which could be recommended to the brotherhood. Burnet was made chairman and the four other committeemen were Moss, Kendrick, Scott and Pendleton.[62]

Burnet, with Challen and Scott as fellow committeemen, was named chairman of a committee to "prepare a concise and appropriate address" to the Christian churches and brethren in general, setting forth the sentiments, principles, and measures agreed upon by the convention.[63] This was done later and showed the craftsmanship of Burnet (See Appendix III).[64] Near the close of the convention Walter Scott made a resolution which was unanimously adopted "that the thanks of the convention are due to D. S. Burnet, for the dignified, impartial and able manner in which he had presided over the deliberations of this assembly."[65]

---
[59]*Ibid.*, pp. 36, 37.
[60]*Ibid.*, p. 37.
[61]*Ibid.*, p. 38.
[62]*Ibid.*
[63]*Ibid.*, p. 39.
[64]*Ibid.*, pp. 21ff for a full statement of this "Address."
[65]*Ibid.*, p. 40.

The final act of business in the convention was to direct a letter of sympathy to be written by Brother Burnet, addressed to Elder A. Campbell on account of his recent illness which hindered his attendance at the meeting.[66] The general convention ended with the Saturday afternoon session.

That evening Burnet reconvened the Bible Society. According to his favorite method, he began the session, as almost every other session that had been conducted under his leadership, by reading from the Scriptures followed by a prayer. During the final session of the Bible Society, his friends constituted him a Life Director in that society by contributing the following amounts:[67]

N. T. Marshall,	$20
H. O. Clark,	$10
James Leslie,	$10
A. M. Leslie,	$10
S. S. Clark,	$ 5
C. H. Gould,	$10
Mrs. Bingham,	$ 5
G. S. Jenkins,	$10
Israel Garrard,	$10

This gesture was significant that his friends knew his first love was the cause of the Bible Society. He previously had been made a Life Director in the Missionary Society. It followed that the best reward they might bestow for his skilled and stalwart leadership in the history-making convention would be to recognize by a worthy token their appreciation of his feeling about the Bible Society.

Shortly Burnet called Walter Scott to the chair and then, in accord with the acceptable rules of order, moved that William Morton be constituted a Life Director of

---

66. *Annual Proceedings,* 1849, p. 40.
67. *Ibid.,* p. 71.

the Bible Society in accordance with Morton's prior agreement to pay into the Society treasury $100 in four annual installments.[68] Burnet never missed an opportunity to strengthen the cause of the church where a benevolent use of money was available.

The absence of the activities of Alexander Campbell in these meetings must not be construed as meaning that Campbell did not believe in the societies. He had been a supporter of the Bible Society, having given "his share of the profits from the publication of the Rice debate to the Bible Society, not to Bethany College."[69] Burnet sought the support of the churches for the Bible Society. Campbell sought support of the churches for Bethany College. The Tract Society went forth to gain general support of the brotherhood. Now the Missionary Society was in the field. This rivalry for financial support came into the picture at the very first.

Burnet's plans of stewardship and cooperation were in terms of constituted societies operating within the framework of the general convention. It was calculated that these societies would receive a greater and more stabilized financial support since now they were to be projected and nurtured by a representative assembly of a people presumably eager to cooperate in a magnificent enterprise for Christ and the church.

The historic sessions of 1849 were ended. Inspiration had been high and the work had progressed to the satisfaction of the vast majority of those who participated. Three days after the close of the convention, Dr. J. T. Barclay (son-in-law of Alexander Campbell), of Scottsville, Virginia, in a letter to the Board of Managers of the A. C. M. S., offered with his wife and three teen-age children—two sons and a daughter —to go to Jerusalem as a missionary for the salvation

---

[68]*Ibid.*

[69]Garrison, *Religion Follows the Frontier*, p. 185.

of the "Jews, Mohometans or Pagan Idolators."[70] This connection with the Society was to be one of the unique missionary efforts of history.

Soon after the convention, Burnet set forth an *Address* designed to be informative of what the meeting had accomplished. Challen and Scott were delegated to give some assistance in framing the report to the brotherhood,[71] but the style and the central ideas so reflect those of Burnet that his views are best seen in the exact transcript (see Appendix III).[72]

The *Address to the Churches* is of such far-reaching significance in the formative years of organization of Disciples of Christ that it might be placed along with Thomas Campbell's famed *Declaration and Address* and the *Last Will and Testament of the Springfield Presbytery*. It explains many of the actions of the brotherhood. It helps clarify the idea of fostering the first foreign mission to Jerusalem, and why such action was taken.

Dr. James T. Barclay, of Virginia, was one of the vice-presidents of Burnet's Bible Society board. The dream of Jerusalem as a center in which to send forth Bibles was primarily that of Burnet and his contemporaries in the early days of that institution. Part of the business of the Bible Society was carried on through income from Bibles. Burnet and James Challen placed a notice in the first Year Book of Disciples of Christ, saying,

> For the present, applications, accompanied with the cash, for Bibles and Testaments, and transmissions of donations, should be made to the President or Corresponding Secretary.[73]

After all, the societies which emerged from the first general convention were very much in accord with the

---
[70] *Annual Proceedings*, 1849, p. 90.
[71] *Ibid.*, p. 39.
[72] *Ibid.*, pp. 41-46.
[73] *Ibid.*, p. 51.

views of Alexander Campbell. It remained for the executive genius of Burnet and his influential followers to enlist Campbell's leadership in the further program. Campbell insisted on a general convention which would have no authority over matters of faith, ordinances or worship.[74] This is exactly what was achieved. Burnet saw these new institutions as the center from which could be cultivated the benevolent spirit of the members. Campbell held that the form of the organization ought to be left to be determined as any other expedient.[75] This, also, was done. Campbell advocated that a general convention could bring about some agreement among Disciples of Christ on such matters as the press, missions, Bible translation, religious tracts, and moral agencies of every sort "necessary to the prosperity of the churches and the conversion of the world."[76] This was done.

Both Campbell and Burnet had personal interests which could not be overcome in a single gesture. Campbell was not disposed to turn the work of Bethany immediately to a committee or board of the general convention, or to any group of messengers the convention might elect; nor was it necessary. Burnet had similar publishing interests. Neither was he disposed to weaken the already achieved structure of the Bible Society which was under his guidance.

Also the fear of ecclesiasticism always confronted these men in their dilemma. If they yielded to a national organization, what were the guarantees against authoritarian ecclesiasticism taking over at the top? If they yielded to extreme independency, what was to prevent erratic sectarianism from depleting all the resources for doing the work of the church? Whether Campbell would

---
[74]Cf. *Millennial Harbinger*, 1849, pp. 272, 273. Also, quoted in A. R. Moore, *Alexander Campbell and the General Convention*, p. 46.
[75]*Ibid.*
[76]*Ibid.*

have been as willing as Burnet to yield to some kind of compromise, as was the case, is surely speculation. Logically, Campbell would have done something very similar to that achieved by those at the convention, or the convention would have ended in utter confusion and an impasse between editors, preachers, educators.

Allen R. Moore believes that a weak spot was in the organization convention because of the publishing interests. There were more than twenty periodicals among Disciples of Christ at that time. Burnet and Campbell were not the only editors and publishers. Most of the editors were present for the convention.[77] The amazing diplomacy of Burnet is the more signal achievement because no general convention could have controlled the independent action of these men. They, because of the movement to which they were committed, were allowed the high privilege of volunteering their cooperation.

The sanest and most profitable action was that which made a move in the direction of total brotherhood stewardship and cooperation. This was the basic structure and function Burnet had sought in the Bible Society. It must be recognized distinctly that Burnet led in a movement to seek to control and administer only what belonged to the churches jointly. It was to be done in the cooperation of these national societies, each responsible for cooperation with the other very much as local churches maintain a fellowship and similar to the working together of one Christian person with another.

In 1932, H. Leo Boles in his *Biographical Sketches of Gospel Preachers* is very laudatory of the work of D. S. Burnet except at one point. He says, "It is to be regretted that he [Burnet] went off into the meshes of human organizations known as 'missionary societies.' "[78] This reflects the uncooperative spirit which ultimately

---

[77] A. R. Moore, *Alexander Campbell and the General Convention*, p. 61.
[78] Boles, *Biographical Sketches*, p. 144.

led to the division, in 1907, between the Christian Church or Disciples of Christ, and the Church of Christ.

Independency was present at the founding convention, but the majority of leaders in that generation knew the efficient and scriptural means employed for cooperative enlistment of funds for religious causes was in the process of development. They, a hundred years ago, realized that only a superior financial stewardship, made possible by a voluntary association, could validate the claims that Christian churches were wanting "Christian union" and "to save the world."

Immediately following the annual meeting, Burnet sent the letter which the Convention instructed him to write to Mr. Campbell. There was a significant absence of any stress on the idea of a Publication Society and there was a double reference to the other two societies. No reference whatever was made to a relapse from recovery from illness which might have made Campbell's absence necessary. The emphasis was upon the success of the work. The letter follows:

Hygeia, Mt. Healthy, O., Oct. 29, 1849.

Bro. A. Campbell—*My Dear Sir:* We were much disappointed that you were not at the Bible Society Anniversary and the General Convention. Indeed, we expected you to be with us at Christian Chapel the Sunday preceding. When Bro. Pendleton appeared in the Convention, and informed us that your absence occurred in consequence of illness, from which you had recovered before his departure, we felt gratified for your recovery, though compelled to sympathize with you in an affliction which was a disaster to us, as it deprived the Convention of your society and counsel. The Convention, over which you were elected President, has requested me to assure you of their sympathy and prayers—a duty most genial to my feelings, the more especially as I can, in the same communication, contribute to your joy, by announcing a happy issue of our meeting. About five thousand dollars were raised in money, and pledges for our various enterprises, but especially for the Bible and Missionary Societies, which shared about equally in the munificence. I never knew so fine a meeting. It lasted one week, and filled us full of joy and love. The representatives of the churches from abroad, amounted to about two hundred.

Suffer me, then, my dear brother, in behalf of the Convention, to express their sympathies with your sorrow, and their joy at your recovery; and through you, to your numerous readers, the joyful news of our incipient success in the kindred enterprises of the Bible and Missionary causes.

For the Convention,
D. S. BURNET,
First Vice President, but
acting President

1850: NEGOTIATIONS WITH A. CAMPBELL

Some of those who are familiar with the thought of Alexander Campbell are of the opinion that his views on church organization and cooperation were clearly unheeded in the formation of the society system. Campbell had wished a plan of cooperation of delegated representatives who, in national meetings, had no authority to legislate for the churches.[79] Burnet also favored the delegated convention idea which never seemed to materialize because the national meetings from the first were more or less mass meetings which brought forth the societies. If Campbell and Burnet wanted a cooperative body that had neither power nor authority to legislate for the churches, they certainly achieved that end in the organizational pattern that followed.

By 1850 the organizing of functioning systems was an achieved reality. Burnet had given the talents of his genius for such matters wholeheartedly to the purpose of harnessing the powers of cooperation. If the structure of the expedient for doing cooperative work was not

---

[79] Cf. *Millennial Harbinger*, 1845. Also, Garrison and DeGroot, *Disciples of Christ*, p. 517.

everything Campbell desired, neither was it all that other brethren wanted. But it was a step in the direction of saving the movement from disintegration; a step very much desired by Burnet.

The problem most apparent to Burnet was to enlist Campbell's blessing upon these projects. Of the three societies which Burnet had led into existence, only one had in it a major threat to Campbell's private Bethany enterprises. It was the Tract Society. This society was the one which logically could become a denominational publishing house, a challenge to private publishing enterprises abroad among Disciples of Christ.

The Bible Society at that time was considered the vital work of the brotherhood. More than half of the sessions, as we shall see, were devoted in October, 1850, to its interests. The Missionary Society as a means of implementing the spread of biblical knowledge was suitable to Campbell's purposes because Bethany College could train missionaries. The ambitious achievement of a vast mission to the world was generally envisioned by all; besides, Dr. J. T. Barclay, groomed to be the first foreign missionary since he offered himself in 1848 for that work, was Alexander Campbell's son-in-law. Inasmuch as Barclay had been sent to Jerusalem as a missionary, and inasmuch as world mission work demanded implementation, it was necessary that some kind of centralism and connection with the churches should be developed. Burnet saw clearly the financial responsibility needed for such a vast enterprise as that which was under construction.

It is highly probable that he must be credited with the diplomacy that took for himself a secondary position in the organizational movement. He seems clearly to have fostered Campbell's position with the societies in order that Disciples of Christ might cooperate to better advantage in their general stewardship and enlistment of funds. This view is substantiated by the events of 1850.

Burnet's statement of the purposes of the three societies[80] claimed in that year first place for the American Christian Bible Society, not for the Missionary Society. In an "Address to the Churches of Christ in North America" he says:

Beloved Brethren:

You are aware that certain Christian associations have originated with the disciples,[81] meeting from time to time, in conventions, at Cincinnati, with the express object of carrying out the benevolent design of the Christian religion, in the conversion of the world, and the union, prosperity, and peace of the churches of the saints. Among these is the *American Christian Bible Society;* which recognizes the Hebrew of the Old Testament, and the Greek of the New, as the only authoritative standard; and that it is the duty of Christians to acquaint the human family with the revelations contained therein, by faithfully translating and circulating them throughout the world.

Also, the *Christian Tract and Sunday-school Society;* the objects of which are to diffuse the knowledge of the Christian religion, by the publication and circulation of religious tracts, and a Sunday-school Library, with special reference to the wants of our brotherhood, and the interests of our children.

Also the *American Christian Missionary Society;* the object of which is to promote the preaching of the gospel in this and other lands. It is designed for home and foreign purposes; to meet the wants of our own population, in such destitute portions of the country as may stand the most in need of our aid; and to send the gospel to other lands, not only those sitting in darkness, and in the region of the shadow of death, but in those but partially enlightened in the great matters pertaining to the Christian religion.[82]

---

[80]*Annual Proceedings*, 1850, p. 3.

[81]Note Burnet's use of "disciples" not as a proper name, but without the capital "D."

[82]*Annual Proceedings*, 1850, p. 3.

From the relationship existing between these societies in 1850 it may be argued with considerable effectiveness that Burnet as president of the Bible Society was regarded as the leader of the Christian Church movement. This view is further observed in the review of other factors in the total situation.

Early in May, 1850, Burnet House, an elegant new Cincinnati hotel, had been opened with a grand soiree, beginning the era of one of the magnificent public places of its time. Burnet House was described as "more like a palace than a house of public entertainment,"[83] and Uncle Jacob, the owner, was very proud of it. Cincinnati continued to be the hub of political and religious agitation.

The antislavery discussions were not pleasant topics because of the growing commercial and social relations. However, the slavery and sectionalism issues largely determined the course of politics in Ohio.[84] The dreams that Cincinnati should be the literary heart of the nation suffered a severe blow when Alice and Phoebe Cary moved to New York City after their fifteen years of weekly receptions for the writers and artists of the world.[85]

The educational life of Disciples of Christ went forward rapidly. Even though Bacon College, where Burnet had been president, was discontinued temporarily,[86] many other schools were springing up; e.g., at Midway, Kentucky; Hiram, Ohio; Indianapolis, Indiana; Eureka, Illinois; Columbia, Missouri; Abingdon, Illinois; Jacksonville, Illinois; Oskaloosa, Iowa; and in Arkansas.[87] The rivalry for educational leadership reached new heights in much the same way that the competition for leadership in

---

[83] *The Ohio State Archaeological and Historical Quarterly*, Vol. 59, No. 2, p. 143. Cf., Vol. LVI, 1947, pp. 36, 37.

[84] "Ohio," *Ency. Amer.*, XVI (1951), 618.

[85] Goss, *Cincinnati: Queen City*, p. 201.

[86] Garrison, *Religion Follows the Frontier*, p. 169. Cf. Garrison and DeGroot, *Disciples of Christ*, p. 224.

[87] *Ibid.*, p. 218.

the publication field continued unabated. Burnet entered into a publishing partnership with Benjamin Franklin in which they produced the *Reformer* and the *Christian Age* for one year (1850).

Franklin was an experienced editor and publisher, having started his editorial career in January, 1843, as editor of the sixteen-page *Reformer* which was first published at Centerville, Indiana, then moved to Milton, Indiana. He was for some seven years editor of this publication before joining into partnership with Burnet.[88] Franklin resembled Burnet in his belief that wholesome controversy was a means of arriving at ultimate truth. Of about twenty-five public debates, Franklin succeeded in publishing and circulating five of them.[89]

But in physical appearance he was considerably different from Burnet. He was a six-foot, 190-pound individual. His large gray eyes and prominent mouth gave the impression of sincerity of purpose, as his broad chest suggested he was equal to all kinds of heavy tasks.[90] He was neither the writer nor speaker that Burnet had proved to be, although he became author of a tract, *Sincerity Seeking the Way of Heaven,* which had the largest sale of any such tract published prior to the Civil War among Disciples of Christ.[91] Franklin was a writer for the masses, Burnet was a writer for the leaders of the masses.

Theirs was a significant partnership. Burnet had come into possession of the *Christian Age* which had been started in 1845 by T. J. Melish. The *Age* absorbed Walter Scott's *Protestant Unionist* in 1848. Burnet began in 1850 to use this journal for promoting and reporting the new national societies.[92]

---
[88]Moore, *Living Pulpit,* p. 340.
[89]*Ibid.,* p. 339.
[90]*Ibid.,* p. 340.
[91]*Ibid.*
[92]Garrison and DeGroot, *Disciples of Christ,* p. 257.

While these journals were maintained by free enterprise they advocated cooperative stewardship of funds. The logical conclusion from their own announced policies and to their position among Disciples of Christ was that they should be owned and operated by the brotherhood. But that ownership was not transferred until 1853 and it did not last long after transferral.

When the Bible Society meeting proceeded with its business, Tuesday afternoon, October 22, 1850, there were three items of business which offered occasions for controversy: (1) the proposal to amend the constitution in order to eliminate the money basis of membership in the societies; (2) the matter of Bible translations and the consideration of plans whereby a cooperative translation might be made and financed; and (3) the establishment of a press for the use of the societies.[93]

The first item was thrust into the convention with the usual straightforwardness of John T. Johnson, of Kentucky, who offered an amendment to the A. C. B. S. constitution:

Resolved, That the subject be referred to a committee, with instructions so to amend the constitution of this society, as to abolish life memberships, and memberships the basis of which is money.[94]

The convention unanimously set aside the money basis of membership. Generally the thought seemed to be that by making the "widow's mite" acceptable there would be no need for traveling agents and thus it would be possible to spend for other purposes the money previously used in sending agents to raise funds.

There were several difficulties with the new requirement for membership. Those who had paid a hundred-dollar membership the year before now found they might

---

[93] *Annual Proceedings,* 1850, p. 16. See report of committee on business.
[94] *Ibid.*

become members for nothing. Those who thought the dismissal of the emphasis on money would enlist greater generosity were due for a shock. But Burnet was able to steer a course that eventuated into harmony. His work is reflected in the revised Article III of the Bible Society constitution which neither abandoned the pursuit of funds nor made membership a simple dollars-and-cents proposition. The revised Article III read:

> Art. III. Any church, Bible co-operation, or other Christian organization, placing its surplus funds in the treasury of this Society, shall have the right to appoint one member, for each annual contribution, and for every fifty dollars contributed by it, it shall be entitled to another member, and all persons heretofore constituted life members, or life directors, shall continue in the enjoyment of their rights.[95]

This was a very different proposal from the one of John T. Jones, of Illinois, that the constitution be so amended as to entitle each and every congregation to a delegate, upon the payment of a stipulated sum. It was in such discussions that the whole matter of the delegate manner of organization came into the open. Some had attacked the delegate system of organization. Burnet, like Campbell, saw the weakness of mass meetings.[96]

The convention attacked the problem of a new Bible translation in a resolution offered by Jacob Burnet, Jr., David's brother, commending the work of the "Bible Union" plan and urging the convention to appoint a committee to get information from the "Bible Union" and other sources and make a report at the next annual meeting. This committee was appointed Thursday evening, October 24, 1850.

Alexander Campbell had arrived at noon that day and had presided over the afternoon session of the Mission-

---
[95] *Annual Proceedings*, 1850, p. 16.
[96] Garrison and DeGroot, *Disciples of Christ*, p. 248. Cf. *Proclamation and Reformer*, 1850, p. 371.

ary Society. He participated in the discussions of the Bible Society at the night session, over which Burnet was presiding. Campbell's interest in such a translation was reflected in the fact of his own contribution to a published New Testament text, *The Living Oracles* (1832).[97]

Not much was said on the floor of the convention about the establishment of a press. It was in the mind of all, no doubt, that Campbell opposed a publication society. A brotherhood press, owned by the societies, would aid and expand the work of cooperation. But the large number of editors and publishers present caused some willingness to move slowly in that direction, in sympathy with the cautious and obviously antagonistic position taken by Campbell. The outstanding enthusiast for such a project was D. S. Burnet. On this matter Burnet and Campbell were poles apart in their views.

The clear relationship of Bethany College with the infant Missionary Society is reflected in a motion made by James Challen on the last afternoon of the convention—after Campbell had arrived upon the scene. Challen moved, and it was adopted, that, in view of the destitution of the home and foreign field, the convention "recommend to the churches everywhere, to select, train up, and educate pious young men, under the auspices of Bethany College, for the great work of missions, and of the ministry of the word."[98]

At the Friday evening session of the Bible Society meeting, James Challen presented an even stronger resolution in behalf of Bethany to the effect that the convention recommend to the brethren generally that they take efficient steps to aid in endowing fully the college, on the proposed plan of scholarships in that institution. This final session had recessed long enough to hear an

---

[97] See pp. 117ff for further discussion of translation work.
[98] *Annual Proceedings*, 1850, p. 45.

address by Campbell. It was the session in which Burnet, the diplomat, had enlisted the cooperative efforts of Campbell, the leader.

It will be remembered that Campbell was not present the previous year at the organizational meeting of the Missionary Society. In his absence he had been made president. A glance at the schedule of the meetings in 1850 indicates the lateness of Campbell's arrival, as well as the importance of Burnet's chairmanships.

SCHEDULE OF 1850 CONVENTION MEETINGS

SOCIETY	DATE		TIME	PRESIDING
CCTS	Mon.,	Oct. 21, 1850	P. M.	Burnet opened meeting by reading Scriptures
ACBS	Tues.,	Oct. 22, 1850	10 A.M.	Burnet
ACBS	Tues.,	Oct. 22, 1850	2 P.M.	Burnet
ACBS	Tues.,	Oct. 22, 1850	7 P.M.	Burnet
ACBS	Wed.,	Oct. 23, 1850	8 A.M.	Burnet
CCTS	Wed.,	Oct. 23, 1850	10 A.M.	This special meeting of the Tract Society, which was to be the Publication Society, met for naming a new committee to revise the society's constitution. Note the committee named: A. Campbell, chm.; D. S. Burnet; J. T. Johnson, James Challen; and T. J. Melish
ACMS	Wed.,	Oct. 23, 1850	2 P.M.	Burnet presided "A. Campbell, of Bethany, Virginia, not being present."
ACBS	Wed.,	Oct. 23, 1850	7 P.M.	Burnet
ACBS	Thurs.,	Oct. 24, 1850	8 A.M.	Burnet
ACMS	Thurs.,	Oct. 24, 1850	2 P.M.	"President A. Campbell in the chair." He had arrived only shortly before.
ACBS	Thurs.,	Oct. 24, 1850	7 P.M.	Burnet
CCTS	Fri.,	Oct. 25, 1850	A.M.	Society met according to appointment.
ACMS	Fri.,	Oct. 25, 1850	2 P.M.	A. Campbell
ACBS	Fri.,	Oct. 25, 1850	7 P.M.	Burnet

From the above schedule it is seen that Campbell presided over two of the fourteen sessions. The president of the Tract Society presided over three of them. Burnet presided over nine of the sessions, including one of the American Christian Missionary Society before President Campbell arrived. On the basis of Campbell's apparent reluctance to attend the meetings of the societies and the obvious gestures of favor which Burnet's intimate friends made toward Bethany College, it becomes a fair assumption that the chief business of the meetings of the societies in 1850 was to integrate Campbell into a place of recognized leadership in the cooperative fund-raising and disbursing plans of Disciples of Christ. From the record it is quite clear that the strategy which achieved this end was conceived and executed primarily by Burnet.

What was the real reason that Campbell was reluctant to identify himself with the cooperative societies? The answer to that question seems clearest when one studies the works and purposes of D. S. Burnet. The primary reason for Campbell's caution was not his recent illness and not the delays encountered by travel on the Ohio River. It was plainly his strong disfavor of the arising publication plans of the brethren.

When Pendleton, president of Bethany, delivered the silver anniversary address of the American Christian Missionary Society (1874), he said, in answer to the critics who claimed that Campbell was hoodwinked into his relationship with the Missionary Society:

> This was the work of no faction; of no ambitious, scheming demagogues; of no unsound progressionists; of no clique, conclave or club. It was the ripened fruit of twenty-five years of prayerful growth under an ordeal of persecution and misrepresentation and multiplied conflicts with friends false within and enemies fierce without; it was the wisdom of the heroic pioneers of the Reformation whose lives had been stamped with many and

signal evidences of providential guidance; it was the united voice of leaders than whom none truer or braver ever bore in the battle's front the battle of our King; it was an open field movement when Israel's hosts arrayed themselves for nobler achievements, and foremost in the ranks rang the veteran voices of Campbell and Scott, Burnett and Johnson, and Smith and Challen, and Allen and Rogers, and Fall and others who are of the immortal few whose names a grateful brotherhood will not suffer to be forgotten or defamed."[99]

The truth about Campbell's absence in 1849 and his late arrival in 1850 seems ultimately to have been expressed by Pendleton himself. That is, that Campbell had sent as his personal representative his son-in-law, President Pendleton, of Bethany, "to keep the Bible Society out of the publications field and to convey his determination not to accept the presidency unless his prescribed bounds were honored."[100]

In his address before the twenty-fifth anniversary meeting of the Missionary Society, the principal speaker, W. K. Pendleton, had in his audience the venerable James Challen who was the first corresponding secretary of the convention and who in Campbell's absence delivered the first annual address. Pendleton recalled to Challen's memory the events by saying:

A few of us who were younger twenty-five years ago are here, and, I thank God, still standing by the flag which the fathers unfurled; but you, our venerable Challen, you were our first corresponding secretary; and when, through the caprices of Ohio river navigation, our first president was prevented from reaching the first anniversary of the society in time to open the proceedings, you were appointed by the Board to deliver the first annual address. Do you remember your first words on that

---

[99] L. C. Woolery, *Life and Addresses of W. H. Woolery, LL.D.* (Cincinnati: Standard Pub. Co., 1893), p. 425.

[100] Dwight E. Stevenson, *Walter Scott: Voice of the Golden Oracle* (St. Louis: Christian Board of Publication, 1946), p. 198. Source, Benjamin L. Smith, *Alexander Campbell* (St. Louis: The Bethany Press, 1930) pp. 254-58.

memorable day? "The cause of missions is the cause of God. It is the chief instrumentality in the propagation of the gospel." So you said then, and so you believe now.[101]

But Pendleton is said to have explained Campbell's views in a very different manner to Benjamin L. Smith shortly before the Bethany College president's death.[102] Some had said that Campbell's poor health was the reason for his absence, but Burnet's letter following the 1849 convention (to tell Campbell of his election to the Missionary Society presidency) indicated that all were aware that poor health was not the total reason. Others had said that recent bereavement in his family prevented his presence.

Although it is impossible to prove a point by what one man says a deceased person told him, the close examination of other factors indicates a strong probability that Smith was very accurate when he said:

> W. K. Pendleton, with whom I discussed this matter just a short time before his death, told another story: that Mr. Campbell felt a newly organized tract and publication society was a slight on his own work of publication, and that he therefore refused to attend the Cincinnati conference. Instead he sent Mr. Pendleton as his personal representative, bearing his protest that if the tract and publication society were dissolved, then only would he accept the proffered presidency of the missionary society.[103]

If that were so, Campbell accepted his place in the leadership of the Missionary Society without having destroyed at once the emerging Publication Society. When members made Campbell chairman of the constitutional revision committee of the society, they placed him in a strategic position to strike whatever blow he might wish at the plans for cooperative publications.

---

[101] Francis Marion Green, *Christian Missions and Historical Sketches* (St. Louis: John Burns, 1884), pp. 72, 73.
[102] Smith, *Alexander Campbell*, pp. 254, 255.
[103] *Ibid.*

The years that followed told the story. The fact remains that Burnet and the others created a situation which made it difficult for Campbell not to accept a place of leadership in the societies.

Now that the Bible, Tract, and Missionary societies had been organized, Burnet saw that there would follow a period of testing. He said:

These several enterprises, brethren, are thrown into the bosom of the church of God, to be nourished "as a nurse cherisheth her children." The hour of our associated strength has arrived, the hour which shall demonstrate our union to be more than uniformity of sentiment, a oneness of mind, and of effort arising from the nature, power and exaltation of the holy truth believed. This year is to prove us. It will be decisive of our character and our destiny. The spirit which we shall now exhibit will be the augury of our fate.[104]

---

[104] Green, *Christian Missions*, pp. 119, 120.

CHAPTER IV

Deserved Leadership

1851-1854: AMERICAN BIBLE UNION PROJECT

DURING THE WINTER OF 1852-53 a new publishing venture was taking form under the leadership of Burnet and some of his brethren associated closely with the publication of *The Christian Age*. This new concern was to be a $40,000-stock company which would seek support of the brotherhood and would divide its profits between the causes acclaimed by Disciples of Christ and the stockholders. It was designed to be similar in structure to the Methodist Book Concern (with a branch in Cincinnati) which turned its proceeds to the support of retired and disabled ministers. However, among the Christian Church enterprises the work of the Bible Society and that of the Missionary Society were to have first claim if and when the "Bible Union" publishing concern made a profit.

The American Bible Union aimed to foster the revision and perfecting of the English version of the Scriptures among its other plans. No special interest seemed to be directed toward accepting Alexander Campbell's version of the New Testament as sufficient to meet the needs of the times. It was an era when all over America the need for revision seemed imperative and Campbell's *The Living Oracles* had been in print for twenty years.

Later, Burnet went to New York where he addressed the Bible Union meeting, October 6, 1854. He made a strong plea for the correction of the English version at the hands of the American Church. "Our common version," he said, "though defective, was good when made, and notwithstanding Criticism and Hermeneutics have been born since, is good yet, but as a good thing is susceptible of improvement it is our duty to make it better. Without re-performing the oft-repeated labor of detailing the errors of the common version, I shall proceed to the consideration of the proposition 'that the correction of our English version is demanded at the hands of the American Church.' "[1]

He believed that there were four adequate reasons why a new translation of the Bible should be made by the American Church: (1) because the Christians of the New World were free, inventive, and untrammeled and had never yet engaged in such an enterprise; (2) because America was the divinely chosen theater of new measures as well as of new men; (3) because the American Church was the Congress of all Churches—a Congress of full representation and equal rights (even though he recognized that most of the supporters of the Bible Union were immersionists he did not favor excluding any denomination); and (4) because America was developing some initiative in popular free education and as Americans learned to read they ought to have access to a pure classic translation of the Bible.[2]

It was a strong conviction with D. S. Burnet that God has a right to be heard through his Word in the vernacular by both immersionists and nonimmersionists. He expressed before the Bible Union his views of divine revelation. He viewed the Bible as "the light of life."[3] In a masterful use of illustration and figure of speech, Burnet said: "Let us lay off the armor of the English Saul and taking the sling and five smooth stones of David, let us meet the giant Goliath (Romanism), trusting in the living God." He compared the English version of the

[1] *Annual Proceedings*, 1854, p. 13.
[2] *Ibid.*, p. 14.
[3] *Ibid.*, p. 18.

Bible with the cumbersome and unwieldy armor of Saul as David arrayed himself for battle against Goliath.

Not only in the battle with Romanism did he see the need for a revised American version; he thought that the horde of skeptics also might be silenced. The peculiar position held by the Bible deserved and demanded a pure version as could be had in America. He said:

> The Bible is the fundamental law of Christianity; the original law of the Church. In it God has defined his own rights and ours, and has set the bounds of all duty and privilege. It is clothed with the majesty of Law and the loveliness of Grace. It develops God, our Father, and Jesus the Son of the Father and our elder brother, by the Spirit of all truth and purity and power. Christ's paraclete and our sanctifier. It is our guide-book in life, our solace in death and our promise of life and glory.
>
> "Most wondrous book! bright candle of the Lord!
> Star of eternity! the only star
> By which the bark of man could navigate
> The sea of life, and gain the coasts of bliss securely!"
>
> This book and this book only is the bullion of religious commerce. It is of value, and of equal value, in every Christian clime, in the chamber of the conscience, in the church, and in the consistory; all assume to bow before its majesty, and seek an inspiration of its spirit. It is the true foundation of the Church. In assuming these Living Oracles, we assume all truth, without mixture of error; in rejecting every other foundation, we reject all error, without discrimination in favor of any. It is the shortest way of cutting bad acquaintance, and the best method of getting into good company. Here, I am "in Abraham's bosom," and have Isaiah for my familiar teacher; I weep with Jeremiah and sympathize with Job, in strains of the loftiest tempo and the most stately measure, I join Daniel in his visions of empires, and John in his views of the celestial city and palace of the Divine Holiness. Companion of Adam by faith, I am Jehovah's auditor, and by the Creator I am initiated into the mysterious origin of things. From the sun, I see this spark of fire stricken out, and around its central heat, mouded

a green and beautiful earth, and glorious skies, replete with life, life in the sea, life in the land, and life in the air, each form of existence, vegetating, breathing, or thinking in harmony with its sphere, deriving light from a far-off sun and elaborating life from the air. I learn more than Milton sung of Paradise enjoyed, Paradise lost and Paradise regained. The two eternities, 'twixt which our narrow neck of time is interjected, like the northern prairies and southern pampas of our own magnificent continent, spread out before me, in scenes of primeval glory and sempiternal bliss.[4]

There was nothing in the speech which referred directly to the fact that the Bible Union was in the process of undergoing a severe criticism by one of the editors of the *Millennial Harbinger*. W. K. Pendleton was busy at Bethany prejudicing Disciples of Christ against not only the Bible Union project but the Publication Society as well.[5] Almost immediately the Bible Union stock company suffered financial losses.

In 1851 the annual convention of Disciples of Christ had approved the plan of obtaining and perfecting a new version of the Scriptures according to the plan of the American Bible Union. Furthermore, the churches were invited to make liberal contributions to the funds of the American Christian Bible Society for the express purpose of cooperating with the Bible Union. Still further, the board of managers of the American Christian Bible Society were instructed to appropriate as many other funds as could be spared for the same purpose.

Disciples of Christ were at first well pleased with the design of the Bible Union. Mr. Campbell translated the *Acts of the Apostles* for them and the Union at first looked favorably upon gaining control of his other translation work. The Bible Union was looked upon with such favor at first that the idea of getting a revised version by cooperative effort had much to do with the

---

[4]*Annual Proceedings*, 1854, pp. 21, 22.
[5]Garrison and DeGroot, *Disciples of Christ*, p. 257. Cf. *Millennial Harbinger*, 1854, pp. 338-47, 451-53, 531-33, 625-31.

ultimate abandonment of the American Christian Bible Society. Finally the Baptists secured completed control of the Bible Union, however, and they manipulated the new version to conform with Baptist theology. Disciples of Christ withdrew and ceased any hope of having even a modified version of *The Living Oracles* fully adopted by the Bible Union.[6]

Therefore, by discrediting the work of the Bible Union as a denominational enterprise, Campbell's *Millennial Harbinger* editors were able not only to kill the plan for a new interdenominational version of the Scriptures, but in the long run they weakened the Bible Society of Disciples of Christ to a point where it led a financially feeble existence because of fewer supporters.

Such financial losses required Burnet to turn again to the use of the *Christian Age* as his chief means of expression and the American Christian Publication Society as his hope for the future. If a new translation were to be completed it would have to come from a less complicated and pretentious venture than the one offered by the American Bible Union.

1851-1856: THE UNMARKETABLE BROTHERHOOD PUBLISHING HOUSE

"Opportunities and appliances for the propagation of Christianity are to be accounted for, as is the Gospel itself," urged Burnet in his speech to the fifth annual meeting of the Bible Society. "Before we had any Societies for concentrating our means, and applying them to the conversion of the outcasts of Israel and the sinners of the Gentiles, it was our duty to organize such, a duty felt by some years before, a duty to which we vowed to give ourself on the sick bed, and in the apparent prospect of death, if God should be pleased to spare our life."[7]

---

[6] Rowe and Rice, *Elder Benjamin Franklin*, pp. 37, 38.
[7] *Annual Proceedings*, 1851, p. 6.

Burnet looked upon the Societies as institutions for circulating the Bible and other religious writings, and for the purpose of supporting preaching in mission areas at home and abroad.[8] These institutions, he believed, were God's gifts to the Church and every Christian should accept full responsibility for them. "They cannot live and thrive without our cooperation and support."[9] Like other great enterprises, Burnet thought the Societies should be developed on a practical and sound business basis.[10]

Because many of his brethren thought that the Societies were intended to be the source of brotherhood power, Burnet was careful to repeat so that they understood that these organizations were not the "generators" but the "distributors" of Christian power. To him the Christian enterprise was the deliverance of Christian doctrine to the world. It was a magnificent task.

His own appeal for the use of good business judgment is reflected in his proposal:

> The enterprise is great, and requires, from its inception to its triumphant issue, the richest gifts of wisdom and the most copious effusions of the spirit of sacrifice, self-denial, and consecration—the spirit of benevolence—the Spirit of God. Like all other great enterprises, these require calculation and practical business capacity. Educated labor must be employed and sustained in the various departments at home and abroad, at an expense bearing a strict relation to the magnitude of the undertaking. Great as must be the outlay in such a cause, we must bear in mind the expense of war, of standing armies, of fortifications, of the navy, and all the other details of a peace establishment.
>
> . . . .

---

[8] *Annual Proceedings*, 1851, p. 6
[9] *Ibid.*, p. 6.
[10] *Ibid.*, p. 7.

Give me the means which are gathered from the hard earnings of the world into the coffers of their governors, and I will build a temple of science and a temple of religion on every hill and in every valley now unclaimed by the ocean, and install within them teachers and pastors, filled with more than the learning of the Egyptians; and the sound of the hammer and the voice of revelry shall cease, one day in seven, and the people shall rejoice in the Lord every day of the week. . .[11]

At the annual Missionary Society meeting, October 22, 1851, Alexander Campbell delivered the president's address without special preparation, not expecting it to be published.[12] Later, in publishing the address as he remembered it, he called attention to the fact that Disciples of Christ had ample means for carrying forth the missionary tasks lying before them.[13]

However, that year the Missionary Society had spent only $1,622.59.[14] The low rate of income perhaps stimulated Elijah Goodwin to give notice that at the next annual meeting he would offer an amendment to the constitution which would make it possible for any believer in Christ who contributed one dollar annually to the funds of the society to be a member. This would raise once again the money basis of membership. The needs for money were constantly before them. As corresponding secretary of the Missionary Society, Burnet pointed out that there had been "calls for missionaries or evangelists from Boston to Texas."[15] There were two reasons the calls could not be met: (1) there were insufficient funds; (2) men for the task were not properly qualified.[16]

---
[11] *Ibid.*, pp. 7, 8.
[12] *Ibid.*, p. 59.
[13] *Ibid.*, p. 34.
[14] *Ibid.*, p. 13.
[15] *Ibid.*, p. 38.
[16] *Ibid.*

Funds had come slowly into the treasury during the past year, and in small amounts. This condition was attributed to several antecedent factors. Some thought that the doing away with Life Memberships, Life Directorships and similar subscriptions the past year when the constitution was changed had something to do with the situation. Burnet thought certainly that was one of the reasons, but he was inclined to think also that the drop in income was due to the adjoining states having formed state societies, preferring to manage the Bible and Missionary causes in their own way.[17]

Burnet's journal, the *Christian Age,* was an organ of the Societies. It published and promoted the new national organizations. Organized in 1845 by T. J. Melish, the *Age* became the property of Walter Scott in 1848 and later, in 1850, was taken over by D. S. Burnet and Benjamin Franklin as joint owners and editors.[18] It was published at Cincinnati by Jethro Jackson, who bought it from Burnet and Franklin in 1852, and until May, 1853, when it was officially purchased by the American Christian Publication Society.[19] But the *Christian Age* was primarily Burnet's journal in 1851 when it was adopted as the sanctioned voice of the new Societies.[20] Friends of the Societies were pledged to support the building up of the circulation of the journal. The *Age* replaced the idea of tract distribution. Hence, less than $100 was donated for tract distribution in the year 1850-51.[21] The Bible Society saw the need for a brotherhood press and put the plan in the agenda for the 1851 convention.[22]

The story of the ''Publication House of the Brethren,'' established in October, 1852, at the third annual conven-

[17] *Annual Proceedings*, 1851, p. 13.
[18] Garrison and DeGroot, *Disciples of Christ*, p. 257.
[19] *Ibid.*
[20] *Annual Proceedings*, 1851, p. 54.
[21] *Ibid.*, p. 67.
[22] *Ibid.*, p. 19.

tion of Disciples of Christ, was short but lively. A notice appeared in Campbell's *Millennial Harbinger*, June, 1853, as follows:

THE PUBLICATION HOUSE OF THE BRETHREN[23]

The American Publication Society, established by the Convention, having abandoned their idea of a "Book Union" as its organ, in order to throw the publication and sale of all books and papers issuing from Cincinnati, the seat of its operations, with all the profits, into the hands of the brotherhood, to whom they rightfully belong, have purchased from Jethro Jackson the *Christian Age, Sunday School Journal*, all his books, stereotype plates, and the right to publish; and having enlarged their rooms and their stock, have on hand a good assortment of literature demanded by our churches, including all the works of Bro. Campbell and our best writers. They have now in press a *History of the Jerusalem Mission*, gotten up in superior style of letter-press and binding, illustrated with plates, portraits of Dr. Barclay and Mrs. Barclay, and a view of Mount Zion and the mission premises, from the pencil of Sarah Barclay. The price of the work, first edition sold at cost, will not exceed 75 cents, sent by mail free of postage.

The *Selected Sunday School Library* is ready for delivery. It consists of sixty volumes of the beautiful works of the American Tract Society, selected from some hundreds, by a committee of the A. C. Publication Society. A limited number of indigent schools can have this library at half price. The *Original Sunday School Library*, of 50 volumes, advertised sometime since in the *Age*, is in preparation, and will be issued as soon as possible. Loans of $5 are solicited for this work, to be paid by a set of the Library when it is done. Send in your money, brethren. It will be receipted in the *Age*, and faithfully appropriated. We also solicit loans of $100 and contributions of any sums, as our operations require a capital of many thousands.

Address, American Christian Publication Society, corner Eighth and Walnut streets, Cincinnati, Ohio.

Both the *Christian Age* and the Publication Society maintained headquarters in the basement of Burnet's

---
[23]*Millennial Harbinger*, 1853, p. 359.

church. The above notice, sent probably by Burnet from Cincinnati to Bethany for inclusion in the *Millennial Harbinger,* seemed self-explanatory. The brotherhood publishing house was a "going concern." But appended directly below this *Harbinger* notice was a stinging editorial critique of the "Publication House of the Brethren" idea. It was signed "A. W. C." Probably it was the work of Archibald W. Campbell, one of the co-editors of the *Harbinger.* It carried selected criticisms of the "progress" of the managers of the Publication Society, inferring that their actions had degenerated into a mere "idea." A. W. C. professed that he could not understand the wisdom of repeated changes in the policies of the managers. He called the publishing house idea an experiment awaiting a more perfect plan of operation.

Burnet had a phrase which he used often in his vocabulary—"active benevolence." It was, therefore, a direct jibe at Burnet when A. W. C. said he hoped "that what their *active* benevolence has now proposed may be fully realized."[24] The italics emphasizing "active" was the Bethany editor's means of accentuating his scorn and sarcasm.

The response of the Ohio brethren to the attitude of those of Virginia was as caustic as what they had received. They sent from Burnet's headquarters a notice to the *Harbinger,* fairly bristling because of the adverse criticism which had been leveled at them. In part, the notice said:

"A. W. C." in the last Harbinger, styles the above (A.C.P.S.) an *"idea* of a publication house." So it is, and quite a substantial idea, too; six times as large as the Methodist Book Concern of this city, at its origin, though we hope, through the prayers and patronage of the brotherhood, it is truly but an idea (image) of what it is yet destined to be. This, too is *progress—*

[24]*Millennial Harbinger,* 1853, p. 359.

commendable progress, the results of a proportionate "*activity.*" As to experiments, none have been made. The Publication Society is a fixed fact, pursuing the even tenor of its way, and according to a law well known, accelerating its force as the distance from the salient point increases.[25]

The new 319-page book, *The Jerusalem Mission,* by Burnet, was nearing completion. The author and editor was confident. He smarted under the slur on his appeals for "active benevolence." He stressed the need for greater progress. However, he closed his missive to the *Harbinger* with an almost wistful prayer: "The Lord aid us to appreciate the labors of each other in the kingdom and patience of Jesus Christ."[26]

Another thunderbolt from Bethany certainly must have shaken Burnet severely; it was in the September issue of the *Harbinger* (1853). Again the invective was handled by "A. W. C." It was a slight mention of the Bible Society with the stinging rebuke, "This Society has no special mission. She has nothing to do, as yet, which is not as well done by the A. and F. Bible Society."[27]

Tame criticisms, such as the above from Bethany, were followed by much wilder ones. In June of the next year (1854), W. K. Pendleton in a lengthy statement accused the Publication Society of misappropriation of funds.[28] That the Publication Society had used nearly $1000 of the Missionary Society funds, that Bible Society funds had been misappropriated in the same way, and that the society was deeply in debt after the brethren had perverted their sacred trust, were a few of the devastating accusations. Burnet could hardly wait for the October convention.

[25] *Ibid.,* p. 414.
[26] *Ibid.*
[27] Ibid., p. 534.
[28] *Ibid.,* 1854, p. 345.

In the meantime, Campbell made a move to put an end to the furore that arose between his own editor, Pendleton, and Burnet. Campbell thought he had succeeded in stopping the discussions. In fact, both Pendleton and Burnet had signed an agreement to cease discussions of the policies and actions of the Bible and Missionary Societies in the public press.[29] But Burnet's Bible Society board refused so neat a settlement. So an even greater editorial battle developed before time for the fall convention. Campbell sought some kind of way out of the incongruous situation in which he found himself as president of a national organization undermining the effectiveness of national organizations. So A. Campbell simply affirmed in capital letters: WE HAVE NO ORGANIZED CHRISTIAN PUBLICATION SOCIETY. He made his customary one, two, three arguments so clear and reasonable that intelligent readers would conclude that there was no such society indeed.[30]

On the same arguments it could have been said that there were no Bible or Missionary societies. The real situation was much different from that argued by Mr. Campbell. There was a Publication Society. But the Bethany leader had signaled thumbs down. It was not long before both Bible and Publication Societies were out of existence. Only the Missionary Society remained, and Alexander Campbell was president of it.

Burnet refused to allow the stigma of bad business methods and dishonesty to hang as a shadow over the Societies. On Thursday morning, October 19, 1854, Brother Burnet presented a resolution to the annual convention:

Whereas certain statements have appeared in the *M. Harbinger*, calculated to unsettle the confidence of the Brotherhood in the American Christian Publication Society, and whereas a

[29]*Millennial Harbinger*, 1854, p. 470.
[30]*Ibid.*, pp. 470, 471.

former clerk of the Society has been given as the author of those statements, Therefore

Resolved, That a committee of five be appointed by the President to investigate the grounds of those charges, and report to this meeting.[31]

The investigation committee examined the books of both the Publication Society and the Missionary Society and decided "there are in our judgment, no just grounds to question the ability, or integrity of the managers of said society."[32] The investigating committeemen signed their names: Jno. Rogers, Ky.; Elijah Goodwin, and L. H. Jameson, Ind.; S. W. Irvin, Ky.; and A. E. Strickle, O.[33]

Then the convention heard a report of Burnet's activities for the past six months, preceded by a defiance of the *Millennial Harbinger's* intimations and accusations. Part of the report follows:

> During fifteen or sixteen months, I have visited parts of Ohio, New York, Maryland, Virginia, Pennsylvania and Kentucky twice, and Indiana, Illinois, Iowa and Missouri once, collecting nearly all the $4,607.00, received of life members and by donations. I obtained pledges to the amount of $9300.00, (for which services, I received $1,093.00,) collecting also, at the same time, large amounts for the American Christian Bible and Missionary Societies. In connection with this labor, I preached continually, and witnessed the obedience to the faith of between three and four hundred persons of various ages and both sexes.
>
> The labors of the Publication Committee, have consisted mainly in the examination of more than twenty manuscript books, of which a goodly portion have been stereotyped, and others of them are now undergoing that process. These works are calculated to do good service. Some of our favorite writers are engaged on them and others are under promise. Of the most captivating, several are written by Christian women, the

[31]*Annual Proceedings*, 1854, p. 5ff.
[32]*Ibid.*
[33]*Ibid.*

delicacy of whose perceptions, and the generosity of whose natures, eminently qualify them for this most responsible task.

It is desirable that those persons who are engaged on manuscripts for the Sunday School Library, should complete them at an early day. Our cause is suffering for a want of this Library. Schools have been discontinued in default of this supply, and others are discouraged. Many brethren have, for more than a year, contented themselves with promising to write. The Lord quicken their consciences!

In the assumption of the *Christian Age, Sunday School Journal* and stereotype plates, formerly held by Jethro Jackson, the Board incurred a formidable obligation, not only for the original purchase, but also by the faithful supply of an unexpectedly large number of papers to subscribers who had prepaid. This of course cramped their efforts during the past year, as all the labor performed on the Sunday School Library, has been faithfully compensated. The Board is yet personally liable for some considerable amount. As soon as a sufficient series of Sunday School books can be prepared and stereotyped, a heavy outlay will be required to furnish paper, print and bind them. This expense will be large and calls for a rapid accumulation of funds.

In the history of our movements, one important fact has escaped the attention of some. The members of the board resident in Cincinnati and vicinity, by the law of Ohio, are personally responsible for the obligations contracted by them—a fair guaranty of their vigilance and faithfulness.

The board, its agents and officers, earnestly solicit the sympathy, and prayers, as well as the substantial support of the Brotherhood. Our work is great and the results are to be momentous. Let each take hold and try the virtue of the long pull, the strong pull, and the pull altogether. All of which is respectfully submitted.[34]

D. S. BURNET, *General Agent*

The first full-length book published cooperatively by Disciples of Christ was Burnet's *The Jerusalem Mission,*

---

[34] *Annual Proceedings*, 1854, p. 64. (From Burnet's report on "General Agency, Sunday School Library, Future Duties, &c." for the A. C. Publication Society).

as previously indicated. It was an extremely popular volume because of its timely relation to the first missionary enterprise of Disciples of Christ, the sending of the Barclay family to Jerusalem in Palestine. Its publication was a signal to the religious world that Disciples of Christ aimed to have a "Book Concern," with the center of publication not in West Virginia but in Ohio.

Burnet prefaced the volume by calling attention to the nineteenth century as the time of emergence of remarkable benevolent institutions. Bible and missionary societies formerly had been little more than "enthusiastic dreams."[35] He estimated the distribution of Bibles in the first half of the century as thirty or forty millions. To him it was a glorious advancement that Christian missionaries could almost shake hands around the globe. Disciples of Christ had sent their first foreign missionaries to add power to those of other denominational groups already abroad. Burnet was enthusiastic in his report: "The first foreign Mission of the churches denominationally called Christian, in the United States, was commenced in Jerusalem, in February, 1851."[36] He had called the body a denomination! Such terminology was highly distasteful in some quarters among the churches which claimed to be nondenominational.

The sending of this mission to Jerusalem was probably the occasion for more earnest prayer, deep-felt solicitude, and hearty rejoicing and gratitude than any cooperative undertaking which had been heretofore undertaken by these churches. The letters sent from the mission field by Dr. Barclay and those exchanged by the A. C. M. S. officers, particularly Burnet, formed a substantial part of the volume. The preface contained a view of Mount Zion and an illustration showing where

---

[35]D. S. Burnet, *Jerusalem Mission, Under the Direction of the American Christian Missionary Society* (Cincinnati: American Christian Publication Society, 1853), p. 1.

[36]*Ibid.*, p. 1.

the Jerusalem mission was located. Also pen portraits of "Rev. James T. Barclay and Mrs. Julia A. Barclay," husband and wife, were printed.[37]

Burnet traced the beginnings of the Jerusalem mission back to October 5, 1848, when Dr. Barclay addressed a letter to the corresponding secretary of the Bible Society, offering his services, with his family, should the Society's deliberations result in the establishment of a foreign missionary society or department.[38] As soon as the Missionary Society was organized, Dr. Barclay addressed from Cincinnati, on October 30, 1849, another letter to the board of managers of that body. In it he repeated the offer and explained more fully the devotion and qualifications which he believed his family possessed and would be helpful in the missionary enterprise.[39]

An anonymous article had appeared in the *The Christian Age* proposing that Jerusalem should be the field of the first mission of Disciples of Christ. The article was entitled, "Where Should We First Establish a Foreign Mission?" Obviously designed to influence the Board of Managers and the brotherhood at large to a favorable consideration of Jerusalem, the article is included in Burnet's book with his certain knowledge that Dr. Barclay had written it. Furthermore, Burnet's editorial connection with the *Age* indicated that it was originally published with his consent. It was in this planned publicity that the successful choice of Jerusalem was made by Dr. Barclay with the cooperative guidance and approval of Burnet.[40]

The Scottish Burnet kept his eye on frugality and good stewardship in connection with the launching of the Jerusalem mission. When on their way to the Holy

---
[37] Burnet, *Jerusalem Mission*, frontispiece.
[38] *Ibid.*, pp. 5, 6.
[39] *Ibid.*, pp. 6-9.
[40] *Ibid.*, pp. 10ff.

Land Dr. Barclay and his family arrived in London, they addressed a letter to James Challen, October 28, 1850. In it Dr. Barclay told of taking "the cheapest lodgings that could be found of a respectable character," also that he sought to travel at the lowest rates possible.[41]

From this letter, Burnet saw that the heart of the Barclays was indeed in their work and that they were operating under a policy of "enlightened frugality." Burnet said of Barclay: "He supremely realizes that he is a trustee of the funds placed at his disposal, and he most obviously keeps a conscience void of offense in their management."[42]

In January, 1851, Dr. Barclay was on the site of ancient Melita, and nearly in the same condition there as the Apostle Paul once experienced. Burnet compared Barclay's journey with that of Paul and pointed out that the missionary of Disciples of Christ "was in perils oft, yet the good Lord delivered him out of them all."[43]

The first published letter of Burnet to Barclay was written from Hygeia, Ohio, July 18, 1851, following the arrival of the missionary family in Jerusalem and their report of first converts. It was in that letter that the wisdom of Burnet concerning that abortive missionary adventure of Disciples of Christ under the sponsorship of the American Christian Missionary Society is most clearly seen. The following extracts of the letter are indicative:

... I have always feared that you would find a barren and ungenerous field, in a land which though it peculiarly belonged to the Messiah, received him not, but hung him on a tree. The inveteracy of habit has been illustrated by no people more than by the various nations which have descended from Abraham,

[41] *Ibid.*, p. 35.
[42] *Ibid.*, p. 34.
[43] *Ibid.*, p. 48.

and among whom you have chosen to labor. . . . The mixing of races in the motley population of one city, the conflicting interests which obtain among them, but especially among the Franks, and most especially among the missionaries, give rise to a peculiar moral condition quite unfavorable to genuine conversion. The rival sects are liable to severe temptation, to unfair dealing and an unchristian spirit, in the management of the discussions which inevitably arise . . . the worst of all is the exhibition of deep depravity on the part of those who would sell themselves to the highest bidder in the ecclesiastical market. . . . I fear, my dear brother, that the trials which you have already experienced are not the last which may arise from these causes.[44]

Mr. Burnet was a little more cheerful, however, with the belief that Barclay could meet his competitors in Jerusalem with a superior presentation of the gospel. And he was sure that the missionary venture had excited a benevolence of feeling and giving in the United States of America which indicated that Disciples of Christ had a lively appreciation of the needs and miseries of "the dying world."[45]

Churches among Disciples of Christ soon began to expect news from their mission field. Burnet wrote Dr. Barclay and asked that each member of his family in Jerusalem should keep a diary as a system for providing the churches with news. This letter, sent August 1, 1851, was the second one of Burnet's to the mission field. The topics about which he inquired made it evident that a new interest in missions was awakening on the field and in the churches. The questions Burnet asked were legion. News from the field was essential, he believed, to the furtherance of the program.[46]

Mrs. Barclay addressed a letter to Mrs. Burnet, December 5, 1852, which may rightfully be noted as the be-

[44] Burnet, *Jerusalem Mission*, pp. 183, 184.
[45] *Ibid.*, pp. 184, 185.
[46] *Ibid.*, pp. 186-190.

ginning of the women's missionary society work among Christian Church women. Mrs. Barclay pleaded for the rights of women in the church to support the missionary enterprise. The history of the women's Christian missionary movement among Disciples of Christ rightly stems from the correspondence and activities initiated by these two women. Mrs. Burnet had sent some presents to the Barclay family and the letter from Mrs. Barclay was in the form of grateful acknowledgment of the missionary family's having received them. The articles sent had been greatly damaged, particularly the items of food and clothing.

A dress had been sent by Mary Burnet's mother, Mrs. Gano, who was regarded by Mrs. Barclay as "our aged 'mother in Israel.' "[47] A Bible in the package had not been damaged as much by sea water. Most significant in the first letter of a woman missionary of Disciples of Christ was that part of the correspondence which centered about the status and plight of "degraded females" in the Near East. The low estimate of women abroad in the world was a topic of great concern. The worship carried on by Moslem ladies and their curiosity about American customs, the practice of polygamy and the customs of the harem, caused Julia Barclay to speculate what might be done in an educational program for women at home and abroad. The question Mrs. Barclay had raised was, "Cannot some of our wealthy sisterhood support such a school on Mount Zion for the benefit of the daughters of Israel?"[48] The idea of a girls' school had a strong appeal to Mrs. Burnet who had been associated with her husband at Hygeia.

Women in the Cincinnati church rallied quickly to the new aspect of missionary work, sometimes called

[47] *Ibid.*, p. 273.
[48] *Ibid.*, pp. 277, 278. Cf. *Millennial Harbinger*, 1853, p. 352.

"women's work." Mrs. Burnet was determined to secure the cooperation of other women in fostering the Jerusalem Mission. It was advertised that funds for that object could be sent directly to Mrs. Mary G. Burnet and that she would acknowledge and properly appropriate them. This avenue of securing financial aid received the unqualified support of her husband.[49]

The latter part of the book, *Jerusalem Mission,* is composed mainly of letters of the missionary, Barclay, to the corresponding secretary, Burnet. Appropriately enough, the first full-length book from the presses of the brotherhood Publishing Society delineated the first missionary adventure of the churches. Many other smaller volumes went on sale from the Cincinnati headquarters, but Burnet's *Jerusalem Mission* was the first cooperative book publication.

Among the smaller volumes was the *Sunday School Library,* also edited by Burnet. His educational interest was reflected in his development of *The Christian Sunday-School Library,* which went into repeated editions. It was published expressly for Christian Sunday Schools and Christian families. Each of the volumes (32mo, cloth) was neatly and substantially bound in cloth with gilt back and the set sold for $12.00.[50] These volumes claimed to be free from sectarianism and infidelity and suited to the wants of various ages. Some idea of the contents which Burnet believed necessary to include in such a library may be surmised from the list of titles below:

Goodness of God
Miracles of Christ
Childhood of Jesus
Great Preachers. Part 1

---

[49]Burnet, *Jerusalem Mission,* p. 279.
[50]Green, *Christian Missions,* catalog supplement, p. 6. Cf. Moore, *Living Pulpit,* p. 38. Also, Power, *Sketches of Our Pioneers,* pp. 126, 127.

Great Preachers. Part 2
Young Teachers. 2 Vols.
The Air We Breathe
Our Duties
Mary and Martha
Old Testament Facts
Rare Testimony
Maternal Influence
The Great Teacher
Uncle Harlin's Voyages. 2 Vols.
Week-Day Readings. 2 Vols.
History of David
Law of Love
Apostle Peter
Battle of Life
Plea for Sunday Schools
Searching the Scriptures
Americans in Jerusalem. 3 Vols.
Lessons for Teachers
Law of Beneficence
The Israelite
Lectures for Children
Our Lord and Saviour
Jesus Is the Christ
Broken Household
Weeping and Tears
History of Jesus. Part 1
History of Jesus. Part 2
History of Jesus. Part 3
The Chinese. 3 Vols.
Wonders of the Atmosphere
Fanny Manning
God's Goodness
Vegetable Creation. 2 Vols.
Outward Man
Life of Paul
The Happy Day
Evidences of Christianity

The Publication Society was located in the basement of Burnet's church at Eighth and Walnut Streets, Cincinnati,[51] and it was there that the bookstore sales of the *Sunday School Library* took place. Burnet had an idea to see Brother A. Campbell about publishing Campbell's *Hymn Book*. A Sunday School hymnbook was published in 1853, but Campbell gave his hymnbook rights later to the Missionary Society. Other publications by the Society included a work by Dr. L. L. Pinkerton and the issue of a new edition of the *Life of Barton W. Stone*.[52]

After the devastating criticism from Bethany, to which we have referred earlier, the Publication Society fell upon hard times. At the 1856 convention October 21, at 11:00 A.M. a motion was made to merge "the three societies into one." That motion was tabled. But the meeting could hardly overcome Brother W. K. Pendleton's resolution: "*Resolved,* That it is inexpedient to continue the existence of the American Christian Bible Society, and that it should be dissolved."[53] Before the annual meeting was finished, both the Bible and Publication societies were also finished. Garrison and DeGroot say that it "was not to the interest of the Bethany enterprises to attempt to allay criticism of the Publication (Tract) Society." Obviously, it was not!

Two primary factors put the Bible Society and Publication Society out of existence: (1) the seeds of distrust of the financial management sown by Campbell's *Millennial Harbinger;* (2) and the too rapid expansion of the cooperative publishing ventures which involved the societies in indebtedness upon which it was unable to survive. Of the first factor it may be noted that the *Millennial Harbinger* criticisms were not well founded. The societies vindicated their actions and their business integrity. But it was too late. The seeds of distrust had been sown.

---

[51]Shaw, *Buckeye Disciples,* p. 178.
[52]*Annual Proceedings,* 1853, p. 51.
[53]*Ibid.,* 1856, p. 6.

It may be observed also that the experience at that time was helpful in requiring the highest kind of business honesty in the surviving Missionary Society, as well as the kind of operational caution which would keep the expense within the budget:

> The idea of a brotherhood publication concern had its premature birth and early death in the decade of the 1850's. Mr. Campbell and his associates at Bethany, who had the most to lose by such a venture, opposed it...[54]

> He [Campbell] considered the publishing of books and periodicals one of his prerogatives.[55]

Failure is always difficult to meet courageously, and even if the Missionary Society survived there was a mark of failure written across D. S. Burnet's most diligent efforts. He was hurt and baffled because those who preached love and brotherhood were unready for a kind of action that would prove it, such as pooling their efforts in publishing the gospel.

1852: MAKING CAPITAL OUT OF THE OPPOSITION'S DESIGNED CONTEMPT

"Ministers are men, and men are not angels," said Burnet when he found himself the object of the intended slight and asperity of the Ohio Evangelical Association.[56] The "Evangelicals" walked out of a city-wide meeting in Cincinnati when they learned that Burnet had been chosen to give a welcome address to a national guest, Louis Kossuth.

Kossuth had come to America directly from the cells of a Turkish fortress, not seeking sanctuary as an exile

---
[54] Garrison and DeGroot, *Disciples of Christ*, p. 256.

[55] Shaw, *Buckeye Disciples*, p. 185. He cites *Millennial Harbinger*, pp. 207-15, 451-53, 469-72, and 599. [Brackets mine.]

[56] D. S. Burnet, *A Discourse on the Question: Is the Christian Church (Sometimes called the Reformation) Truly Evangelical?* (Cincinnati: American Christian Publication Society, 1852), pp. 3-10.

but aiming to enlist the sanction and support of "republican opinion" in an effort to arm Europe and America against political aggression then manifested by incumbent Turks. In his lecture tour Kossuth had been highly honored by governments and by huge crowds which flocked to hear him. The admirers of Kossuth were the admirers of liberty to the extent that such admiration crossed party lines. The popular feelings stirred Whig and Democrat, judge and juror, lawyer and client, physician and patient, farmer and mechanic, merchant and trader, rich and poor, men and women, boys and girls. There was a lofty emotion of genuine patriotism abroad in the land, resembling in many ways what Burnet and his contemporaries among Disciples of Christ hoped might be accomplished among the sectarian denominations.

When Kossuth reached Cincinnati in his American tour, the benevolent enthusiasm suddenly came to a close. A newspaper notice called for a meeting of the clergy of the city. Some efforts were planned to raise money in order to foster the success of the efforts of Kossuth. Burnet was not informed as to what person or persons published the notice for a meeting of the ministers, but he had been invited to make a speech of welcome to Louis Kossuth, the distinguished visitor.

Upon arrival at the scene of the meeting at Smith and Nixon's Hall he learned that someone was taking responsibility for the called meeting independent of the Cincinnati "Evangelical Association." He learned that the members of the Evangelical Association had turned out *en masse*, thinking the newspaper announcement was a call of their body. They had made plans to receive Kossuth and to do the honors themselves.

Burnet was not a member of the Evangelical Association which was composed of Methodists, Baptists, Presbyterians, Congregationalists, Episcopalians, and English Lutherans. That body called themselves "The Protestant Evangelical Association of Ministers" and had originated from the older London "Evangelical Alliance." They had appointed a committee to invite and honor Kossuth.

When it was clear that Burnet was expected by the citizens' committee to be the main local speaker, the members of the Evangelical Association promptly withdrew. They had no desire to be counted as having the heretical Mr. Burnet, regarded by them as "unevangelical," as their spokesman on this occasion.

The editor of the *Central Christian Herald* proceeded to publish an article under the headlines "THE CLERGY AND KOSSUTH," in which he presented the Evangelical Association's side of the story. He presumed that the members of the Evangelical Association had withdrawn from the meeting at Smith and Nixon's Hall for two reasons:

> First, having made other arrangements to call on Kossuth, they had no need to remain. Second, the evangelical clergy of the city have long since determined, and have carried their determination out on several occasions, not to recognize as ministers of the Gospel those who do not preach the Gospel, but who preach errors calculated to subvert it.[57]

In short, Burnet had been snubbed because he was regarded as not only a heretic but one who did not preach the evangelical gospel.

Enmity against him and Disciples of Christ was publicly expressed despite the fact that Burnet had declined the nomination to be the speaker who should make the welcome address when Kossuth should arrive. He furthermore had moved to turn the called meeting of ministers over to the officials of the Association. He

---
[57] *Is the Christian Church Truly Evangelical?* p. 5.

withdrew himself from support of either the Evangelical Association or the movement which was represented as being independent of that body. Burnet had no taste for strife.[58] On the one hand he would not align himself with a minority, on the other he could not align himself with the majority.

He was much more in agreement with those who styled themselves "evangelical" than any who may have been "unevangelical." It turned out that Kossuth's coming to Cincinnati was one of the crises in which the theological test of fellowship was projected into a nontheological situation. Burnet saw no propriety in dividing religious bodies on this occasion. He said he would have been better pleased with the outcome of things if Catholics and Protestants, "all who bore the Christian name, had been called upon to honor the Providence which had brought safely to our shores an embodiment of Christian Republicanism, in the person of our city Guest."[59]

That he should have been styled by his peers as "unevangelical" irritated Burnet no less than the accusation of heresy. That the Evangelical Association ministers should not recognize him as a gospel preacher stirred his blood. For such reasons he decided to preach a sermon to his own Walnut Street congregation on Sunday entitled, "Is the Christian Church Truly Evangelical?" This he did on March 28, 1852.

At the close of the services the church called a congregational meeting and addressed an affectionate letter to their pastor:

Dear Brother: Believing that the publication of the Sermon delivered by you this morning, in answer to the question, "Are we Evangelical?" will conduce to the diffusion of knowledge and truth, we, the congregation, respectfully request a copy of

---

[58]*Is the Christian Church Truly Evangelical?* p. 6.
[59]*Ibid.*

the same for publication and general distribution. Affectionately, Your Brethren.

The church voted that their committee should provide for the proposed publication. Dr. Joseph Ray, author of the famed *Ray's Arithmetic* and member of Burnet's congregation, made the motion that the sermon should be published by the committee working through proper agencies. In the course of events it was learned that the Publication Society could publish the manuscript. Burnet had presented what he believed to be the most ecumenical basis of the Christian faith and order. While with all Protestants he disclaimed the epithet Roman Catholic, he accepted the position of catholic in "the true and usual sense of that word."

"We are true Catholics," he said, "and are laboring to restore the true Catholic Church of God, by restoring the true and primitive grounds of faith and fellowship."

He said furthermore: "We hold no sentiment, adopt no formula, observe no ordinances, and practice no duties not sanctioned by all evangelical denominations, whether we employ the term evangelical in its ecclesiastical, or its etymological and true sense."[60]

The portion of his sermon which set forth his views of Scripture and orthodoxy was presented as a clarification of his interpretation of the views of Disciples of Christ. The ordinary use of the Scriptures during the middle portion of the nineteenth century was to prove certain doctrinal views by citing proof texts. The footnotes to the *Westminster Confession of Faith* are a notable example. Burnet recognized such an approach to the use of the Scriptures as an indiscriminate eclecticism which would "select a few favorite portions and array them against the remainder of God's Word." Burnet's aim was to read his views from the Scriptures, not prove his views by the Scriptures.[61]

[60]*Ibid.*, p. 10.
[61]*Ibid.*, p. 11.

His arrangement of the materials of the gospel, although outlined with considerable arbitrary simplicity, nevertheless suggests an honest struggle to find a common ground for Christendom (See Appendix V).

At the time of publication of the sermon in answer to the rebuff of his "evangelical" brethren, Burnet was editor of the *Christian Age*. This was a weekly journal, devoted "to original Christianity, family religion, and a pure literature." The assistant editor was Benj. Franklin, with whom W. K. Pendleton of Campbell's staff in West Virginia ultimately disputed many of the issues among Disciples of Christ.

The publication of Burnet's booklet, describing Disciples of Christ as being evangelical in their outlook, did not at once lift the stigma which the sextet of denominations of the Association had placed on them. It did, however, indicate that Disciples of Christ aimed to place emphasis upon the four Gospels and the Acts of the Apostles as the most significant portion of their Scriptures. It insisted by this emphasis that the movement was in the true evangelical stream of Protestant and Catholic Christianity.

1852: Missions Organized in Ohio

The desire for educating leaders in Ohio resulted in a move to establish another school of higher learning. First meeting was held at Hiram, Ohio, December 20, 1849. Western Reserve Eclectic Institute, which later became Hiram College, was founded. The proposal had been made earlier that year, May 1, by the Ohio association meeting at Wooster.

In the resolution by the Hiram brethren was the strong desire that other and foreign subscriptions for colleges and seminaries should be frowned upon by Ohio Disciples of Christ. They would seek Ohio funds with Ohio avenues of publicity. Brother Burnet had claimed that the *Millennial Harbinger* refused to print the announcement about organizing the Bible Society in 1845. The Ohio brethren would not try to use the columns of the Bethany, West Virginia, journal again. Instead, they voted to publish the notes concerning their activities in the *Christian Age* and the *Protestant Unionist*.[62] Henry K. Shaw has indicated many facets of the struggle for a shift in leadership from West Virginia to Ohio. Ohio was growing strong with awareness of the necessity to develop some kind of centralism which would prevent the movement of Disciples of Christ from fragmentation and degeneration.

Attending the Bedford and Wooster, Ohio, "Yearly Meetings" in 1851, Burnet and T. J. Melish represented the southwestern district of the state with the proposal that they invite all Ohio Disciples of Christ to a convention in Wooster the following year.[63] It was to be a missionary convention to which all the brethren of the state were subsequently invited. The proposed meeting was favored by the northeastern Disciples of Christ and a *Circular* was sent out to notify the churches.

This meeting was called May 12, 13, 1852, at Wooster and fifty-five churches of the state were represented. Burnet, with A. S. Hayden and T. J. Melish, formed the temporary group of officers until a constitution for the new society could be formed. Chosen for the business of drawing up the constitution for the Ohio Christian Missionary Society were David Staats Burnet, Isaac Errett, Charles Brown, A. S. Hayden, and R. R. Sloan.

Shaw, in *Buckeye Disciples,* gives some excellent insight into the divisive elements which were present in the formative days of the Ohio missionary organization.

[62]Shaw, *Buckeye Disciples*, p. 129.
[63]*Ibid.*, pp. 170-175.

He points out that the issues most debated among Disciples of Christ were the issues of the slavery question and those of church polity. He says:

> Two divisive elements were present at Disciple gatherings for many years. The first was the slavery issue with its legal, moral, and spiritual ramifications; and the second, an acute fear of even the simplest form of ecclesiastical organization. To use a coined word, the brethren were victims of *ecclesiastiphobia*, a complex never quite eradicated from the Disciple mind. No doubt the dread of external control has been largely responsible for determining the peculiar pattern in which church life functions within the traditional framework of what is called the Disciples' brotherhood. Being primarily a laymen's movement, it apparently didn't seem incongruous to the brethren when so-called "popery" developed and flourished on the local church level.[64]

Evidently Mr. Burnet was something of a genius at forestalling an outbreak of the emotional slavery arguments in meetings of Disciples of Christ. The issues were kept out of the business sessions, or at any rate found no place in the publication of the *Annual Proceeding*. Doubtless unofficial expressions were given on the subject because Ohio was teeming with men who faced the insistent problem of forming societies among religious peoples who disclaimed "any form of ecclesiasticism."

Alexander Campbell made a hurried trip to Wooster for the founding meeting of the Missionary Society which took the name, The Convention of the Churches of Christ in the State of Ohio. He gave the keynote address, wrote his autograph conspicuously across a whole page of the minutes, and departed. Later, in the *Millennial Harbinger*, he told of his visit to Ohio and the "happy effort, to institute a great home missionary operation."[65] An-

---
[64] Shaw, *Buckeye Disciples*, p. 170.
[65] *Ibid.*, p. 170ff. Cf. *Millennial Harbinger*, 1852, pp. 351, 352.

other distinguished person present at the founding convention in Ohio was William Lillie who had unwittingly baptized, two years before, a future President of the United States, James A. Garfield.[66]

The work of Burnet can be seen in the composition of the constitution for the Ohio missionary society. It bore great similarity to the constitutions of other societies formed under the same guiding hand. Composed of nine articles, it provided for the society's name, object, representation, authority of each church, officers, managers, proximity of board members to the proposed Bedford headquarters, time of meetings, and provision for amendment.

Under the new constitution the regular officers were elected and Burnet was chosen as president. From the following chart may be seen the important function of Burnet in the formative days of the organization that later became known as the Ohio Christian Missionary Society:

O. C. M. S. ANNUAL MEETINGS

YEAR	PLACE	PRESIDING OFFICER	CORRESPONDING SECRETARY
1852	Wooster	D. S. Burnet	Lee Lord
1853	Mt. Vernon	M. S. Clapp, *pro tem*	Lee Lord
1854	Bedford	D. S. Burnet	Isaac Errett
1855	Akron	D. S. Burnet	Isaac Errett

By 1854 the experiences of Disciples of Christ indicated something of the important functions being assigned to the corresponding secretary. The names "bishop" and "presiding elder" were generally frowned

[66] *Ibid.*

upon by the Disciples of Christ because of similar executive offices in other bodies which they believed to smack too much of ecclesiasticism. Naturally the offices of "president" and "corresponding secretary" soon fell under similar condemnation. At the same time, practical necessity forced upon these officers more and more obligations. The load grew particularly heavy upon the office of corresponding secretary. It is curious that a brotherhood which claimed biblical names for biblical things should have steered clear of biblical titles for the offices which ultimately became so heavily laden with responsibility.

Isaac Errett was on the Board of Managers of the Ohio society from the first. He assisted in drawing up the charter under which the society operated. His close association with Burnet was of increasing importance because it was upon Errett that fell the leadership of Disciples of Christ following the death of Burnet.

At this point it is possible to draw some broad generalizations which may be apparent in this context: the Campbells and Barton W. Stone led in the formation of the thought of the movement; Walter Scott led the publicity of it, making the reformation ideas popular and simplifying the brotherhood tenets; then the leadership of the movement swept westward from its focal point at Bethany, West Virginia, to Cincinnati, Ohio; D. S. Burnet gave leadership to cooperative organization; and Isaac Errett led in the period of conservation of the movement, catching it up in a program of sustained operations.

When Isaac Errett became corresponding secretary of the Ohio missionary society, with headquarters at Warren, Ohio, the position required that he should have much in common with Mr. Burnet.[67] They became close friends and co-workers as long as Burnet lived.

---

[67]Moore, *Living Pulpit*, p. 470.

While these men labored to introduce among Disciples of Christ the development of a kind of connectional polity which would aid them in raising and administering missionary, educational and benevolent funds, Harriet Beecher Stowe finished and published her highly influential *Uncle Tom's Cabin* (1852). This stirred up the problem of a different color. If Disciples of Christ in Ohio had been able to keep the slavery controversy out of their annual meetings in the past, there was no assurance that it would be so in the future.

1853-1854: Ohio in Africa

David Burnet's uncle, Judge Jacob Burnet, in April 1848, was leader of a clever plan to make popular the idea of American colonization of Africa. With a group of fellow citizens of Cincinnati, he aimed to develop a portion of northern Liberia as a special African attraction to Ohio freed Negro emigrants. The plan was to be known as "Ohio in Africa."[68]

Cincinnati newspapers carried items which suggested that a mortal blow might be struck at the slave trade if some ready and easy provision were made for the settlement of Negroes from Ohio in a purchased plot of territory on the African coast. Judge Burnet was busy raising funds for the purchase of colonial lands in Liberia.

D. S. Burnet's understanding of the move of his uncle and other Ohio leaders toward colonization in Africa prompted him to interest Disciples of Christ in opening a missionary front in that area. When he was visiting the Ninth Street Christian Church in Hopkinsville, Kentucky, in 1853, he chanced to hear a slave named

[68]*Ohio State Archaeological and Historical Quarterly*, LI. (1942), No. 2, 79-88. Art. by Edward Wesley Shunk.

Alexander Cross deliver an address on temperance.[69] A possible work in Africa seemed advisable and it occurred to Burnet that here was a man who would be capable of serving his own people in that needy land. It was understood that he would be educated for the Christian missionary enterprise in Liberia, in order to evangelize among his people.[70] The missionary, Cross, sailed from Baltimore, November 5, 1853. He was accompanied by his wife and eight-year-old son. They landed in Monrovia early in January (1854) where they spent two months in preparation for the labors.

Burnet believed that the zeal and great efforts in making ready for the task caused the missionary to overexert himself.[71] Cross had been instructed particularly not to expose himself to the intense rays of the Africa sun and always to carry an umbrella for protection. But the Negro family was intensely concerned with building a house on the St. Paul's River. Also on one occasion the man poled a canoe fourteen miles up the river in the scorching tropics. However, he soon fell victim of fever and died. His small son, unprotected and inexperienced, suffered the same fate.

The mission had to be suspended while the brotherhood of Disciples of Christ sought elsewhere for a volunteer and for funds to make another attempt in Africa. Burnet reminded the annual meeting of the Missionary Society in October (1854) that "Alexander Cross was a man of good logic, ready utterance and burning zeal. His fine voice, impressive delivery and ardent piety fitted him for a wide field of usefulness."[72] Obedience to the laws of health and recognition of the providence of God be-

---

[69]Robert Gilbert Nelson, *A Historical Study of the American Christian Missionary Society and Its Work in Jamaica,* British West Indies (Thesis, Texas Christian University, 1953), p. 13.

[70]Garrison, *Religion Follows the Frontier,* p. 190.

[71]*Annual Proceedings,* 1854, pp. 48, 49.

[72]*Ibid.,* p. 49.

came significant to Disciples of Christ in their first thrusts at the staggering task of foreign missions.

It was Walter Scott's connection with Alexander Cross and other Negroes which caused him to feel so keenly the slavery issues. He said, "Bro. Cross, in the estate and rank of a slave, had yet the feelings and heart of a man—a man of God."[73] D. S. Burnet had some of the same feeling, because only one year prior to the 1854 annual meeting Burnet and the other executive leaders had presented Alexander Cross to the assembly. There had been some tears shed as the brethren gave to the Negro the "right hand of fellowship that he should go to the heathen."[74] He went like other missionaries, he contracted fever like other missionaries, and he died like other missionaries. Thus Burnet developed a great concern for Negroes—north, south, east and west.

---

[73] *Ibid.*
[74] *Ibid.*, p. 49.

CHAPTER V

Apparent Failure

1857-1860: GETTING AWAY FOR AWHILE

JOSEPH RAY, AUTHOR of *Ray's Arithmetics*, died May 24, 1857.[1] He was a member of the Christian Church of Cincinnati, at the corner of Eighth and Walnut Streets, where Burnet was pastor. Burnet preached the funeral discourse of the famous textbook writer whose third part of his famous books ran into more than 10,000 editions. John T. Johnson had died five months before. Two of Burnet's near friends had fallen in the onslaught of time.

It was in this same year (1857) Burnet was called to New York City to work with the church on Seventeenth Street.[2] He remained in the New York pastorate only one year. Succeeding him at the Cincinnati church was Thomas Munnell, who gained some reputation as a house-to-house visitor, especially among the poor of the congregation. Burnet's being of a family of considerable wealth and his concern for writing and preaching caused some of the congregation to infer that he neglected to call on the poor.

The disturbing turn of affairs at the 1856 annual meeting in which Burnet's beloved Publication and Bible Societies were merged into Campbell's Missionary Society created considerable embarrassment even for the officers of the Missionary Society. Benjamin Franklin was acting as corresponding secretary at the opening

---
[1]*Ohio State Archaeological and Historical Quarterly*, XLVI (1937), 42-50. Art. by Jerry Dennis.
[2]Moore, *Living Pulpit*, p. 40. Cf. Boles, *Biographical Sketches*, p. 143.

session of the 1857 meeting, October 20, 1857, in Cincinnati. He realized that the previous bad fortune of the other societies had raised the question abroad about what might happen to the Missionary Society.[3] Funds were extremely difficult to raise among those who questioned the course to be pursued in the future. There was a great need for agents to do fund-raising in the field.[4] They were unable to induce a single man to enter the field of fund-raising for the Society. Burnet had demonstrated conclusively that missionary, educational, and benevolent funds were raised most adequately by personal contacts with the donors. But rising war clouds and the absence of Burnet cast gloom over the situation.

Burnet did not attend the 1857 meeting. He was dropped completely from the roster of officers for the ensuing year. Although he was not present, there were men in the group deeply respectful of his abilities and conscious of his absence. On October 21, J. P. Robison brought to the floor a resolution, "Resolved, That we raise the means, and send Bro. D. S. Burnet to Great Britain as our Missionary." The resolution might logically have been referred to the Board of Managers, as a Brother Fillmore proposed. But those present would have it out in the open and adopted the resolution. Nothing ever came of it, but the action showed the high esteem in which he was held.

On October 22, 1857, the convention introduced a new Article into the Constitution of the Missionary Society. Article XII stated the duties of the corresponding secretary as follows:

ART. XII. It shall be the duty of the Corresponding Secretary to conduct the correspondence of the Society; to collect and digest information for the Board and for the Society; to

---
[3] *Annual Proceedings*, 1857, p. 4.
[4] *Ibid.*, p. 5.

solicit and otherwise procure funds for the support of the Society; to superintend the general conduct of its evangelical and financial affairs; and to devote himself to the private and public advocacy of its interests and aims.[5]

Isaac Errett, of Michigan, made an extremely impressive speech during the convention and was elected to the office of corresponding secretary. Benjamin Franklin, the acting secretary, was of the opinion that the Society should have a person who could give his undivided attention to the interests of the Society. It had been general talk for some time that such an office should be a salaried position. It was quite obvious that Burnet was the man for the task, but he had been left with his Sunday School Library and hardly a word of appreciation for the long services he had rendered. Mr. Errett could do the work very effectively instead.

Before the year had passed, Mr. Errett prevailed on Burnet to travel a few months as a solicitor. Errett was a publicity agent and reporter, but neither he nor his Board had plans of finance comparable with those of Brother Burnet.[6] For these reasons the aid of Burnet was again sought.

Burnet was not easily influenced to return to Cincinnati. He spent the year, 1858, following along the seaboard from New York to Texas.[7] Preaching from city to city along the coast, Burnet went to Texas to visit his famous uncle, David G. Burnet.

Uncle David also was an orator; but his interests were political rather than religious. He had the same persuasive ability when upon the platform as did many of the Burnet clan. Especially was he famous for the short but colorful oration at the funeral of John A. Wharton. When D. S. Burnet visited his uncle in Texas the oration

---

[5] *Annual Proceedings*, 1857, p. 10.
[6] *Ibid.*, 1858, p. 13.
[7] Moore, *Living Pulpit*, p. 40.

was twenty years old but was still recited in the schoolrooms and printed in history books of Texas.

The next year (1859) Burnet toured Kansas and Missouri in his evangelistic activities.[8] Interest in Burnet's preaching developed everywhere he went. For several weeks in a community he held what religious people then called a "protracted meeting." Preaching services would be held both morning and evening.

One of the remarkable meetings held was at Paris, Missouri, where community interest grew to the point that local merchants closed business from mid-morning until noon each day in order to attend the church services.[9] His pulpit power during this tour of the Midwest was said to have reached magnificent proportions.

An interesting report of his activities was published in the *Harbinger:*

Platte City, Mo., 27th January '59.[10]

Brethren Editors:

When I wrote you twelve days since, I had delivered one or two discourses here on this, my second visit. Since then, I have preached thirteen discourses, to all whom the house would contain, including a fair representation of all classes of the community, especially of the more intelligent. My closing discourse, last night, resulted in six confessions, making *fifty-eight* in eleven days. I closed the meeting in full strength and with an undiminished audience, moved with an intensifying interest, because two other denominations, by standing agreement, commence to-night, and because the unpaved streets are now temporarily impassable from a flooding rain last night. Among the converts, is the President of the Male High School. His pupils, by their own suggestion, marched under one of the teachers to the water to see him baptized. Thus Bro. Gaylord has put his

---
[8] Moore, *Living Pulpit*, p. 40. Cf. Boles, *Biographical Sketches*, p. 143. Also, *Millennial Harbinger*, 1859, p. 116.
[9] *Ibid.*
[10] *Millennial Harbinger*, 1859, p. 116.

armor on for the war. Bro. T. F. Campbell, for whom I sent, for that purpose, assisted me to baptize yesterday. I baptized the remainder to-day. There is great joy in this town. This makes 76 additions to this church in two visits.

Yours in the Lord,
D. S. Burnet.

Among the places visited in the fall was Weston, Missouri, from which he addressed a letter to the Missionary Society to be read at the October meeting.[11]

Isaac Errett read the letter from Burnet at the fall convention but said also that Burnet, while traveling a few months as a solicitor for the Missionary Society, had made no detailed report of his labors. Errett said, "We know enough of his eminent ability and zeal to be assured that his efforts, while in the employment of the Board, have been highly useful to the cause at large."[12] Probably Burnet had agreed to seek contributions from the churches where he held evangelistic meetings.

The 1858 Annual Meeting decided to put Burnet back among the officers of the Society as second vice-president.[13] The next year he was back in Cincinnati and registered in attendance at the convention with his two brothers, Jacob, Jr., and S. G.[14] Almost immediately he was appointed on a committee of three set up to study the "mode of raising funds."[15] This was another testimonial to his ability in the matter of institutional stewardship. The committee reported,

> That they would commend to the attention of the Executive Board the propriety of appointing an agent to labor in each of the following states, viz.: Ohio, Kentucky, Virginia, Tennessee,

---

[11] *Annual Proceedings*, 1858, p. 19.
[12] *Ibid.*, p. 10.
[13] *Ibid.*, p. 15.
[14] *Ibid.*, pp. 3, 4.
[15] *Ibid.*, p. 14.

Illinois, Indiana and Missouri, and in such other places as they may think proper, all of whom are expected to be acceptable preachers of the Christian church.[16]

Isaac Errett as corresponding secretary of the Missionary Society board continued to be harassed by accusations of Disciples of Christ that the Society sought to exercise ecclesiastical authority. Obviously there were disturbances being raised relative to questions of doctrine, discipline, and themes of local and sectional interest.[17] One of the most vocal reactionaries was T. Fanning, of Tennessee. He spoke with some scorn of the organization at the 1859 convention, reporting on conditions in Tennessee:

> Our plan of laboring, as churches, without the aid of a Missionary Society, Executive Board, President, Vice Presidents, or able and efficient traveling Secretary to get subscriptions, has succeeded to our satisfaction; and whilst we are resolved to cooperate with the disciples of our Lord Jesus Christ every where, in every good work, yet till we can be convinced there is a better way, we shall likely endeavor to do all that may be in our power, as Christian kings and Christians priests—as churches of Jesus Christ, striving together for the conversion of the world, and building up to saints in the faith, as it is written in the Oracles of God.[18]

The execution of John Brown at Harper's Ferry (1859) threw the country into intense political excitement. It was early in 1860 that Burnet returned to Cincinnati, where he resumed the pastorate of Christian Chapel, corner of Eighth and Walnut Streets.[19] It was a year of much excitement in Cincinnati. The social event of the year was the visit of the Prince of Wales, who was elaborately entertained by Cincinnati society

[16] *Ibid.*, p. 17.
[17] *Ibid.*, 1859, p. 14.
[18] *Ibid.*, p. 25.
[19] Moore, *Living Pulpit*, p. 40.

leaders. He made his headquarters at Burnet House. Miss Edith Burnet, an aunt or cousin of D. S., was the last of six ladies to dance with the Prince.[20]

At the 1860 Annual Meeting many of the brethren determined that D. S. Burnet should be persuaded to take the work of the corresponding secretary for the American Christian Missionary Society. On the evening of October 23, President Alexander Campbell took the chair but called to his aid Mr. Burnet[21] (who was not the first vice-president but only a vice-president), to do the actual function of presiding. This testimony to his legislative talents was only part of the picture. Burnet was being pushed to take the helm of a war-threatened institution at a time when the financial reports suggested that it was practically on the rocks.

Burnet accepted the secretaryship which placed him once more in the general field. He resigned again his pastoral care of the Cincinnati church and took upon himself additional travels.[22] The convention closed with a vote of thanks to "the President, and Bro. D. S. Burnet, the acting President, and the Secretaries, for the dignified and faithful manner in which they have discharged their duties."[23]

First evidence of the work of Church Extension, raising common funds among churches for the building of meetinghouses, is directly traceable to the activities of Burnet. It will be remembered that Burnet spent some time in Kansas and Missouri. Most of the church houses built before 1860 were very simple in structure. There were protests recorded against the sinful show of "great cathedrals costing forty thousand dollars."[24] By the fall of 1860 the Board was soundly convinced that

---

[20] Goss, *Cincinnati: Queen City*, pp. 197, 198.
[21] *Annual Proceedings*, 1860, p. 3.
[22] Moore, *Living Pulpit*, p. 40.
[23] *Annual Proceedings*, 1860, p. 24.
[24] Garrison and DeGroot, *Disciples of Christ*, p. 340.

... while we have always desired to see the churches schooled into systematic benevolence, so as to avoid the cost of agencies in the collection of moneys, we are satisfied that this is impracticable.[25]

So the solicitors went out to collect funds. With such an appeal there had been funds raised to build the meetinghouse at Leavenworth City, Kansas. The Board explained that the Leavenworth City project was strictly outside the duties of its purposes but that Leavenworth City was considered "so important a point for future influence, as well as for present good" they dared not hesitate.[26] For the present we can only speculate that it was Burnet who made the board see the place of that kind of work which finally became the chief function of the Disciples Board of Church Extension.

1861-1864: ADDING HEARTBREAK TO FAILURE

Burnet was corresponding secretary during the first year of the Civil War, at which time the Missionary Society income dropped off more than half.[27] Isaac Errett left the secretaryship to become editor of Mr. Campbell's journal, the *Millennial Harbinger*. Many adjustments were necessary in the civil struggle in which the agricultural South was pitting its strength against the industrial North.

The area of Cincinnati in 1861 had increased in less than forty years to more than double its population when chartered as a city. Its area now covered about seven square miles. In the war, Cincinnati, by force of circumstances and desiring union for reasons of trade more than to solve the slavery problem, joined the Northern forces. Many homes were open in the city for

[25] *Annual Proceedings*, p. 8.
[26] *Ibid*.
[27] Garrison and DeGroot, *Disciples of Christ*, p. 518.

escaping slaves, as abolitionists were numerous and active in operating the Negroes' "underground railway."

Disciples of Christ did not divide over the slavery issue. Much speculation has been done as to why the war issues did not cause a rift in this brotherhood. It has been pointed out that slavery was a political issue in the realm of opinion rather than a religious issue in the realm of faith.[28] Their theory of scriptural and church authority is said to have made it impossible for them to divide over war and slavery.[29] But the Board of Managers, reporting to the annual convention through Mr. Burnet, pointed out that, "Almost no funds have been sent in without solicitation, and but very few persons have responded to the call of the secretary's letters."[30] The war occasioned an acknowledged setback. One could look at the report of income for the year and see the situation. The Missionary Society collected $8,863.25, including $1,218.39 in funds carried over from the previous year.[31] Disciples of Christ held no property North or South worth dividing.

The heartbreak of Burnet over the "unnatural war" situation is reflected in a letter which he sent across the lines to John Rogers of Kentucky. In it he said, "Though hostile armies tread down our fields and array friend and brother against friend and brother, Christ is not divided and his church reigns over every zone."[32]

Burnet continued his evangelistic preaching. In North Eaton, Ohio, a church sprang into existence under the leadership of a devoted woman, Mrs. Chloe Tucker.[33]

---

[28] Shaw, *Buckeye Disciples*, p. 194.
[29] Garrison, *Religion Follows the Frontier*, p. 180.
[30] *Annual Proceedings*, 1861, p. 7.
[31] *Ibid.*, p. 13.
[32] Shaw, *Buckeye Disciples*, p. 196. Cf. *Ohio Proceedings*, 1861, pp. 15, 16.
[33] Hayden, *Disciples in the Western Reserve, Ohio*, p. 443.

Burnet conducted a meeting for this congregation in 1861,³⁴ which resulted in the meetinghouse becoming too small for their needs. The new building was completed and dedicated by the next fall.³⁵ But everywhere he went he was hurt by the tragedy of the war. Due to the sudden disturbance of the public tranquillity he urged everyone to "pray for all that are in authority, that we may lead a quiet and peacable life in all godliness and honesty."³⁶

The most significant work attempted by Burnet at the outbreak of the war was an effort to establish a National City church in Washington, D. C. In his report for the Board that fall he said:

> We had thought that the establishing of the gospel in the Federal City, preached by a brother of our own choice, in a good house of worship, the gift of the brotherhood to the infant church there, was a fixed fact; but when all was ready, the insecurity of the city forbade its accomplishment. A similar plan in reference to the erection of a house of worship and the establishment of a church in New Orleans, failed for the same reason.³⁷

It seemed that one after another of his plans met with rebuff. But the greatest blow was his ultimate failure to keep the war issue out of the brotherhood Convention meeting. A loyalty resolution was presented by Dr. J. P. Robinson of Ohio, at the Cincinnati meeting, in behalf of the Union cause, October 1861. The resolution was as follows:

> Resolved, That we deeply sympathize with the loyal and patriotic in our country, in the present efforts to sustain the Government of the United States. And we feel it our duty as

---
³⁴*Ibid.*, p. 448.
³⁵*Ibid.*, p. 447.
³⁶*Annual Proceedings*, 1861, p. 8.
³⁷*Ibid.*

Christians, to ask our brethren everywhere to do all in their power to sustain the proper and constitutional authorities of the Union.[38]

Robinson's resolution came at the close of a morning session and since he expressed a preference to speak on his motion at the afternoon session it was held over. At the 2:00 P.M. session, Robinson called for his resolution to be acted upon. Immediately Brother Burnet raised the question whether, in view of the second article of the constitution, it was in order to entertain such a resolution in the body. Isaac Errett was presiding, at Campbell's request, and Errett decided that the resolution was in order. A Brother John Smith then moved an appeal from the decision of the chair to the vote of those present. So much discussion ensued that Smith withdrew his motion. But it was immediately back on the floor again, renewed by R. M. Bishop. When the vote was taken, the appeal was sustained and the resolution declared out of order.

The action of the body seemed at first like a victory for Burnet in his attempt to keep the war question out of his beloved organization. But L. L. Pinkerton moved for a ten-minute recess. During the recess Mr. Burnet was called to the chair and requested to serve as presiding officer for a called "mass meeting." As chairman he would not be formally allowed to discuss the proposition! Dr. Robinson's resolution was read again, and a few remarks were made by Col. James A. Garfield. The resolution was passed with only one negative vote.[39] As presiding officer Burnet did not vote but he probably would have had the same sentiment as the resolution. He simply did not want the cooperating organization threatened by fostering the civil warfare in any way. More than once he found it necessary to satisfy his conscience

---

[38] *Annual Proceedings*, 1861, p. 20.

[39] *Ibid.*, p. 20. Cf. Garrison and DeGroot, *Disciples of Christ* pp. 335, 336.

by avoiding participation in the strife.[40] His views were much the same as those of Benjamin Franklin who said, "We will not take up arms against, fight and kill the brethren we have labored for twenty years to bring into the kingdom of God."[41]

Burnet centralized his labors in the spring of 1862 in the State of Ohio, attempting to build up the Sunday schools. His aim, as expressed May 20-22, 1862, at Wooster, was to establish such schools in every neighborhood "to benefit the church and the world."[42] In behalf of the Missionary Society he was finding it impossible to employ agents to raise funds. Consequently, he traveled widely himself during the summer and fall, visiting Maryland, Pennsylvania, New York, Kentucky, Virginia, Connecticut, Indiana and Ohio.[43] Up and down the country were the marks of war tragedy.

The city of Cincinnati became dangerously threatened by the Confederate army under General Kirby Smith in the campaign of 1862. Accordingly, it was necessary to establish martial law in the city for a short time. These conditions were reflected also in Burnet's address to the annual meeting on the state of the Missionary Society cause:

> The year just closing has been one of most stirring incident. A rebellion, the gravest in character and most colossal in proportion which history records, has swept from the area of our co-operation some of the States, from which we realized a heavy pecuniary support...[44]

The use of the word "rebellion" was quite obnoxious to some of those present. Elijah Goodwin moved that the

---
[40]Garrison and DeGroot, *Disciples of Christ*, p. 335.
[41]*Ibid.*, pp. 335, 336.
[42]Shaw, *Buckeye Disciples*, p. 199. Cf. *Ohio Proceedings* 1862, p. 12. Also, Wilcox, *Disciples of Christ in Ohio*, pp. 294-296.
[43]*Annual Proceedings*, 1862, p. 6.
[44]*Ibid.*

word be struck out of Burnet's report. J. W. McGarvey offered as a substitute "attempt at revolution." After a brief tempest over the matter, W. T. Moore succeeded in getting the matter tabled, but the word appeared in the report. They were stormy days for a man who sought, with all his strength and mind, to steer the course of the infant Society through the stormy seas of war. The weight of it was equivalent to adding injury upon injury, heartbreak upon failure. Now his brethren were squabbling over terminology! His feelings in the midst of the war are indicated in an address made shortly before giving up the work with the Missionary Society:

> The disaster of the nineteenth century has come, which white-haired sire and fair-browed son prayed never to see! But it has come, like some splendid and blighting comet, driving commerce and trade from their channels, and the blood out of our hearts! The world gazes on the scene aghast! and the religion of Christ, made for man, not knowing his distinctions of tribe and nation, nor his ocean and mountain boundaries, visits alike the field golden with harvest or incarnadine with human gore, and still brings her pardon-bearing mercy to all. Our work then is unchanged, except by the difficulties which it is the victory of faith to overcome.[45]

---

[45] *Annual Proceedings*, 1863, pp. 12, 13.

CHAPTER VI

Recognized Success at Last

1863-1864: BALTIMORE AND RESIGNATION

WAR CONDITIONS WERE PRIMARILY responsible for Burnet's acceptance in 1863 of the Baltimore, Maryland, pastorate. It was at Baltimore that his most effective pulpit and pastoral ministry attained its fullest fruition. The church there like others in the country, was beset by the problems of the Civil War. Everything seemed set against permanent progress. But Mr. Burnet took the church and went to work with his usual zest for peace and good will. He hoped that good results would come by and by.

In 1863 Burnet was in the midst of an evangelistic meeting in Philadelphia when a committee from the Paca Street Church, Baltimore, Maryland, came to him with a request that he become pastor of their congregation.[1] Burnet had held a meeting in Baltimore in 1834 at the old North Street Church. During the thirty years that had passed, Burnet experienced great success, but the old North Street Church had some highly developed schismatic tendencies until in 1840 many of the Christian members had withdrawn from it. The persons with cooperative spirit seem to have withdrawn rather than to continue in strife. On July 26, 1840, the scattered Disciples of Christ met in Trades Union Hall, at Baltimore and Gay Streets.[2] After meeting for a while in the New Assembly Rooms, Fayette and Holiday Streets, and

[1] Andrew W. Gottschall, *Across a Century, Being the History of the First Christian Church,* Baltimore, Md. (Baltimore: Hess Ptg. Co., 1932), p. 54.
[2] *Ibid.,* p. 33.

at Warfield's Church, on St. Paul near Fayette Street, the congregation secured the church building on Paca Street from the Dunkards.³ The building was remodeled and was dedicated by Alexander Campbell on May 26, 1850.⁴

Following J. D. Benedict as pastor of the Paca Street Church, Burnet moved to Baltimore. It was a historic church, with a unique appeal for rational and family-like religion, to which he had gone.

The Baltimore church became noted for its very liberal passion for brotherhood and unity. The church had been organized largely by a young man from the Haldane school in Edinburgh, Scotland, which also had influenced the young Alexander Campbell before his coming to America. This young man was Charles Farquharson. He settled in Baltimore about 1817.⁵

In organizing the church, December 22, 1833, the congregation of sixty-three persons was headed by elders, deacons, and deaconesses. Farquharson, William Carmen and Hugh Bell were elders. Deacons were John Thomas, Jr., Edward Sweeney, and James G. Henshall. Not all the churches recognized the function of deaconesses, but this church began its work with Ann Bell, Martha Sweeney, and Sarah Sands serving in this capacity.⁶

Farquharson served as elder of the church until May, 1850, at which time he withdrew from the North Street Church, sending a notice to A. Campbell of his action. Mr. Campbell said that the reasons Elder Farquharson withdrew from the church was because of "the debates, the strifes, the emulations, the cold and lifeless forms and ceremonies of that *no soulism,* or destructionism,

---
³Gottschall, *Across a Century*, p. 37.
⁴*Ibid.* Cf. *Millennial Harbinger*, 1850, pp. 404-408.
⁵*Ibid.*, p. 10.
⁶*Ibid.*, p. 14.

sown amongst them some time since. . . . .'"⁷ The Paca Street Church came into being as a gathering together of the liberal and generous spirit of freedom. The members built a suitable meetinghouse and occupied it May 26, 1850.

Campbell attended the opening of the new church and described the building as follows:

They have, indeed, in the midst of a venerable and beautiful grave-yard, at the corner of Lombard and Pace Streets, erected a commodious and handsome meetinghouse, which, when well packed, will seat some seven or eight hundred persons. It has a very neat and comfortable basement under it, well fitted up for Sunday School and Library. Its principal room, in all its arrangements for convenience and real beauty, is regarded by the tasteful as an architectural gem; and yet there is nothing in it of that affected grandeur or ecclesiastic magnificence indicative of that lordly pride and prelatic arrogance, so often copied, in the eastern cities, from the world beyond the Atlantic.[8]

Having been founded by those who had a deep and sublime passion for brotherhood, the ministers were free to preach, teach and expound the truth as they saw it.[9] Burnet contributed his part in helping this family of God to live and work together as brethren.[10]

Denominational exclusiveness, the acceptance of sectarianism as divine, divisions among Christians that kept people apart who ought to be together, mutual suspicion, misunderstanding and distrust never were given the sanctions of divine approval.[11]

This was the Baltimore church to which Burnet gave his most mature leadership. Good results came as the fruitage of his devotion. Numerous additions to the membership and the development of a strong faith in

---
[7] Ibid., p. 33.
[8] Millennial Harbinger, 1850, pp. 404-408. Cited in Gottschall, Across a Century, p. 38.
[9] Gottschall, Across a Century, p. 63.
[10] Ibid., p. 62.
[11] Ibid.

kindness, mercy, and peace were firmly established in Baltimore.

The final proclamation of emancipation of all slaves living in the seceding states, except in Tennessee and some districts of Virginia and Louisiana, came Jan. 1, 1863. The war issues had been more sharply drawn and the tension ran higher in the Disciples of Christ annual meeting the following October. A new "Loyalty Resolution" was proposed from the floor of the convention. The new resolution was more bitter than the one two years before when Burnet tried to keep the question out of the discussions. In the new resolution was the reference to "the attempts of armed traitors to overthrow our Government."[12] When the resolution came up, a motion to adjourn failed. The president remembered two years before and turned it immediately to a vote of the group. They reversed themselves from the previous decision and another motion to adjourn failed to keep them from adopting the loyalty resolution with but few dissenting.[13]

Burnet as corresponding secretary made a strong plea for centralism. He saw the weakness of independent congregationalism which sometimes refuses to give its support to any worthy cause but operates for its own sake. He desired a kind of Christian congregationalism which volunteers its power and support in a confederation of free churches on the basis that the Spirit of Christ should be held in common. He said:

"Indeed, a system of independent congregationalism, like ours, needs the centralism of massive attraction and diffusion—attraction to the great work of the Messianic commission and the diffusion of its power, thus concentrated, in ministrations of love to the farthest verge of human society. For all such purposes, this society is the hand, the tongue, the voice, the heart, of the great brotherhood. We have no other point of

---

[12] *Annual Proceedings*, 1863, p. 24.
[13] *Ibid.*

contact. The gospel is God-given, and the government is laid gracefully upon the Savior's shoulders. Preaching to all the world, is the work of Christian men, and those Christian men have united their energies in this association for the labor, conceding the obligation which weighed upon the bosom of the apostle through life—I am *debtor* both to the Greeks and to the Barbarians, both to the wise and the unwise; so much as in me is, I am ready to preach the gospel.''[14]

Almost the last act of D. S. Burnet as corresponding secretary of the Missionary Society was near the close of the 1863 meeting in Cincinnati. After a few remarks he took up pledges and money ''to the amount of some eight hundred dollars.''[15] It was his custom to strike while the iron was hot. He never passed an opportunity to stir up the benevolent spirit of those seeking to carry on a great cause. It is doubtful that any other man in the convention could have raised that sum so well as Burnet.

He sought funds for evangelization of the Negroes, especially the multitudes of freedmen resulting from the war. On January 20, 1864, Burnet announced that but one contribution was received for that purpose, and unless other funds came in, the amount would be returned to the donor.[16] Burnet seemed habitually to have expected generosity from his brethren for which they were unprepared to respond. Then in March (1864) he resigned his office with the American Christian Missionary Society because he had accepted the call to the Paca Street Christian Church in Baltimore. There was considerable speculation as to why Burnet decided to resign as corresponding secretary. His own statement presents some of the more prominent reasons. B. W. Johnson, who later took the work of that office, reported to the 1864 Convention that Elder Burnet's health would not

[14]*Ibid.*, p. 14.
[15]*Ibid.*, pp. 23ff.
[16]*Millennial Harbinger*, 1864, p. 93.

permit him to do such rigorous work, that "he found himself physically unable to endure the duties of financial agent in the field."[17] This was not the exact reason, as Burnet's letter to the *Millennial Harbinger* indicated:

RESIGNATION OF BRO. D. S. BURNET, CORRESPONDING SECRETARY OF THE A. C. MISSIONARY SOCIETY[18]

Early last autumn I communicated to many persons in several States my intention to decline a re-election to the position of Corresponding Secretary. Indeed, I mentioned the subject to some persons in the summer. Prominent among the reasons for this step, were these: That Mrs. Burnet's health no longer permitted her to adhere to her determination to accompany me in all my extended tours. Long since, she had exceeded the demands of duty in her sacrifices and exposures. My own health had at times materially suffered by continued travel; and my constant preachings, physicians have told me, would entail upon me permanent disability. I am thus particular in my statement, lest it should be supposed that I had grown weary of, rather than in, the work of evangelizing, which I always associated with my official duties, or in the other work of the Society. From the time I urged the scheme of associated evangelical action upon the brethren, in 1845, to the present, the work has commanded my heart, my best energies, and my means.

When waited on by the committee of nomination last October, I adhered to my declination. Yet when their report containing my name was read at the last afternoon session, owing to the exciting character of the debates of the morning, I made no public objection, preferring to communicate with the Board, to whom I stated that I had at least a provisional engagement with the church in Baltimore, and that I should spend the winter East. In my report of March 1st, I again urged upon the Board my resignation, and it was accepted.

---

[17] *Annual Proceedings*, 1864, p. 9.
[18] *Millennial Harbinger*, 1864, p. 185.

The policy of the Board requires a traveling Secretary, and it is desirable that a competent person be secured, in time to improve the opening season. I quit the more public field with many regrets, especially at this juncture, commending to God an association so vital in its relation to the cause of primitive Christianity. May God bless all the co-operants in this work! I shall still aid the Society as occasion may require. For the present, Bro. H. S. Bosworth, Recording Secretary, Cincinnati, Ohio, should be addressed by agents and others. My post-office address is Baltimore, Maryland.

D. S. BURNET.

Even though Elder Burnet was absent from the 1864 annual meeting in Cincinnati, he was made chairman of a committee to raise funds for a monument to the grave of Elder Walter Scott.[19] The death of Scott, Burnet's dear friend and co-worker, was a severe blow to the movement. In the heat of civil strife the great preacher and evangelistic teacher had passed away. The realization that some funds should be raised brought the convention's memory around to the fact that Burnet was one of the most skilled in that kind of work. In his grief at the loss of his friend, he accepted the challenge to place a monument over the last remains of the man who made the five-point sermon on the "Plan of Salvation" famous across America.

1865-1866: PRESIDENT OF A GOING CONCERN

The surrender of General Robert E. Lee at Appomattox and the assassination of President Abraham Lincoln were high lights of the crisis of 1865. For approximately a century the political gospel of the country had been that of "rugged individualism."[20] The strain upon those conceptions of the social situation came about by the urbanization of many areas east of the Mississippi

---

[19] *Annual Proceedings*, 1864, pp. 29, 30.
[20] T. Walter Wallbank and Alastair M. Taylor, *Civilisation—Past and Present* (Chicago: Scott, Foresman and Co., p. 232.)

River. But the end of the frontier was not in sight. There were lands to be settled farther west. Peace meant that there would be opportunity for still further pioneer developments.

Although the annual meeting of Disciples of Christ in 1865 sounded a note of hope, there were two men who were very conspicuous by their absence, D. S. Burnet and Alexander Campbell. Isaac Errett took the chairmanship in Campbell's absence. However, when officers were elected for the next year both Campbell as president, and Burnet, as vice-president, were retained by the Missionary Society.[21]

Bacon College, of which Burnet once was president, became Kentucky University and was moved to Lexington "where it became heir to the property and the historic tradition of Transylvania University, the name of which it later restored."[22] Burnet was seeing a good number of his enterprises gain strength and come into greater prominence. But Western Reserve Eclectic Institute (Hiram), one of the Ohio interests of Disciples of Christ of that state, fell into such financial difficulties that it was offered to the state missionary society in 1865. The aim was to adopt the seminary idea. A few lectureships were given by Isaac Errett, Robert Milligan, H. T. Anderson, and D. S. Burnet, but the school was reorganized two years later at the college level and named Hiram College.[23]

W. T. Moore was called as a professor of Kentucky University (Transylvania) and as part-time pastor of the Eighth and Walnut Street Christian Church of Cincinnati, in 1866. Moore was in his early 30's when called to the church which Burnet had held as pastor for many years.

---

[21] *Annual Proceedings*, 1865, pp. 2, 4.

[22] Garrison, *Religion Follows the Frontier*, p. 169. Cf. Garrison and DeGroot, *Disciples of Christ*, p. 224.

[23] Shaw, *Buckeye Disciples*, p. 207.

Isaac Errett began to publish the *Christian Standard* in the spring of 1866. The first issue in April carried the news that Alexander Campbell had died on March 4.[24] It was not long before this journal, which was first published at Cleveland (but moved to Cincinnati, July 31, 1869),[25] boasted significantly that "it is the only weekly among us that advocates organized effort for missionary purposes."[26] At a time when the need for practical righteousness and the spirit of Christian obedience was more important than conformity to legalistic and theological tenets, the brotherhood were extremely fortunate to have a man in their leadership such as Isaac Errett. He understood Burnet and Campbell and he understood why Burnet was regarded as being among the minority, which will be explained later.

At the annual meeting in 1866 Mr. Campbell was characterized as "the man of the age."[27] Few, if any Disciples of Christ wished to detract from the significance of his leadership. His importance in the nineteenth century is avowed in the vast number of books, sermons, and articles which have extolled his virtues.

Mr. Campbell was president of Bethany at the time of his death. D. S. Burnet was called to Bethany to hold an evangelistic meeting and to deliver the memorial address following the death of Alexander Campbell. The meeting was successful in adding thirty to the church,[28] and at Commencement Burnet delivered his second memorial tribute to the memory of Campbell. His oratorical ability[29] especially equipped him for the laudatory speech. Bethany College published the address and dis-

[24]Garrison and DeGroot, *Disciples of Christ*, p. 357.
[25]*Ibid.*
[26]*Ibid.*, p. 356.
[27]*Annual Proceedings*, 1866, p. 15.
[28]Frederick D. Power, *Life of William Kimbrough Pendleton*, LL.D. (St. Louis: Christian Publishing Co., 1902), p. 253.
[29]Errett Gates, *The Story of the Churches, the Disciples of Christ* (New York: Baker and Taylor Co., 1905), pp. 189, 190.

tributed it widely in pamphlet form at 10 cents a copy. It was a work showing magnificent insight into the character of Mr. Campbell and of a most objective view of the Bethany leader's relation to the program of Disciples of Christ. Because Burnet was a growing man, known to try to make each sermon better than the one before, it is possible in the memorial tribute to see the fertile mind of a great man at work with great power.

But the memorial address given by Burnet from the pulpit of the Baltimore church one week after the death of Campbell is far less laudatory, and indicative of the real relations between Burnet and Campbell. Most histories have relied heavily upon the Bethany address. It is instructive to read also the one he made at Baltimore (see Appendix IV).

After delivering the Baltimore address the Christian church there published it in pamphlet form, March 12, 1866. Burnet evidently polished the speech and softened it for delivery at Bethany in June. These addresses contain the letters "M.A." after Burnet's name, evidently in order to indicate an academic master of arts degree. Where Burnet obtained such a degree is not clear.

A short quotation from the June address at Bethany indicates the style in which Burnet characterized Mr. Campbell's later life with less bold lines.

What was the character of his intellect? I do not know to whom to compare him. If I could, I would be, for the nonce, a Plutarch and raise aloft my social balance and weigh him with other men. But first we must weigh Alexander Campbell with himself—Campbell with Campbell. Campbell of the *Christian Baptist* and early *Harbinger,* and Campbell of the later *Harbinger* are in equipoise but for a moment. The former preponderates. Of his debates, those held in Cincinnati, preponderate. His Lexington debate would have been his best, for he was quite perfect in preparation, had he not permitted the side issue of his uniform consistency as a writer, to come into the arena. The Campbell of the last fifteen years never compared with the Campbell of the preceding thirty-five. But with the partial and almost imperceptible decay of the intellectual power discerned by but few, there was an increased evolution of the sentimental and spiritual—a gracious compensation.

Three events, more than any others, contributed to the breakdown of Mr. Campbell's overtaxed powers. The labors of the College superadded to "The care of the churches" and incessant literary labor—the sudden death of his darling boy Wycliffe—and the translation for the American Bible Union, of "Acts of Apostles." Before the last he staggered, then he fell, no more to rise to the height of his former power.

Now with whom can we compare the Alexander Campbell during the thirty-five or forty years of his prime? In dignity and solid judgment he was both Moses and Solomon...[30]

It is interesting also to note from the Bethany address that Burnet thought of Campbell as comparable with Luther and Zwingli, but not Calvin. He characterized Campbell as follows:

There are many points of resemblance between President Campbell and Luther. Vigorous intellect, imperturbable confidence in God, an aggressive nature, a life of prayerful toil, and a tendency to conservatism in later life, were common to them.... With Calvin he had nothing in common but a towering intellect. He more resembled Zwingle.[31]

After the death of Alexander Campbell, many adjustments began to be made. One of the strange turns of events was the action of Benjamin Franklin, formerly in partnership with Burnet in the publication of the *Christian Age*. After his association with Burnet in the publishing business, Franklin went to the *American Christian Review*. He continued to support the view that Christian Church congregations should cooperate through the Society system. In fact, as early as 1850 in his close friendship with Burnet he supported the organization of brotherhood societies in strong words.[32]

[30]*Millennial Harbinger*, 1866, pp. 314, 15.
[31]*Ibid.*, p. 316
[32]Garrison and DeGroot, *Disciples of Christ*, pp. 353, 54.

Beginning in December, 1866, Franklin began to voice through the *Review* his bitter opposition to the Society system which had developed among Disciples of Christ.

But Brother Burnet never wavered in his belief that the churches of the fellowship of Disciples of Christ needed some means of operating cooperatively. His long-time advocacy of the view was amply signalized by his election to the presidency of the convention following the death of Mr. Campbell.[33]

When the committee on nominations at the October annual meeting brought in a report nominating Isaac Errett, the editor of the *Christian Standard* and great admirer of Burnet, for the presidency, he declined the nomination in favor of his friend. Burnet was then chosen president and was conducted to the chair he had so often occupied as the actual presiding officer without bearing the title thereof. Errett and Robinson escorted Burnet to the pulpit. The new president accepted the office and its duties with deep feeling and with his usual high degree of extemporaneous skill.[34] At last Disciples of Christ had named to the honored office the man who did most to make that office honorable. It was the moment of recognition of the high esteem the brethren had for him, even though he maintained the minority view that Christianity is a tremendous way of life based on a simple doctrine. Many of his contemporaries had it the other way round—that Christianity is a system of biblical doctrine emerging into something of a life.

1867: IN THE MIDST OF SUCCESS

In June, 1867, Burnet resigned his pastoral charge at Baltimore. His resignation was the close of his ministry at a church destined to cling to the passion for

---
[33] *Annual Proceedings*, 1866, p. 16.
[34] *Ibid.*

brotherliness and unity. With such antecedents the church ultimately came to the view that

> ... it could not consistently deny full fellowship to Christians, evidently approved by God in works, stewardship and character. Unity by absorption was an outworn hope. Unity through fellowship became the ideal. . . . Frankly facing the issue, the Church extended its hand and heart, to all who name the name of Christ and walk with him, without reservation. Thus it is that this Church practices "open membership"—what an unfortunate term! It isn't open and it isn't membership, it is Christian fellowship, practiced indeed by all of the Churches of the Disciples of Christ, in every respect except that of a Church roster and the counting of noses. This Church does not believe in a Church membership roll as being in any sense a divine institution, nor does it so look upon the right hand of Christian fellowship that signifies joining a particular congregation as separate and distinct from other local groups of Christians.[35]

Such is the background today of the church once served by D. S. Burnet. Burnet had evidently given to it some of his deep convictions. He preached his farewell sermon on the Lord's Day, June 30, 1867.[36] It was a climax to the most successful pastoral connection of his life.[37] It was thought that perhaps on that day he became victim of a malignant dysentery germ. He had not been well for some time but was not considered seriously ill.[38] When the full force of the disease struck Mr. Burnet, he suffered extremely until the last few hours, although this sickness was comparatively brief.[39]

After a great day of preaching his farewell sermon at Baltimore, before his proposed taking up the work at Louisville, Burnet spent Monday, July 1, in quiet ef-

---
[35]Gottschall, *Across a Century*, p. 64.
[36]Moore, *Living Pulpit*, p. 41.
[37]*Millennial Harbinger*, 1867, p. 427.
[38]Moore, *Living Pulpit*, p. 41.
[39]*Millennial Harbinger*, 1867, p. 427.

forts to control the disease and to be relieved of the distress.⁴⁰ He grew weak from severe suffering, but on Tuesday morning "he insisted on meeting an engagement to administer the ordinance of baptism to two persons who had made the confession the previous Lord's Day."⁴¹ W. T. Moore says that Burnet was so feeble he had to be supported to and from the church where the baptisms were held.⁴² The strong determination of the man is reflected in this last act of his public ministry. The immersion of two persons at the church added something to the strain on his physical self and the next morning (Wednesday) he was too ill to rise.⁴³ Medical treatment began to be applied with fears that it was already too late.

During the rest of the week the family called in the best medical skill available in Baltimore. He was extremely ill on Saturday, his fifty-ninth birthday. On the next day, Sunday, many members of the Christian church went to the pastor's home to be at his bedside during the crisis. They saw how seriously ill he was, but that he retained his vigorous faith. As his friends and family stood at the bedside he said, "Brethren, my faith is strong in God; I die in the faith of the Gospel, and have no fears."⁴⁴ He recited the Twenty-Third Psalm in English and in Hebrew as a testimony to his faith and indication of his clearness of understanding.⁴⁵

He died Monday morning at 11:30 o'clock.⁴⁶ His couch was surrounded by weeping members of the

---

⁴⁰Moore, *Living Pulpit*, p. 41.
⁴¹*Ibid.*
⁴²*Ibid.*
⁴³*Ibid.*
⁴⁴*Ibid.*
⁴⁵Power, *Sketches of Our Pioneers*, p. 127. Cf. *Millennial Harbinger*, 1867, p. 427. Also Moore, *Living Pulpit*, pp. 41, 42.
⁴⁶Moore, *Living Pulpit*, p. 41. Cf. *Millennial Harbinger*, 1867, p. 427. Power, *Sketches of Our Pioneers*, p. 127.

church[47] along with Mary, his wife. His last words, immediately before death, were: "My path is clear before me, and I have nothing against any one."[48] Thus, his passing was at the age of fifty-nine years and two days.[49] The last hours had been very much like his whole life—filled with faith, hope, and love.

A. N. Gilbert, of Syracuse, New York, was called upon to conduct a service in Baltimore before the body was returned to Cincinnati. On Wednesday the service was conducted at the Paca Street Christian Church in Baltimore.[50] Many of his friends came together as the membership of the church paid their respects in his honor. From the report which Gilbert wrote to the *Millennial Harbinger* there is some indication of what was said on that occasion.[51] David Staats Burnet died, said Gilbert,

... in the full hope of a glorious immortality. His sickness was of but short duration in its severe aspects. On last Monday he should have been in bed. On Tuesday morning, supported by the arm of a brother, he tottered to the church building, performed the ordinance of baptism, and went home to the sick room, from which he never again will emerge alive.

He had completed his preparations for removal, preached his farewell sermon, bade his personal adieus to most of the members of the congregation, closed his financial business in Baltimore, and stood at the opening of a new epoch of life, which proves to be the life beyond the grave. The imagination of the poet can scarcely conceive of a more complete closing up of life than is here presented.[52]

The body was then placed in charge of his brother, Jacob Burnet, Jr., and a committee of the official board accompanied Mrs. Burnet to Cincinnati.[53]

[47]*Millennial Harbinger*, 1867, p. 427.
[48]*Ibid.* Cf. Boles, *Biographical Sketches*, p. 145. Moore, *Living Pulpit*, pp. 41, 42.
[49]Moore, *Ibid.*, p. 41. Cf. Boles, *Ibid.*, p. 144.
[50]*Ibid.*, p. 42
[51]*Millennial Harbinger*, 1867, p. 427.
[52]*Ibid.*
[53]Gottschall, *Across a Century*, p. 55. Cf. Moore, *Living Pulpit*, p. 42.

Friday afternoon, July 12, the funeral service was conducted at Christian Chapel, Cincinnati, where he had lived and served so many years, at the corner of Eighth and Walnut Streets.[54] At 2:30 p.m. the coffin containing his body was moved into the church. The immediate relatives, including the wife, mother, brothers and other relatives and friends of the deceased, followed in its train. Inside the church, the casket was placed upon a table draped with cypress. The richly ornamented case which contained the coffin was covered with large and beautiful wreaths of flowers.[55] Soon after the funeral procession entered the church, W. T. Moore began the service by reading a hymn which had been written by John Newland Maffit and which was found only in collections of hymns published by Disciples of Christ.[56] Its timeliness and the fact that it was read by Moore, who was pastor at the church where the funeral was held, makes it worth consideration here:

> Fallen—on Zion's battlefield,
>   A soldier of renown,
> Armed in the panoply of God,
>   In conflict cloven down!
> His helmet on, his armor bright,
>   His cheek unblanched with fear—
> While round his head there gleamed a light
>   His dying hour to cheer.
>
> Fallen—while cheering with his voice
>   The sacramental host,
> With banners floating in the air—
>   Death found him at his post.
> In life's high prime the warfare closed,
>   But not ingloriously;
> He fell beyond the outer wall
>   And shouted, Victory!

---

[54] Moore, *Living Pulpit*, p. 42.
[55] *Millennial Harbinger*, 1867, p. 428.
[56] *Ibid.*

Fallen—a holy man of God,
  An Israelite indeed,
A standard-bearer of the cross,
  Mighty in word and deed—
A master spirit of the age,
  A bright and burning light,
Whose beams across the firmament
  Scattered the clouds of night.

Fallen—as sets the sun at eve,
  To rise in splendor where
His kindred luminaries shine
  Their heaven of bliss to share;
Beyond the stormy battlefield
  He reigns in triumph now,
Sweeping a harp of wondrous song,
  With glory on his brow!

After Moore finished reading the above hymn, which was later reprinted in the *Millennial Harbinger*,[57] the service continued with his reading a letter from the Paca Street Church in Baltimore. The congregation then learned that A. N. Gilbert and George W. Morling had come to the funeral to represent the Baltimore Christian church; and that the church at Louisville to which Burnet had been called had sent two representatives, James Trabne and William Terry.[58]

The Scriptures were read by Gilbert, the Ninetieth Psalm, beginning, "Lord, thou hast been our dwelling place in all generations."[59] A prayer followed, by Dr. L. L. Pinkerton, of Lexington, Ky. In describing the prayer afterward a Cincinnati newspaper said that it was a simple and fervent petition that those immediately affected by the death might have faith in the midst of mourning and that all might find a hope that is sweeter

---
[57] *Ibid.*, pp. 428, 29.
[58] *Ibid.*
[59] *Ibid.*

than life and stronger than death.⁶⁰ Following the prayer the congregation and choir joined, as was the custom, in singing the hymn which begins "It is not death to die...."⁶¹

The sermon for the occasion was delivered by the eloquent Isaac Errett, editor of the *Christian Standard*. He stood up to preach. His personal appearance was very striking. About six foot one inch tall and muscular, he had dark auburn hair and light gray eyes. Upon this man had fallen the leadership of Disciples of Christ, and D. S. Burnet had valued him in that light. The deceased had regarded the speaker as a close friend. As speakers both had few superiors. Now it was time for Isaac Errett to say something. He began the funeral oration:⁶²

> Death has stricken down, away from home, one in the prime of a glorious manhood, and one dear to many here. This was his religious home, for he never ceased to be a member of the congregation here. But he died surrounded by friends and beloved brethren, and his eyes were closed by the hands of love. I know the brethren of Baltimore, and know they omitted nothing to cheer and comfort his closing hours. It is not wrong for us to sorrow, for even Jesus wept, and we with weak faith and feeble hope may well be pardoned if we too weep when one of our beloved is taken away. It is a dreadful stroke when one great and gifted and wise is laid low in the tomb. The deceased was a noble man, physically, intellectually, and religiously. His death breaks in heavily upon the family circle. In a family of ten children, death, for thirty-five years, has made no invasion until now. It is especially sad that the mother, aged and feeble, should be compelled to give up one who has been her pride and joy for forty years. His wife, too, mourns in sadness and loneliness. A leader of the people is taken away. Much depended upon the continuance of his life. And it is meet that there

---

⁶⁰*Millennial Harbinger*, 1867, p. 429.
⁶¹*Ibid.*
⁶²*Ibid.*, pp. 430, 431.

should be some general sorrow. In his public capacity I propose to consider the departed.

It is seldom a public man, especially if breasting the current of public opinion, goes through his work without reproach. Our brother, however, did so. When he commenced to preach, religion was largely a system of doctrines, and an easy religious life was to subscribe to some system and throw in your fortunes with those who were its cold disciples. The deceased could not consent to this. He believed Christianity to be a life, rather than a system of doctrines. Not the subtleties of theological speculation were to be the bond of union, or the terms of acceptance—but faith in the Lord Jesus, love of Jesus, submission to Jesus as our Prophet, Priest, and King.

His adherence to this view threw him into a minority, and made his life one of crosses and toil. He commenced to preach in this city when he was 16 years old. Before 20 he became pastor of a church in Dayton; and ever after that he labored earnestly either as pastor or minister, or in some capacity to teach men the beauties of a Christian life.

His intellectual powers were great, and he was a man of fine culture, who could throw around his discourses all the graces of rhetoric and eloquence. Reformers are mostly men of somewhat rough and angular characteristics. Bro. Burnet was always well balanced and smooth. He was at home with the most intellectual; and with a heart glowing with love for all, he was always popular with the masses. In the backwoods of Iowa and Illinois and Kansas, his name is revered as much as by those who loved him in Cincinnati and Baltimore. He had much versatility of character, and the circumstances connected with the church of his choice compelled him to accept at different times a great variety of employments. Hence he was at one time pastor, at another evangelist, at another solicitor for benevolent societies; then editor, publisher, teacher, etc.; doing well in all, if he did not attain the highest eminence in any. He was in all things a growing man, being engaged in the study of Hebrew when he died. His power in the pulpit was greater in Baltimore when he was nearly sixty than ever before. It is, indeed, a great sadness that such a man should be taken away.

But there is a bright side to the picture, and I propose to mention a few considerations why this should be a day of triumph and joy. The great mass of lives are failures. Dangers, tempests, and whirlwinds of temptations continually beset us. Hell powerfully seeks our overthrow. Our brother went through all successfully, and *his* life was one of triumph. Kepler was nearly set wild with joy at the success of his astronomical calculations. What inexpressible rapture of soul must be his who has worked out the problem of salvation, and stands crowned before the throne of God! Let us be glad for him and with him to-day. But again, the misgivings and anguish and despairing of a human heart are past, and this too, should be for us a source of joy. He has passed into a world of blissful realization, from which no honors of earth could induce him to return. Why should we not rejoice?

Errett continued the funeral sermon by urging the congregation to remain faithful to the principles they had accepted under Burnet's leadership. It could be seen that those founding leaders of the movement were passing away and the responsibility was now falling upon others. Errett observed that those who died with such a faith as Burnet's had found consolation and hope. "Their faith did not fail them as they approached the grave—it made their last hours their brightest and most glorious."[63] It was almost an evangelistic appeal, which Burnet would have sanctioned on this ocasion.

Closing his address he recited something of the simplicity, earnestness, integrity, singleheartedness, and Christian zeal of Mr. Burnet.[64] Following the sermon, John Shackleford uttered a brief prayer.[65] Then the lid of the casket was opened, the congregation passed by to view the remains, and the family was caught up in that moment of sober grief. The funeral procession moved out of the city to Spring Grove Cemetery where the body was interred in the family burial plot.[66]

---

[63]*Millennial Harbinger*, 1867, pp. 431, 432.
[64]*Ibid.*
[65]*Ibid.*, p. 432.
[66]*Ibid.* Cf. Moore, *Living Pulpit*, p. 42.

A report of the proceedings was sent to various newspapers and journals, including the one to the *Millennial Harbinger.* The Walnut Street Christian Church of Louisville sent an announcement of their resolution, voted July 10, to the *Harbinger,* the *Christian Standard,* and to the *Christian Review* for publication.[67]

RESOLUTION[68]

This congregation has received with much poignant sorrow intelligence of the death of Bro. D. S. Burnet. The Christian Church throughout the country will feel deeply this sore bereavement, but upon this congregation the blow falls most heavily. He had recently accepted an urgent and unanimous call to the pastorate of this church, and was preparing to enter upon the immediate performance of those duties when the Master, whom he loved and served with devotion, called him to another sphere of worship. His life appeared to be a necessity to us, and a bright future for the cause of our Master in this city was anticipated from his known ability and piety, and we feel deeply grieved that our hopes were not realized. We mourn not as those without hope. In fullness of faith we recognize the fact that our dear brother has gained his crown of immortality. We rejoice in his gain, and bow in humble and pious submission to the event that has bereaved us of his presence among us, of his great instructive ability, and those traits of a Christian teacher in which he was an eminent example.

Elder D. S. Burnet has long been recognized among us as a successful laborer, both as a speaker and writer. His labors in these respects have been fruitful of good results wherever his efforts reached the public mind. He had such full recognition of his every duty as a Christian, and was ever so ready to perform it in all its fullness, that his life was one of the most arduous in labors for the renovation of humanity through the teachings of the Holy Spirit. We look back upon those labors with a sense of profound gratitude, and are thankful that he was so long spared to preach to the world "the unsearchable

---
[67] *Ibid.*
[68] *Ibid., pp.* 432, 433.

riches of Christ," and to influence his brethren to love and good works. Our memories are filled with records of his faithful endurance as a soldier of the Cross.

We deeply sympathize with the brethren throughout the land in the loss of such an able advocate of pure Christianity and such an humble, pious, and genial co-worker.

This congregation affectionately condoles with sister Burnet in the affliction that has separated her from the cherished companion of her joys and Christian graces, but we rejoice to know that she looks forward to a blissful re-union where partings are at an end.

John Carr, John Patterson, Wm. Terry *Elders*

The October annual meeting in Cincinnati's Christian Chapel was one of gloom. Disciples of Christ were at the threshold of a new epoch indeed. On Thursday morning, October 24, 1867, a committee on obituaries made its report in the form of two resolutions memorializing the death of John Rogers and of D. S. Burnet.[69] Rogers had been a member of the Board of Managers and Burnet was president of the Society. Concerning Burnet, the resolution read:

Resolved, That the death of D. S. Burnet, the President of the Society, has removed from our midst a faithful and devoted Christian, an eloquent and powerful preacher, a gifted and earnest champion of the truth, and a steadfast friend and advocate of the missionary enterprise.

The committee proposing the resolution was composed of L. L. Pinkerton, O. A. Burgess, Isaac Errett, and Joseph Wasson. Both Gilbert and Errett made laudatory remarks about the life of Burnet.

The young preacher, William Thomas Moore, newly married and enjoying the first successes of his ministry, had become pastor (1866) of the historic church of Disciples of Christ at the corner of Eighth and Walnut Streets, Cincinnati, where Burnet had served. He

---
[69] *Annual Proceedings,* 1867, p. 20.

planned to be a pastor to the church as much time as possible, considering that he had been elected to a professorship in Kentucky University (Transylvania). Also he intended to do some editorial work on religious books which he thought worth publishing. When Alexander Campbell died, Moore set to work in earnest to compile a book of sermons, with some biographical sketches of their authors. He aimed to include in the volume a representative sermon from some of the living preachers, beginning the new epoch in Disciples history. Among the most important would be one by the minister at Baltimore, Maryland, David Staats Burnet. The youthful preacher, Moore, was busy preparing a short sketch of the life of the distinguished Brother Burnet, which sketch was to be used as a preface in the book to the sermon entitled, "The Good Confession." Burnet had preached that sermon many times in his evangelistic tours from New York to Texas.

While the manuscript for the book was nearing completion a letter had come from Burnet, February 28, 1867, in which the Baltimore pastor said, "I consider the inauguration of our Society system, which I vowed to urge upon the brethren, if God raised me from my protracted illness of 1845, as one of the most important acts of my career."[70] Within less than five months, before the publication of Moore's book, D. S. Burnet had died. Moore entitled his book *The Living Pulpit* and published the works of twenty-seven living preachers and the sermon and obituary of Brother Burnet. It was an act of good judgment and intuition. There are many good reasons to believe that Burnet deserved first place among those who remained after the death of Campbell, if not before. Furthermore, there is reason to believe that the fruition of his projected labors may well compare with any of the brilliant performers in what Disciples of Christ chose to call the Reformation of the

---

[70] Moore, *Living Pulpit*, p. 45.

Nineteenth Century—including such names to conjure with as Campbell, Stone, Scott, and Errett. Although the modern history books have lost to a large extent the record, he is much alive in the organizational antecedents of enterprises of Disciples of Christ.

Moore expressed his personal sense of great regret that a leader like Burnet should be cut off in the midst of such a useful life; but it was equally great satisfaction to know that such a life of self-denial and labor had closed at the summit of success.[71] The death of both Campbell and Burnet caused Disciples of Christ to evaluate clearly the purposes of their labors. Moore said,

> ... Luther restored *Conscience* to its proper position, Calvin restored the *Divine Sovereignty*, and Wesley, *Human Responsibility*, as parts of the remedial system. Two things yet remained to be done. THE WORD OF GOD MUST BE RESTORED TO ITS PROPER AUTHORITY, AND SUCH AN ADJUSTMENT MADE OF THE ELEMENTS ELIMINATED BY THE REFORMATIONS JUST REFERRED TO AS WOULD SECURE A RAPID AND HARMONIOUS DEVELOPMENT OF THE RELIGION OF CHRIST IN THE WORLD.[72]

The importance of placing the person of Christ above creeds and human opinions was a distinctive feature of the purposes of D. S. Burnet and his peers. To many of his contemporaries, the Scriptures came to be a near approximation of a creed, but Burnet was familiar with textual criticism and rather regarded the sacred Book as a guide to the knowledge of Christ and the way of the Christian life. This view was clearly set forth by Burnet in his sermon on "The Good Confession" (See Appendix VII).

---
[71] Moore, *Living Pulpit*, p. 46.
[72] *Ibid.*, p. 13.

Burnet, like his contemporaries, was beginning to question the strange actions attributed to the Holy Spirit. He came to the view that the Holy Spirit in the process of human conversion operates through truth, and never without truth. Persons are won to Christianity in accordance with the Holy Spirit's instrumentality of truth. Thus it became important to teach Scriptures, because Scriptures were religious Truth. The wild and visionary notions abroad among the denominations had attributed to the action of the Holy Spirit certain magical and unpredictable conversion power, so as to create highly emotional circumstances in the programs of evangelism. Burnet's posthumously published sermon indicated that its author had stressed the significance of the spiritual importance of truth. He had concentrated the strongest efforts to uphold an intelligent approach to Christianity. The sermon was a re-echoing of his own conversion experience upon reading Romans 10.

Another gift of his which came to view after his death was something more concrete than a published sermon. It was a fund of $10,000 left for the purpose of educating the ministry. The fund finally came into the hands of the Ohio Christian Missionary Society for its administration.[73] Burnet's Last Will and Testament was a revelation of the earnest view of the cause to which he had given his life. It was contained in the will that "half of his property should be invested in a permanent fund, the interest of which to be expended for the education of young men for the ministry."[74] Furthermore, should the trustees decline to administer the funds, the Ohio Christian Missionary Society should do so.

After some legal difficulties involved in settlement of the estate, and after the named trustees declined their assignment, the heirs offered $10,000 for a quit-claim upon his properties. The Ohio Christian Missionary

---

[73]Garrison and DeGroot, *Disciples of Christ*, p. 298.
[74]Shaw, *Buckeye Disciples*, p. 220.

Society then established the "Burnet Fund." Henry K. Shaw says that the "interest on this fund has been used for the purpose specified since that time."[75] Burnet was not a visionary. He was a practical Christian.

His death, as well as that of Alexander Campbell, left the brotherhood with many unsolved problems. The leadership of the movement, as we have seen, fell upon the shoulders of Isaac Errett. Among the problems which presented themselves for the new generation to solve were the continued postwar concern about slavery, the beginning of the question whether to use instrumental music in worship, the attitude Disciples of Christ would take relative to open or closed Communion, and the continued support or nonsupport of missionary societies.

The slavery issue continued after the war because Dr. Barclay had been a slave owner before his appointment as a missionary to Jerusalem. Those who held strong feeling on either side of the slavery issue offered or refused to offer their cooperation in accordance with their views. A long struggle for unity and stability was threatening because of the manufacture and sale of organs for homes, schools, and churches in a changing cultural order. The purchase and use of organs for churches often did violence to accustomed worship patterns and was regarded as an expensive innovation. Much of the argument began to be centered around New Testament proof-texts.

Having come from a strong Baptist background, Disciples of Christ widely practiced closed Communion at first. It was unreasonable to them at first that nonmembers, especially the unbaptized, might be in a group invited to participate in the Communion. To close or open the Communion was the problem and its general solution in favor of neither open nor closed practice was a long process of development to which Errett gave leadership.

---

[75] Shaw, *Buckeye Disciples*, p. 220.

Support of the Society system for missionary work was widely debated following Burnet's death and it was also Errett, with the power of the *Christian Standard* to back him, who stood for cooperation instead of independence.

Ten years after his death Burnet's sermon on "The Poverty of Jesus, the Wealth of the Saints" was published as the leading sermon in Mathes' volume, *The Western Preacher*. Like much of his preaching, it was a sermon in consideration of the Christian use of money. Some extracts are enclosed in Appendix VII.

1954: Undeserved Obscurity

Burnet was doubtless the single individual most to be credited for bringing Disciples of Christ organization through its rudimentary stage. There has been much achieved since his beginnings, and there is certainly much to be desired today, but the practical and intelligent actions of this man ought not to be eclipsed by the brilliant performances of his contemporaries. He was skilled in conducting congregational polity negotiations without arousing hostility. He was father of organized cooperative benevolence, missions and education among Disciples of Christ.[76] He understood better than others that the movement would squander its energies without some form of organization which embraced the voluntary support of all the churches.[77]

Such findings as are disclosed in this volume provide an impressive list of distinctions which may be credited to the silver-tongued exponent of organizational fellowship among Christians. A review of the findings discloses that he was a descendant of the family of the great seventeenth-century reformer, the Bishop of Salisbury, Gilbert Burnet; a nephew of Judge Jacob Burnet, of Ohio; a nephew of David Gouverneur Burnet, first presi-

[76] *Ibid.*, p. 155. Cf. Moore, *Living Pulpit*, p. 45.
[77] *Ibid.*, p. 219.

dent of the Republic of Texas; and the oldest son of Isaac G. Burnet, mayor of Cincinnati six successive terms.

He believed that the simple confession of faith should be the only doctrinal test of Christian fellowship and that such a simple test should entitle disciples of Jesus to ask for all which the church might offer doctrinally, and functionally in theory and practice. Burnet led both the church at Eighth and Walnut Streets, Cincinnati, and the church at Dayton, to break with the Baptists almost two years before Campbell's final severance in 1830. He was editor of the earliest periodical distinctively for Disciples of Christ, *The Evangelical Enquirer;* editor of the one-volume edition of *The Christian Baptist* which he regarded as Campbell's most influential work; editor of the *Christian Preacher,* the first journal among Disciples of Christ specifically to face the problem of ministerial training.

Mr. Burnet ventured forth as president of the first actual college among Disciples of Christ, Bacon College; he was the first settled pastor in the movement; but probably most significant of all, founder and president of the first cooperative organization of the brotherhood —the American Christian Bible Society. His leadership was the main factor in organizing the Tract (Publication) Society, the Missionary Society, and the National Convention, the latter being organized with Burnet as acting president in 1849. His influence was responsible for gaining Mr. Campbell's blessing on the missionary work of the brotherhood by accepting the presidency of the A.C.M.S. in 1850.

Tremendously interested in a revision of the Bible, Burnet aided in launching the American Bible Union project which aimed in 1852-53 to foster the revision and perfecting of the English version of the Scriptures. Failing to get satisfactory support for that project, he became the principal figure in establishing the cooperative publishing house of Disciples of Christ at the October, 1852, annual meeting in Cincinnati. The first book published cooperatively by Disciples of Christ was Burnet's volume, *Jerusalem Mission*. Business of the Publication Society centered around the circulation of the Bible, a fifty-volume *Sunday School Library* which Burnet had edited, and the publication of books.

As co-editor, with Benj. Franklin of the *Christian Age*, Burnet had much experience in writing and editing. He published several volumes of *Christian Family Magazine*, and other journals with special purposes, insisting that a journal should have a specific function and that it was impossible to print an all-purpose magazine which would meet all the needs of the growing fellowship.

His wife, Mary, and Mrs. James Barclay, wife of the Jerusalem missionary, were the originators of the first organized Christian women's missionary work among Disciples of Christ. Burnet, with T. J. Melish, began the organization of the Ohio Christian Missionary Society. With his Uncle Jacob's program of "Ohio in Africa," a project for buying land in Africa for the resettlement of freed Negroes, Burnet was chief leader of Disciples of Christ in an attempt to establish the Liberian missionary work. He probably did the first actual construction of a church house in Leavenworth City, Kansas (1859), under the auspices of a National Board, which is a type of work regarded today as the function of the Board of Church Extension of Disciples of Christ. In October, 1861, he reported on his first efforts to establish a Federal City Christian Church in Washington, D. C., heralding the present National City Church.

Often described by his contemporaries as the most eloquent pulpit orator of his day, he preached the memorial address at Bethany College after the death of President Alexander Campbell in 1866. He was made president of the Missionary Society, succeeding Campbell, out of respect for his leadership, but died a few months after

Campbell's passing. Isaac Errett, in his memorial address at Burnet's funeral, identified him as a liberal-spirited person who suffered because of his liberality.

His emphasis upon preaching was illustrated in his publication of the journal *Christian Preacher,* his support of Bethany College, and his provision of a trust fund in his will for the training of ministers. His emphasis upon financial stewardship was amply illustrated by his definite financial plans and programs as well as his personal activities in various capacities as brotherhood leader. His emphasis upon cooperation is best illustrated by his contribution to the formative work in connection with the Bible, Tract, Publication, and Missionary societies. As an evangelist he was especially successful in the cities[78] at a time Disciples of Christ were primarily a rural people.

As a speaker he mastered the art of elocution and emphasized it beyond rhetoric. His pulpit manner was easy and unstrained and his voice was described as rich and melodious.[79] Moore said that Burnet's control of the interest of an audience in some situations was "unsurpassed by any preacher in the ranks of the Disciples."[80] Especially was his magnetic speaking power most effective in an evangelistic meeting. Inspired, he seemed to have something of a "divine eloquence."[81] He spoke with evangelical zeal and urgency, drawing the source of the dominant portion of every message from the Bible and from church history. His simple style of verbal usage was in the vernacular of religious persons on the frontier. The frame of reference was clear to the hearers and thus they understood the issues at stake. His message was primarily one that made appeal to the intelligence of his audiences, although the emotional and

---
[78]Power, *Sketches of Our Pioneers,* p. 126.
[79]Moore, *Living Pulpit,* p. 44.
[80]*Ibid.*
[81]*Ibid*

pious elements were not altogether lacking. What he said gave the impression that he was a conscientious, earnest, serious man. Preachers of his day who had aligned themselves with the movement of Disciples of Christ had no clear-cut set of doctrine, institutes, or creed to promulgate, but they bore the kind of sincerity which was much like that of Elder Burnet.[82]

He had the drive in the pulpit characteristic of great preachers. This was due partly to the fact that he was well balanced between the extremes of expansion and reclusion, between extroversion and introversion. He loved people and understood them. This insight gave him the ability to get his message across. He knew the things for which people hungered in such a complex and migratory society. His insight into the ways of city people made him understand when he had ascendancy over their views and when he was required to be submissive.

His writing was not equal to his speaking talent.[83] However, in the remarkable number of publications which he fostered he showed considerable literary skill.[84] His best work as a writer was in the editorial judgment which he exercised in such volumes as *The Christian Baptist* and *Jerusalem Mission*. The smoothest literary skill is found in his published addresses, particularly those constructed in the midst of heated discussions.

Scholarly attainments were always part of his interest. He made considerable progress in the studies of Greek and Hebrew. His interests in the sciences and his progress in the field of natural and church history can be noted.[85] His career as an educator was partly due to his standing as a scholar, although the schools needed him as one who had the ability to raise money.

---

[82]Cf., *Ibid.*, pp. 30, 31.
[83]*Ibid.*, p. 38.
[84]*Ibid.*
[85]*Ibid.*, p. 44.

Burnet was an extremely intelligent man. Only a person of high intelligence could have solved the problem that existed for Disciples of Christ in the period when a national organization was so desperately needed. One does not need to give him all the credit in order to pay him deserved respect for his intelligent way of proceeding. His memory was acute and his learning ability was a growing part of his character even until the time of his death. He could recall historically significant factors with great ease. One of the most evident marks of his intelligence was his constructive imagination. He saw that it was possible to have a governing body at the helm of a great movement which could arise out of the cooperation and group stewardship of churches freely willing to do so. His special abilities were those requiring acumen and intellectual adaptability. A parrot never makes a vital orator; and Burnet was not simply an echo of the Campbell movement. He spoke and wrote out of his own intelligence and conviction.

Final and irrevocable evidence of his great intellect lies in the soundness of his judgment. He never misjudged the strength and character of Alexander Campbell. Had he done so it is not conceivable that the Convention would have retained men with such variance in viewpoint as Tolbert Fanning and Campbell. Burnet's good judgment was evidenced in locating the cooperative basis upon the shoulders of the Bible Society and the Missionary Society, in which one would serve the other to the fullest extent.

In personal control Burnet developed a wholesome balance between his impulses and his inhibitions. He showed great impulsiveness in his youth, smarting under the social compulsion of a family determined he should learn law. In his later years he edited the *Christian Baptist* although it contained searing denunciations of the idea of organizations which were beyond the level of the local church. Burnet's view was wholly committed to cooperation.

The tenacity of the man was equaled only by his skill in accomplishing the ends to which he bent his energies. It is no easy task to edit a fifty-volume set of Sunday school materials. Such a tenacity was a part of existence as a successful preacher on the expanding American frontier. His long settled pastorate in Cincinnati and a similar experience in Baltimore indicated the tenacious and skillful motility which held him fast to a task until completed.

Burnet was susceptible to the social situation. It was often said of him that his best sermons were under the right audience conditions. People stimulated him to do his best. But his socialization was not a complete loss of self. Like Campbell, Scott, Errett, and the others with whom he had intimate working relationships, he had certain self-interests for the attainment of status. His clash with Campbell over the relation of the Bible Society and Bethany College to the total brotherhood of Disciples of Christ indicated that he was not so completely absorbed in the Reformation that he would deny the rights of his own character. The same would necessarily be said for the vast majority of these leaders. But it can be said also that their self-interests were often set aside for the common good, and Burnet many times proved most unselfish.

He lived "long enough to see his brethren, who were so heartily despised at first, rise to be one of the most powerful and influential religious people in all the land."[86] A survey of the findings of this volume suggests that none of those who worked in this cause devoted himself more wholly to its accomplishments.

Let us not say that Burnet was right and Campbell wrong about many of the practical aspects of working

---
[86]Moore, *Living Pulpit*, p. 37.

out a plan of cooperation among Disciples of Christ; let us say rather that each had an emphasis which was valid and in due course both were tested in the crucible of Time. If Alexander Campbell was the great figure of the early movement, leaving his "impress upon the brotherhood,"[87] then D. S. Burnet ought to be placed in a class with him.

It was Burnet who enlisted the genius of men like John T. Johnson, Walter Scott, James Challen, Benjamin Franklin, Isaac Errett, Elijah Goodwin, even Alexander Campbell himself, in the high purposes of stewardship and cooperation as a brotherhood of Christians. He led them into this cooperative adventure upon the basis of a simple confession of faith in Christ. It was Burnet who made the ways and means of missions, benevolence, and education a rudimentary reality among Disciples of Christ as he called upon all to volunteer to work together.

Eclipsed by a famed family—his father as mayor of the Queen City, his Uncle Jacob as judge, senator and author, and another uncle, David G., the first president of the Republic of Texas—Burnet quietly made a place for himself in history that a century of perspective brings into much clearer focus. Eclipsed by famous figures in the beginnings of the movement of Disciples of Christ, such as the constellation of the Big Four—Thomas and Alexander Campbell, Barton W. Stone, and Walter Scott—he is more than worthy of the place of the fifth star in that group.

Making the most of broken dreams and shattered plans, he did not live to see many of his basic views of cooperation and stewardship widely accepted by the religious movement to which he contributed his genius for leading in the integration of peoples.

It is true, nevertheless, that by the time of his death Burnet found himself one of the great leaders of a

---

[87] Allen R. Moore, *Alexander Campbell and the General Convention*, p. 6.

minority. Perhaps the insight has best been given by Isaac Errett's funeral address, when he said that Burnet

... believed Christianity to be a life, rather than a system of doctrines. Not the subtleties of theological speculation were to be the bond of union, or the terms of acceptance—but faith in the Lord Jesus, love of Jesus, submission to Jesus as our Prophet, Priest, and King. His adherence to this view threw him into a minority, and made his life one of crosses and toil.[88]

But today there is a growing surge of religious leaders throughout the world who express his viewpoint. It is very significant indeed that the basis of membership in the World Council of Churches is almost identically the plea which Burnet made for membership both in local churches and in the national Societies.

The neglect or disregard which Disciples of Christ have had for the place of Burnet in their history was not the willful ignoring of a great man. Nor was it due to the failure of Burnet to impress himself upon the minds of his contemporaries. A combination of natural reasons may be observed for the absence of due attention to this hero of the faith. However, most of the biographers and historians among Disciples of Christ have passed over his record with haste and have exercised a lack of care in studies of the brotherhood's cooperation and stewardship organizations. Contributing to a situation not quickly realized by the historians are the following factors which might be regarded as causative: (1) His writings were widely scattered and inadequately preserved; (2) his proximity to the great leader of the movement, Alexander Campbell, both in life and in death, had a tendency to obscure his significance; (3) his lack of children of his own who might have passed along the family story was unfortunate; (4) his having a genesis from a family of other illustrious persons living at the same time tended to obscure him; (5) and his advocacy

---

[88]*Millennial Harbinger*, 1867, p. 430.

of ideas a century before their more general acceptance left him, like Wyclif, as the morning star of a new day, especially his views on centralism in organization, the office of the pastor, the importance of ministerial training, the proposals for a Federal City church and other such projects, and his liberal views toward the Bible and toward other religious bodies within Christendom. Many of his views are not widely accepted even today among Disciples of Christ, especially those on membership and stewardship.

Students of the history of Disciples of Christ will find a vigorous challenge lying before them if they set themselves in earnest to study the kind of Christian program advocated by David Staats Burnet. They will be criticized sharply if they contribute strongly to the kind of noble liberty and liberality for which he lived and died. Somehow, in the end, it seems to me that the centuries will vindicate those who carry the banners of truth and brotherhood. The stature of the man has improved with age. His was undeserved obscurity.

Appendix I

CHRONOLOGY

1640. Emigration of Thomas Burnet, David's great-great-great-grandfather, to Massachusetts.
1643-1715. Life of Gilbert Burnet, English Bishop of Salisbury.
1684. Birth of Ichabod Burnet, David's great-grandfather.
1729. Death of Daniel Burnet, David's great-great-grandfather (July 8).
1730. Birth of Dr. William Burnet, Sr., David's grandfather.
1768-1857. Life of Mrs. John Gano, mother of David Burnet's wife, Mary.
1770. Birth of Judge Jacob Burnet, David's uncle (Feb. 22).
1784. Birth of Isaac Gouverneur Burnet, David's father.
1788. Birth of David Gouverneur Burnet, David's uncle (Apr. 4).
1806. Marriage of David's parents, Isaac Gouverneur Burnet and Kittie Winn Gordon.
1808. Cincinnati political address by David's father (July 4).
1808. Birth of David Staats Burnet (July 6), in Dayton, O.
1816. Beginning of steam navigation on Ohio River.
1818. Development of Presbyterian New Light "Second Church" in Cincinnati by Judge Jacob Burnet and others.
1819. Cincinnati chartered as a city (David's father becomes mayor).
1821-1824. D. S. Burnet studies law in his father's Cincinnati law office.
1823-1830. Alexander Campbell publishes *The Christian Baptist.*
1823. National government enacts Monroe Doctrine.
1824. Burnet associated with official conduct of Presbyterian Sunday School in Cincinnati.
1824. A. Campbell visits P. S. Fall in Kentucky (Fall).
1824. P. S. Fall visits in home of D. S. Burnet (Fall).

1824. Burnet received by immersion into Enon Baptist Church (Dec. 26).
1825. Burnet begins preaching among Baptists. Known as "The Boy Preacher."
1825. D. S. Burnet's refusal of appointment to West Point.
1826. Campbell and Burnet cross Ohio River in a skiff. Probably their first meeting.
1827. Mary Gano immersed by Jeremiah Vardeman.
1827. Formation of Sycamore Street Baptist Church in Cincinnati (Autumn or Winter).
1827. Burnet at age of twenty accepted as pastor of a Baptist church in Dayton, O.
1828. Burnet and James Challen create Christian Church at corner of Eighth and Walnut Streets in Cincinnati.
1829. Dayton Baptist Church becomes Central Church of Christ, rejecting written Articles of Faith (Mar. 21).
1829. Campbell-Owen debate in Cincinnati (April 13-23).
1829. Burnet letter to Campbell reporting on dissolution of Todd's Fork Association (Aug. 25).
1830-1831. Burnet publishes *The Evangelical Enquirer,* the earliest Disciple journal.
1830. Campbell begins publication of the *Millennial Harbinger* (Jan. 4).
1830. Lyman Beecher begins preaching in Cincinnati.
1830. Burnet is married to Mary G. Gano (March 30).
1830. Campbell's last issue of *The Christian Baptist* (July 5).
1830. Dissolution of the Mahoning Association (Aug.).
1832. Union of Campbell-Stone followers (Jan. 1).
1832. Cincinnati fire.
1832. Campbell publishes *The Living Oracles,* a translation of *The New Testament.*
1832-1850. Harriet Beecher Stowe in Cincinnati, gathers material for *Uncle Tom's Cabin.*
1832. First Democratic national convention (May).
1832. Burnet begins friendship with Walter Scott of Carthage, O., editor of *The Evangelist.*
1833. Burnet leaves Cincinnati to become full-time evangelist, touring eastern states in company with A. Campbell.

APPENDIX I 203

1833. Burnet attends Dover Association and reports to Campbell (Fall).
1834. An evangelistic meeting held in Baltimore by Burnet raises the question of the youngest age at which one could become a church member.
1834. Judge Jacob Burnet, with 34 others, incorporates Ohio Life Insurance and Trust Co.
1834. Returning to Cincinnati, D. S. Burnet begins editing *The Christian Preacher*.
1835. Burnet edits one-volume edition of *The Christian Baptist*.
1836. First railroad to operate in Ohio.
1836. Campbell publishes *The Christian System*.
1836. Campbell considers suspending publication of *Millennial Harbinger* and devoting full time to writing books.
1836. D. G. Burnet becomes provisional President of the Republic of Texas.
1837. D. S. Burnet becomes president of Bacon College, the first actual college among Disciples.
1838. Burnet expresses in *Christian Preacher* liberal views on who may participate in the Communion of the Lord's Supper.
1839. Burnet becomes principal and proprietor of Hygeia Female Atheneum.
1840. A. Campbell establishes Bethany College.
1840. Aided primarily by Judge Jacob Burnet, W. H. Harrison is elected to Presidency of the United States.
1842. Campbell indicates some change in his views on church organization.
1842. Charles Dickens visits Cincinnati.
1843. Campbell-Rice debate.
1844. Burnet closes work at Hygeia in order to accept again the pastorate of Christian Chapel in Cincinnati.
1845. Organization of American Christian Bible Society (Jan. 27).
1845. Campbell and Burnet dispute the purpose and function of the Bible Society.
1845. Burnet begins publication of *Christian Family Magazine*.
1846. Founding of Cincinnati Tract Society (later the American Christian Publication Society).

Appendix I

1847. Publication of Judge Jacob Burnet's *Notes on the Early Settlement of the Northwestern Territory.*

1848. Judge Jacob Burnet plans "Ohio in Africa" (Apr.).

1848. Campbell criticizes Burnet's proposed address for the Masonic Lodge.

1848. Publication of Alexander Hall's *Register*, creates further disputation between Bethany and Cincinnati.

1848. Dr. James T. Barclay offers services of his family to Bible Society for the purpose of going as missionaries to Jerusalem (Oct. 5).

1849. First national convention of Disciples of Christ. Founding of the American Christian Missionary Society (Oct. 21-27).

1849. Burnet presides at founding meeting of national convention of Disciples of Christ.

1849. D. S. Burnet's letter to Campbell notifying the latter of his election as president of the Missionary Society (Oct. 29).

1849. Meeting to establish Western Reserve Eclectic Institute at Hiram, O. (Dec. 20).

1850. Burnet enters partnership with Benj. Franklin, publishing the *Reformer* and the *Christian Age.*

1850. Burnet House, new hotel, opened in Cincinnati by Judge Jacob Burnet.

1850. Dr. James T. Barclay and family sent to Jerusalem as first missionaries of Disciples of Christ.

1850. Campbell appears late and presides over one afternoon session of five-day convention in Cincinnati (Oct. 21-25).

1851. Burnet and T. J. Melish attend Bedford and Wooster, Ohio, "Yearly Meetings" with the view of organizing a state missionary society.

1852. Burnet asked to welcome Louis Kossuth upon the latter's arrival in Cincinnati (March).

1852. Burnet publishes booklet *Is the Christian Church Truly Evangelical?* (March 28).

1852. First meeting of Ohio Christian Missionary Society, at Wooster; Burnet elected president (May 12, 13).

1852-1853. Formation of American Bible Union stock company.

1852. Establishment of American Christian Publication Society (Oct.).
1852. Julia Barclay's letter to Mary Burnet, the beginning of women's missionary work among Disciples of Christ (Dec. 5).
1853. Burnet edits *The Christian Sunday-School Library*, approximately fifty small volumes.
1853. The *Christian Age* purchased by brotherhood societies.
1853. Publication of Burnet's *Jerusalem Mission*, first book published cooperatively by Disciples of Christ.
1853. Alexander Cross, freed Negro slave, sails from Baltimore to become missionary of Disciples of Christ in Liberia, Africa (Nov. 5).
1854. W. K. Pendleton accuses Publication Society officers of misappropriation of funds (June).
1854. Burnet addresses Bible Union meeting in New York (Oct. 6).
1856. Publication Society and Bible Society merged into American Christian Missionary Society (Oct. 21).
1856. Death of J. T. Johnson (Dec. 24).
1857. Burnet conducts funeral of Joseph Ray (May 24).
1857. Missionary Society convention resolves to send Burnet to Great Britain as missionary for Disciples of Christ (Oct. 21).
1858. Burnet tours American seaboard from New York to Texas.
1859. Burnet conducts two-week evangelistic campaign at Platte City, Mo. (Jan.).
1859. Execution of John Brown at Harper's Ferry.
1859. Burnet tours Kansas and Missouri.
1860. Burnet returns to Cincinnati to resume pastorate of Christian Chapel (Spring).
1860. Leavenworth City, Kansas, church built by funds of national Missionary Society, beginning work later known as "church extension."
1860. Prince of Wales visits Cincinnati, making headquarters at Burnet House.

1861. Beginning of Civil War.
1861. Burnet attempts to establish a Federal City Christian Church in Washington, D. C., as a gift of the brotherhood.
1861. A loyalty resolution creates disturbance in national convention of Disciples of Christ (Oct.).
1862. In behalf of Missionary Society, Burnet tours Maryland, Pennsylvania, New York, Kentucky, Virginia, Connecticut, Indiana, and Ohio.
1862. Cincinnati threatened by Confederate Army under Gen. Kirby Smith.
1863. Proclamation of Emancipation (Jan. 1).
1863. Burnet holds evangelistic campaign in Philadelphia where committee from Baltimore, Md., Paca Street Christian Church, visits him (Spring).
1863. Burnet accepts pastorate of Baltimore, Md., Paca Street Christian Church (Spring).
1864. Burnet resigns office as Corresponding Secretary of the American Christian Missionary Society (March).
1864. Death of Walter Scott.
1865. Surrender of Gen. Robert E. Lee at Appomattox.
1865. Assassination of President Abraham Lincoln.
1866. Death of Alexander Campbell (Mar. 4).
1866. Baltimore memorial to A. Campbell published (Mar. 11).
1866. Isaac Errett begins publication of *Christian Standard* at Cleveland. First issue carries notice of Campbell's death (April).
1866. Burnet preaches at Bethany and delivers memorial address during Commencement (June).
1867. Burnet resigns Baltimore pastorate (June).
1867. Farewell sermon of Burnet at Baltimore church (June 30).
1867. Beginning of Burnet's final illness (July 1).
1867. Death of D. S. Burnet (July 8).
1867. Funeral for Burnet at Christian Chapel, Cincinnati (July 12); Isaac Errett delivers funeral sermon.

1867. Publication of W. T. Moore's book, *The Living Pulpit*.
1869. Move of *Christian Standard* to Cincinnati (July 31).
1870. Death of David's uncle, David Gouverneur Burnet, in Texas.
1874. W. K. Pendleton's silver anniversary address of the American Christian Missionary Society (Fall).
1877. J. M. Mathes publishes *The Western Preacher,* including as the leading sermon one from the pen of D. S. Burnet.

Appendix II

NOTES ON GENEALOGY OF D. S. BURNET

David Staats Burnet was an offspring of a great family lineage, inheriting an ancestory closely aligned with the pioneering and reforming activities of Scotland, England, and the American frontier. A cursory examination of his genealogy indicates an amazing lineage of pioneers in colonization, in medicine and science, in government, and in leading the way toward religious reform. The clan of succeeding Burnets was characterized by reputable leaders who prepared the way for many others to follow. Not only on the paternal side of the house could he recall distinguished forefathers; his maternal grandfather was Capt. George Gordon, of Philadelphia.[1] In order to clarify his connection with Disciples of Christ it is first necessary to consider some rather complicated facts of his paternal genealogy. Although I have found very little record of his maternal ancestry, there are ample sources of the antecedents of his father.

Thomas Burnet[2] was born in Scotland and emigrated to Massachusetts about 1640.[3] After landing in the Massachusetts colony the Scotch emigrant soon removed to Southampton, L. I., receiving there an allotment of land, October 16, 1643. His second marriage was in Lynn, Massachusetts, October 3, 1663, to Mary Pierson. There were eleven children by his two wives, the ninth of which was Daniel. Thomas died in Southampton, L. I., and his will was settled in December, 1684.[4] He was the great-great-great-grandfather of David Staats Burnet. His parentage and family connections back in Scotland are somewhat obscure, but

---

[1] William Thomas Moore, *The Living Pulpit of the Christian Church; A Series of Discourses, Doctrinal and Practical, from Representative Men Among the Disciples of Christ* (Cincinnati: R. W. Carroll Co., 1868), p. 33.

[2] W. T. Moore, *The Living Pulpit*, p. 319.

[3] Isabella Neff Burnet, *Dr. William Burnet and His Sons, Jacob, Isaac and David, A Chart of Their Forefathers and Descendants in America, 1640-1938* (Mimeograph, 1938), p. 1.

[4] *Ibid.*

indications are that he was one of the immediate relatives of Gilbert Burnet, the English Bishop of Salisbury, 1643-1715, probably the grandfather, great-uncle or uncle.

The family across the Atlantic had produced one of the historical figures of the Reformation in England. Gilbert Burnet[5] was born in Scotland. His father was an Episcopalian puritan; his mother was a Presbyterian. Educated at Aberdeen, Gilbert was ordained in 1665 by the Bishop of Edinburgh. In 1669 he became a professor of divinity at Glasgow, and was eager to conciliate the clashing views between the Episcopal and Presbyterian parties in the church. In 1672 he published his *Vindication of the Authority, Constitution, and Laws of the Church and State of Scotland*. It was regarded of such value in Scotland that he was offered a bishopric there, but declined because he soon was to go to London where he preached before King Charles II. The king consequently named him one of his chaplains. It was while there that he made friends with the Duke of York, afterward James II. Even though he soon lost court favor because of accusations from within the national royal families, he settled in London. Contrary to the hostile court, he was appointed by Sir Harbottle Grimstone, Master of the Rolls, as Preacher at the Rolls Chapel and Lecturer at St. Clements. He became a powerful and popular preacher. It was soon after that he wrote the history for which he is best known: *History of the Reformation of the Church of England*. This history appeared in the bookstores of Cincinnati, Ohio, almost 200 years later, in company with Gilbert Burnet's work on *The Thirty-Nine Articles*.[6] The Burnet family must have been aware of the distinguished work of their illustrious ancestor. In the list of books published by Derby, Bradley & Co., publishers of Judge

[5]Cf. Leslie Stephen and Sidney Lee, *Dictionary of National Biography*, 63 vols., and 3-vol. supplement (London: 1885-1901), VII, 394-405. Also, Cf. Samuel Maccauley Jackson (ed.), *The New Schaff-Herzog Encyclopedia of Religious Knowledge* (New York: Funk and Wagnalls Co., 1908), II, 312. Cf. Thomas B. Burnet (son of Gilbert Burnet) *Life* (of his father). The biography is prefixed to the 6-vol. edition of Burnet's *Works*, pub. 1633. Cf. Samuel Austin Allibone, *Critical Dictionary of English Literature* (Philadelphia, 1891), I, 296-298.

[6]Jacob Burnet, *Notes on the Early Settlement of the North-Western Territory* (Cincinnati: Derby, Bradley and Co., 1847). See Appendix, list of books, p. 10.

Burnet's *Notes on the Early Settlement of the North-Western Territory*, was included the following catalog entry:[7]

BURNET'S History of the Reformation. Edited by Dr. Nares. Best edition. 23 portraits. 4 vols. 8vo. _____ 8 00
Nares. Cheap edition, 3 vols. _____ 2 50
BURNET on the Thirty-nine articles. Edited by Page. Best Edition. 8vo. _____ 2 00

Gilbert Burnet was known not only for his historical and critical writings which appeared at the time of a stormy political situation in England. He finally provoked the resentment of the English court to such an extent that his means of living was taken away. When James II became King, Gilbert left the country and ultimately actuated to The Hague where he shared with William of Orange in the intrigues which eventually gained for the prince the throne of England. Burnet accompanied William as chaplain as he took up the rule of the English throne. As recompense for his labors King William presented Gilbert with the vacant bishopric of Salisbury, March 31, 1689. After his settlement in the Salisbury see, Burnet took a large part in ecclesiastical politics, becoming the great champion of the Low Church party. He had advocated the succession of the House of Hanover for a long time and was the logical proponent of that view. His *Exposition of the Thirty-nine Articles*, published in 1699, created a national ebb tide against radical reform ideas.

A loyal Church of England writer[8] is puzzled when confronted with the problem of how to evaluate Gilbert Burnet when he says:

> It is difficult to do justice to such a character; the ability, moderation, and virtues which gave such weight to his ecclesiastical and political action are overlooked by some in their dislike for his ecclesiastical and political principles; while to those who sympathise with his principles, they throw perhaps an exaggerated lustre on his abilities and virtues. His private life seems to have been a model of

---

[7] Jacob Burnet, *North-Western Territory*, p. 10.
[8] Edward Lewis Cutts, *A Dictionary of the Church of England* (Lond: Society for Promoting Christian Knowledge, 1895), pp. 99, 100.

good sense and piety; he was an able and diligent bishop, and spent his revenues upon his see; he stood high in the estimation of his contemporaries for his political ability. Some of his works, especially 'The History of the Reformation' and 'The Thirty-nine Articles,' are still standard works. He can hardly be denied a high place among the great names of a very important period of the national history.

Born in Edinburgh, September 15, 1643, and died in London, March 5, 1715,[9] Gilbert Burnet was an ancestor of distinction, known and imitated by David Staats Burnet, of connection in the nineteenth century with the organizational movement of Disciples of Christ in America.[10]

Not all of the Burnets were sympathetic with the American revolutionary cause. William Burnet,[11] the eldest son of Bishop Gilbert Burnet, named in honor of Prince William of Orange, afterward the King of England, lost his fortune in speculation, but was able to obtain an appointment as governor of the colonies of New York and New Jersey. He arrived in New York, September 17, 1720, aiming to acquire the interior for England against the French claims. In 1722 he established a trading post at Oswego, where, in 1696, Frontenac, the French Governor of Canada, had built a stockade fort. In 1727, Burnet erected there and armed at his own expense a small fort, planting the flag of England for the first time in the Great Lakes region. On April 15, 1728, he was removed and transferred to Massachusetts because King George II gave New York to one of his nearer favorites, John Montgomerie. Governor William Burnet was eventually obliged to recede from his Massachusetts salary claims which created there a significant dispute, and in 1730 was made governor of New Hampshire also. The loyalty to England of a part of the Burnet family and loyalty

---

[9] *Schweizer Lexikon*, 7 vol. (Zurich: Encyclias-Verlag, 1946), Zweiter Band, col. 212.

[10] This connection has not been carefully noted heretofore. Cf. *Millennial Harbinger*, A. Campbell (ed.), Bethany, Va., and Bethany, W. Va., 1830-64 (continued to 1870 by Pendleton, Loos, *et al.*; Vol. 38, Aug. 1867, p. 428.

[11] James Grant Wilson and John Fiske, *Appleton's Cyclopaedia of American Biography* (New York: D. Appleton and Co., 1887), Vol. I, pp. 457, 458.

to the Revolutionary War movement on the part of others, had something to do later with the position which young David Staats assumed in the American Civil War.

David Staats Burnet must have been also in the family lineage of Dr. Thomas Burnet,[12] an extreme Freethinker of the Church of England, who almost became Archbishop of Canterbury at the death of Tillotson. Although there is no clear connection evident in the available genealogies, the fact that King William was anxious to give him certain ecclesiastical preferment makes it clear that he was related to the Gilbert Burnet lineage. Also, these Burnets are part of the family of Burnet of Leys, Aberdeen, originally of Saxon descent, flourishing in northern Scotland in the seventeenth century.[13] It was said of Dr. Thomas Burnet that he was among the clergy the greatest Freethinker with the exception of Dean Swift. In 1691 an English translation of Dr. Thomas Burnet's *The Sacred Theory of the Earth* appeared, heralding some of the modern concepts of geology concerning the stratification of the earth. His *Archaeologia Philosophica* created great opposition because of his challenge to the literal and miraculous conceptions found in Genesis. He died at the age of eighty, in 1715. Because of the nineteenth-century views of David Staats Burnet and because of his evident family interest in the great names of those who were his antecedents it is highly probable that he was strongly influenced by the ideas of the Freethinkers through his knowledge of the works of Dr. Thomas Burnet.

Daniel Burnet[14] (d. July 8, 1729), the ninth son of Thomas Burnet, removed to Elizabethtown, N. J., from Southampton, Long Island, where his parents had settled an allotment of land. Ichabod was the second child born to Daniel and his first wife, Abigail. Daniel was the great-great-grandfather of David Staats Burnet.

---

[12]Charles Bradlaugh, *Biographies of Ancient and Modern Freethinkers* (Boston: J. P. Mendum, 1877), pp. 265-279.

[13]Isabella Neff Burnet, *Dr. William Burnet*, p. 99.

[14]Francis Hazley Lee, *Genealogical and Memorial History of the State of New Jersey* (New York: Lewis Historical Pub. Co., 1910), p. 319. Cf. Isabella Neff Burnet, *Dr. William Burnet*, p. 1.

APPENDIX II 213

Ichabod Burnet, the great-grandfather of David Staats Burnet, was born in 1684 in Southampton, Long Island.[15] He died in Elizabethtown, N. J., September 10, 1783. He was sent as a youth to Edinburgh, Scotland, to receive his professional medical training. Ichabod and his wife Hannah (1702-1758) had two children, the elder of which was Dr. William Burnet, Sr. Always prominent and influential in the affairs of his colonial community, Ichabod traced his lineage to some of the earliest Scotch settlers in America. There are three stones in the graveyard at Elizabeth, N. J., bearing the Burnet name.[16] One of them says:

> Here lies the Body
> of Ichabod B. Burnet
> obi't Sept the 10th
> Anno Domini 1783
> AE tatis Suae
> Lean not on earth, it will
> pierce thee to the Heart.

Dr. William Burnet, Sr.[17] (1730-1791), the grandfather of David Staats Burnet, had a fourth son, William Burnet, Jr., who followed in his father's footsteps in the practice of medicine. Not only distinguished by having a historically significant family, David's grandfather, William, was a pioneer in his own right. Dr. William, the elder, was educated at Nassau Hall during Aaron Burr's presidency. He was graduated in 1749 before the school was moved to Princeton.

Having studied medicine under Dr. Staats, of New York, two of his grandsons bore the name of their grandfather's teacher— Staats Gouverneur and David Staats. When troubles arose between the American colonies and England, Dr. Burnet, Sr., as a Whig, joined the forces of resistance against England. He

---

[15]Lee, *Genealogical and Memorial History*, pp. 319, 320. Cf. Isabella Neff Burnet, *Dr. William Burnet*, p. 2.

[16]Isabella Neff Burnet, *Dr. William Burnet*, p. 50.

[17]Jacob Burnet, *North-Western Territory*, pp. 17-22. Cf. Stephen Wickes, *History of Medicine in New Jersey*. (Newark, N. J.: M. R. Dennis and Co., 1889). Also U. S. Congress, *Biographical Directory of the American Congress*. 1774-1949. (United States Government Printing Office, 1950).

married[18] (first) Mary Camp, January 23, 1754, daughter of Nathaniel Camp, and they had eleven children. The eldest was Dr. William Burnet, the younger; another (the sixth child) was Judge Jacob Burnet, who arose to high esteem in Cincinnati and Ohio.[19] Dr. Burnet married (second) Gertrude Gouverneur, 1783, the daughter of Nicholas Gouverneur and widow of Anthony Rutgers, and they had three children. One was Isaac Gouverneur (Mayor of Cincinnati); another was David Gouverneur (first President of the Republic of Texas).

How Dr. William, Sr., became a delegate to the Continental Congress, 1780, and participated in the founding of the New Jersey Medical Society, the first of its kind, is revealed in Judge Jacob Burnet's account of his father's activities:

> When the judicial courts of the province (of New Jersey) were closed and the regular administration of justice suspended, by a ministerial order, he relinquished the practice of his profession, which was extensive and lucrative, and took part in the political movements of the day (prior to the War of Independence) with great activity and zeal.
>
> The protection of law having been withdrawn, by closing the judicial tribunals of the colony, the people assumed the reins of government from necessity, and administered law and justice as well as they could, circumstances as they were.
>
> In some places it was done by county arrangements, and in others by township committees. In Newark, as a temporary expedient, the power was vested in a "Committee of Public Safety," appointed by the people of the township.
>
> Similar measures of precaution were necessarily resorted to throughout the province; each county, town, or neighborhood, devising and pursuing its own plan. The powers confided to these committees were dictatorial; and the entire Whig population stood pledged to enforce their decisions. The Tories were numerous, and had full confidence that the British troops would overrun the country, and reduce it to obedience, without encountering any serious resistance. They were therefore bold and insolent, and by their move-

[18]Lee, *Genealogical and Memorial History*, pp. 319, 320. Cf. Isabella Neff Burnet, *Dr. William Burnet*, p. 2.

[19]Cf. Isabella Neff Burnet, *Dr. William Burnet*, p. 2. This source indicates he was the tenth child.

ments the public peace was constantly endangered, and was preserved only by the vigorous action of these conservative bodies.

The committee appointed at Newark, of which Dr. Burnet was chairman, was in session almost daily, hearing and deciding complaints, and adjudicating on the various matters referred to them. Some of the most obnoxious of the Tories they banished; on others they imposed fines and imprisonment, and in some instances inflicted stripes. By this bold proceeding the disaffected were kept in check; the Whigs were pacified, and restrained from personal violence on the loyalists, who ridiculed the attempt to resist the Mother Country, and openly justified her tyrannical proceedings.

The Newark committee, which consisted of three members, Dr. Burnet, Judge J. Hedden, and Major S. Hays, continued in the discharge of their duty till the retreat of the American army from York Island, through the Jerseys to the Delaware, closely pressed by the enemy, who overran that state. . . .

Dr. Burnet was in the medical service of the country, from the commencement of the contest, and was the superintendent of a Military Hospital, established on his own responsibility, in Newark, in the year 1775. In the winter of 1776-7, the Legislature of New Jersey elected him a member of the Continental Congress. Soon after he took his seat, the subject of the medical department of the army was taken up in Congress, and a new arrangement adopted. The thirteen states were divided into three districts—the southern, middle and eastern; and provision was made for a Physician-general and a surgeon-general, in each; but in consideration of the strong claims of Dr. Burnet, on the score of past services as well as of qualification, they provided for a Physician and Surgeon-general, in the eastern district, and conferred the appointment on him. He then resigned his seat in Congress, accepted the appointment, and continued in the discharge of its arduous duties, till the peace of 1783.

He was stationed at West Point when General Arnold conceived and matured his plan to surrender that post to the enemy, and it so happened that he, with a party of the officers of the garrison, were dining with the General, when the officer of the day entered, and reported that a spy had been taken below, who called himself John Anderson. It was remarked by the persons who were at the table, that this intelligence, interesting to the General as it must have been, produced no visible change in his countenance or behaviour—that he continued in his seat for some minutes, conversing as before—after which he arose, saying to his guests, that business required him to be absent for a short time, and desiring them to remain and enjoy themselves till his return. The next intelligence they had of him was, that he was in his barge, moving rapidly to a British ship of war, the Vulture, which was lying at anchor a short distance below the Point.

The sequel of that treasonable conspiracy, is as familiar to the American ear, as "household words." All know that it terminated in the execution of Major Andre, the Adjutant-general of the British army, and an Aide-de-camp of Sir Henry Clinton. Very great and strenuous efforts were made, both in Great Britain and France, as well as by the Commander-in-chief of the British army, to save the life of that gifted and highly accomplished officer, who was connected with the most distinguished families in England.

In reply to those applications, General Washington proposed to exchange Andre for Arnold. That offer was manifestly unexpected, and embarrassing; and gave rise to a protracted and animated correspondence between the commanders of the two armies. Sir Henry Clinton denied that Andre was a spy, as he entered the American lines, under the protection of a pass, from the General who commanded in the District; and intimated, that he should feel bound to retaliate, if Washington persisted in his purpose. The American commander maintained, by fact and argument, that, according to the understanding and practice of all nations, Andre was a spy, and that nothing would save him from the penal consequences of his crime, but the surrender of Arnold—on that condition he would release him, and on no other. That proposition not being accepted, the Commander-in-chief of the American Army ordered a board of general officers for the trial of the prisoner of which Major General Greene was designated as the President. That board, after a careful investigation of the facts, reported that Major Andre was a spy, and ought to suffer death. In pursuance of that finding, he was sentenced to be hung on the succeeding day. Two officers were designated by the president of the board, to communicate the intelligence to the unfortunate Andre, and to attend him to the place of execution. One of them was Major Burnet, one of the Aides-de-camp of General Greene, and the second son of Dr. Burnet. When the sentence of the court was communicated to the prisoner, he wrote to General Washington, requesting a change of the sentence, and praying that he might be shot; adding that if that indulgence were granted, he could meet his fate without a murmur; but the circumstances of the case were of a character to convince the Commander-in-chief that he could not commute the punishment, consistently with the established rules of martial law, and without subjecting himself to the charge of instability, or want of nerve. Major Andre heard the failure of his application, with calmness, and when the fatal hour came, he walked with a firm step and composed countenance, to the platform of the gallows, arm-in-arm between the American officers designated to attend him. The multitude, who witnessed the execution, unitedly testified that the unfortunate sufferer met his destiny with a calmness and composure, indicative of a brave, accomplished soldier.

That West Point, the Gibraltar of the United States, might be made a cheap conquest to the enemy, the traitor had caused some of the heavy cannon to be dismounted, and portions of the masonry to be taken down, to be rebuilt, as he pretended, with additional strength. After the arrival of the Commander-in-chief at the post, he caused those treasonable dilapidations to be repaired, without delay.

At the close of the war, Dr. Burnet returned to his family, and devoted himself to agricultural pursuits. He was soon after appointed presiding judge of the court of common pleas, by the state legislature. He was also chosen President of the State Medical Society, of which he had formerly been an active member. Being a fine classical scholar, and desirous of reviving the practice of delivering the annual address in the Latin language, which had fallen into disuse; on taking the chair, he read an elaborate essay, in Latin, on the proper use of the lancet in pleuritic cases.

While in the enjoyment of his usual health, a violent attack of erysipelas in the face and head, suddenly terminated his life, on the 7th of October, 1791, in the sixty-first year of his age.[20]

---

[20]Jacob Burnet, *North-Western Territory*, pp. 17-22.

APPENDIX II

GENEALOGY OF DAVID STAATS BURNET

AMERICA	SCOTLAND	ENGLAND	
	Robert Burnet, Aberdeen,[21] married Rachel Johnston		
Thomas[22] 16??-1684 Amer. Colonial Emigrant		Gilbert 1643-1715 Eng. Bishop	
Daniel ?-d. 1729 Elizabeth, N. J.	Seven others by two wives	5 Children	
		William 1688-1728 Col. Gov. of New York	Thomas Gilbert Nancy & Elizabeth
Ichabod 1684-1774 Physician	David		
Dr. William, Sr. 1730-1791 Delegate to Continental Cong.	Dr. Ichabod 1732-1756		
Isaac 1784-1856 Mayor of Cincinnati	Jacob 1770-1853 Judge, Historian Senator	David 1788-1870 President Republic of Texas	Eleven others by two wives
David Staats Burnet 1808-1867, married Mary Gano Christian statesman, Disciples of Christ			Ten other children
(No Children)			

[21] Isabella Neff Burnet, *Dr. William Burnet*, p. 99.
[22] *Ibid.*, p. 89. As a relative of Gilbert Burnet, see also p. 88.

APPENDIX II 219

The following table shows the immediate family of D. S. Burnet:

FAMILY OF DAVID STAATS BURNET

Isaac Gouverneur Burnet (1784-1856)
Married, 1806, to Kittie Winn Gordon (Jan. 18, 1791-?) the daughter of George Gordon and Sallie Winn Moss Gordon

David Staats Burnet[23] (1808-1867)

Married Mary Gano (No Children)

Mary Thew Burnet (6-20-1814—12-25-1891)
Married William Resor

Julia Ann Burnet (1812-?)
Married Rev. Senaca Austin

Nancy Burnet (1815-1893)
Married Rev. Seely Wood

Jacob Burnet (1817-1889)
Married Mary Lynd

Gertrude Burnet (1821-1910)
Married Rev. Charles Jennings

Isaac Burnet (1824-1904)
Married in 1844, Rebecca Bryant (1824-1901)

Staats Gouverneur Burnet (1827-1888)
Married Isabella Adelia Bromwell

Cornelia Burnet (1831-?)
Never married

Hannah Kinney Burnet (1837-1906)
Married John Hendricks

Kittie Burnet
Died at seventeen

[23]Isabella Neff Burnet, *Dr. William Burnet*, p. 13.

Appendix III

ADDRESS TO THE CHURCHES

The Convention of Christian Churches of various parts of North America, assembled in Cincinnati, O., 23d to 27th Oct. 1849, to the Churches which they represent, and their sister Churches, and to the brethren generally, sendeth Christian salutation: Grace, to you, and peace from God, our Father, and our Lord Jesus Christ.

BELOVED BRETHREN:

A gracious Providence, by various means, has stirred us up to assemble in convention, in this city, from ten different States. Our meeting has been a happy and profitable one. It was characterized by great union of counsel, of feeling, and of action. The Spirit of order, of peace and love reigned in our midst, in sweet concord with "the spirit of power." We never have had such a meeting, though we have had many that were happy and useful. This was general in its attendance, and in its objects, while others have been but local in both. The world-wide field of labor was before the representatives of a young and great people. They felt the importance of their position. Their responsibility was laid before the Great Head of the Church, and his direction and blessing were sought with many prayers. Gratitude for the presence of the concourse of the brotherhood, where so recently death had spread his pall and imposed his awful silence, beamed on every countenance; while the tear trembled in the eye upon the introduction to each other of kindred spirits, previously unrecognized, but by mutual knowledge and esteem of each other's labors, in widely separated localities of the evangelical vineyard. There was an imposing grandeur in such temporary communion of saints. It was a cycle in their earthly period. Many were together for the first and last time, till the meeting of the general assembly and churches of the first-born. It was like the meeting of Jacob and the angel at the gate of heaven; and like that meeting it was interpreted as full of promise of preservations and victories to the true Israel of God. It was a meeting never to be forgotten. The facts, the speeches, the spirit and the acts of these brethren were indelibly daguerreotyped upon all minds; and when many other traces of time have been obliterated from the memory, these life sketches will remain in all their freshness. What was seen, heard and felt, during the convention, was worth a life-directorship. The social and religious feelings are more valuable to us than silver and gold. One such religious week is worth more to us than years of unsanctified social enjoyment.

Not less important is the cultivation of the benevolent feelings. Every human breast has a perennial reservoir of good will, ever ready to burst forth in kind offices at the instance of a fitting occasion; and that occasion is the concurrence of religious tenderness and the forcible presentation of suitable objects on which to exercise it. This convention was pre-eminently characterized by this concurrence. Here we had no dogmas to discuss, oppose or condemn; no abracadabra was to be generated in an ecclesiastical crucible, to break the spiritual chills of any forms of popular error among our fellow Christians. The harmony of our sessions therefore was disturbed by neither "snarlers nor the concision." The passions slept while the affections kept their vigils. The love of the brotherhood, the love of all men controlled all hearts. The feeling of the assembly was a sublime reflection of the love which bled for men on the cross, and proposed an all-sufficient remedy for their woes in the provisions of the apostolic commission.

NARRATIVE OF PROCEEDINGS

The chief measures were, the recognition of certain voluntary institutions previously in existence in our midst, and the formation of a new one. And first; the convention received into its embraces The American Christian Bible Society, and cherished it with an ardent affection. After a fair hearing, all local feelings and all scruples in regard to the time and circumstances of its origin, were extinguished by admiration of the grandeur of its designs, its noble perseverance in the hour of its trial, the good it has done and it now promises in regard to Bible distribution, and by a high appreciation of the good service it had done, in giving birth to this convention and what is to grow out of it. Those who originated the Bible Society felt confirmed in the wisdom of their course, and all others determined to work with them as one man. When the proposition to receive life members and life directors was made, there was an absolute press, and more than two thousand dollars were thus subscribed. Joy unspeakable seemed to prevail at this juncture.

Next, the Missionary Society was organized, the constitution of which appears in the preceding minutes of the convention. All rejoiced in its auspicious birth. Nearly as much was subscribed to its treasury as had previously been conceded to the Bible Society. The whitening fields did not invite in vain. All seemed anxious that we should send forth missionaries who, though they might go forth weeping at the thoughts of separations and hardships, must ere long return with rejoicings, bringing their sheaves with them. Connected with this Convention there was an incident of great interest. Dr. James Barclay, known recently as a beloved evangelist of Eastern Virginia, was present to offer himself and family, consisting of a wife, two sons, and a daughter, all church members, to the Missionary Board as soon as it should be created. This worthy brother, a year before, communicated with the Bible Society on the subject. Time had only served to ripen his feelings and strengthen his determination. He will doubtless be sent to form a mission in "The Holy City," and from the city of David and about the foundations of the ancient house of God, speak of Him whose advent as a babe "troubled Herod and all Jerusalem with him." This is the most venerable and altogether the most reverent spot on earth. An undying interest clings to every locality in and about it. The "eternal city" sinks into insignificance before it, for though the latter was the seat of power of the Caesars, and more lately of the little horn which warred with the saints, a more formidable enduring formative principle "went forth of Sion, and the word of the Lord from Jerusalem." It is now the center of a wider circle than any other place on the globe. "Thither the tribes go up." Nations and races resort here, with a religious devotion which constitutes a more ardent zeal than ever prompted the researches of the antiquary in solution of the question regarding the identity of the sites of Solomon's temple and the mosque of Omar. As a station for the distribution of the Bible and religious books, and for the preaching of the gospel to the representatives of the world, we suppose Jerusalem has not a parallel.

In accordance with the suggestion of the Convention, the Cincinnati Tract Society will doubtless become a general institution, and the union with it, of the Sunday School Library Association, in pursuance of advice from the same source, will contribute largely to its importance and to the good of the cause.

THE CRISIS

These several enterprises, brethren, are thrown into the bosom of the church of God to be nourished "as a nurse cherisheth her children." The hour of our associated strength has arrived, the hour which shall demonstrate our union to be more than uniformity of sentiment, a oneness of mind and of effort arising from the nature, power, and exaltation of the holy truth believed. This year is to prove us. It will be decisive of our character and our destiny. The spirit we shall now exhibit will be the augury of our fate. Can we not raise a fund before twelve months, which shall send the Bible by the hands of men competent to the efficient enforcement of its principles and duties upon the minds of all classes, in the dark places of our country, and of far-off lands?

OUR DUTY

As to the sum to be raised, our own estimates of the urgency of the case and of our means, must be the arbiter. And first, of the urgency of our duty. For every stroke of the pendulum, some one is summoned to his final account. The yawning grave devours for ever! Every Christian, as such, and every body of Christians, by virtue of their association, MUST do something, by the help of God, to prepare these millions accumulating around the judge, for the tremendous issue on which hangs their destiny. If all were done that could be done, there would be room for further efforts. Souls would yet be perishing: the world is half heathen, much of the other half is without any valuable knowledge of religion, and of this knoweldge there is every shade of worth from zero to "the pearl of price immense." How few who profess the true religion in its best form, adorn that profession by godliness and zeal? "The field is the world," and there is reaping everywhere.

OUR MEANS

As to our means, we have enough to do our duty, for the measure of "it is, according to what a man hath, and not according to what he hath not." Thirty thousand dollars is not too much for us to raise before our next anniversaries. This we can do, and that without neglecting the legitimate province of individual churches. The power of the Bible and Missionary Societies must be expended upon the uncultivated fields at home and abroad.

THE PLAN OF RAISING MEANS

According to the constitutions of the societies, any church, or other Christian organization, can become auxiliary to them by contributing annually to their treasuries. The missionary constitution prescribes the payment of ten dollars annually. The Bible and Tract Societies pay back a part, in their issues of Bibles, tracts, and Sunday School publications. Now to meet these conditions, let the churches determine to contribute to each of these institutions, such sums as they can spare, consistent with their obligations, and if they can, also raise a contribution on the day of concerted prayer, to be mentioned in the sequel of this address. Let these funds be sent on promptly and freely, accompanied by such local information as may prove of use and interest. But many can do more than this. Life members and life directors of these institutions can be obtained. Churches, by contributing twenty or twenty-five dollars, can constitute their preacher, or some other deserving person a life member; or by the contribution of one hundred dollars, constitute said person a life director of either of these societies. Legacies can be left, as has been done already. We hope the brethren will be stirred up to do this, to the glory of God.

Do not, beloved brethren, partakers of the heavenly calling, slumber over this subject, nor dismiss it without serious reflection and earnest prayer. Let us be doing while it is day, for the night cometh when no man can work. Have no fears in reference to your funds sent here for evangelical purposes. Every agent and officer, handling the funds, gives bonds and security to large amounts.

DUTIES AND POWERS OF EVANGELISTS

Much interest was expressed on the subject of the general ministry. The cause has been much scandalized by irresponsible and unworthy men. All present, profoundly impressed with the evil, seemed anxious to remedy it, by some means, which should at the same time secure the internal independence of the churches. To all, it must be obvious, that the relation of these same churches to each other, is similar to the interrelations of their several members and equally expressive of dependence. Doubtless more reflection upon these truths, will enable the brotherhood, at some future time, to act harmoniously and effectively, and in perfect good keeping with the New Testament, on this important subject. Our convocations will bring the approved to light. Their names will go forth, and the wolf will creep to his lair in the darkness of the night.

UNION PRAYER MEETING

Concert of prayer has always been a favorite measure with the pious. There is sublimity in the thought that on the Lord's Day the globe is begirt with praying breath, and there is also moral grandeur in a similar union of prayer for the special object of the world's conversion. Most denominations meet for this on the evening of the first Monday of every month, and it is commended to the brethren to do likewise, and at that time they are also requested to take up collections in aid of our societies, and forward them quarterly to the proper officers in this city.

Brethren, suffer this exhortation. Let the magnitude of the cause be our apology for thus burdening you.

The grace of our Lord Jesus Christ be with you all. Amen.

D. S. BURNET,
President of Convention

S. W. Reeder, } Secretaries.
T. J. Melish,

Appendix IV

MEMORIAL DISCOURSE
ON THE OCCASION OF THE DEATH OF
ALEXANDER CAMPBELL[1]

"And I heard a voice from heaven, saying unto me, Write, Blessed are the dead which die in the Lord, from henceforth, yea, saith the Spirit, that they may rest from their labors, and their works do follow them."
—Rev. xiv: 13.

This night one week since, ALEXANDER CAMPBELL departed this life, at 11:45, at his home, Bethany, West Virginia.

The lives of distinguished men are the property of the public; not only of the generation they serve, but of all succeeding generations. Were there no future life, such persons would enjoy a species of enviable immortality in the present world, provided their career secured the commendation of men. The intelligence of a people is in the proportion of the calmness, frankness, and discrimination with which they form their estimation of their public servants. It is a duty to essay the task, and essay it with the determination to profit by their excellencies and be warned by their defects. If we condemn one invention and exalt another into a great instrument of human progress and comfort, we should *a fortiori*, as a man is superior to a machine; as an immortal spirit has a higher value than mere matter; and spiritual qualities are better than material; estimate human usefulness above all meaner things, and carefully select from a great character the true fruits of admiration and imitation.—But peculiar embarrassments beset our efforts in this direction. The world is prone to partisanship, and men are praised or blamed as they assent to our views, or dissent from them. This course is not only unwise and unjust, but is sure to inflict an injury upon the partial and prejudiced examiner. MR. CAMPBELL, by common consent, has filled a larger place in the public mind of this generation than any other theologian

---
[1] D. S. Burnet, *Memorial Discourse, On the Occasion of the Death of President Alexander Campbell, which Occurred March 4th, 1866* (Baltimore: Innes and Maguire, Adams Express Building, 1866). Footnotes in the address are Burnet's.

on either continent, and the views attributed to him have been received by a larger number of religionists, within the last forty years, than those of any other man within the past hundred. No other man of our times could count upon a half million of adherents during the term of his natural life. On the other hand he has been stigmatized as a dangerous heretic. Of course he had his faults, for he was a man; but such success in the conflict of opinions, where the opposing parties were the peers of the most learned and the more pious, must argue great powers and great plausibility, and also must present ground for the presumption of solid merit.

Anthony, over the dead body of his friend said,
"Lend me your ears, . . .
I come to bury Caesar, not to praise him."

I come not to praise ALEXANDER CAMPBELL. I will let his works do that, if they can; but lend me your ears that you may know what those works have been.

In the presentation of the subject, this order will be observed:

I. A short narrative of MR. CAMPBELL'S life and concurrent events.

II. A delineation of his character in his public and private relations.

III. A statement of the closing scenes of his career.

IV. A few reflections suitable to the occasion.

Therefore I ask your attention to

I. A succinct narrative of his life and concurrent events.

The subject of this memorial discourse was the son of the Rev. Thomas Campbell, a relative and classmate of the Scotch Poet, Thomas Campbell. His mother, Mrs. Jane Campbell, was of a French Huguenot family, which fled to Ireland to escape massacre from the Catholics after the bloody St. Bartholomew's day. She was an amiable Christian woman, whom I remember as one who gained my esteem at the first interview.

Thomas Campbell, the father, was a very remarkable man. One of the most devout men said he never knew one so devout as Thomas Campbell. He was several years a Presbyterian minister of the New Market Presbytery in the North of Ireland, and on account of his amiable qualities, was chosen by that body a commissioner to reconcile the Burgher and Anti-Burgher Synods. When an Irish nobleman offered him a lucrative position, he declined it, for fear it would corrupt his children with the vices of society. His house was a house of religious instruction and prayer, and his parish is said to have been the most exemplary in the country. While he adhered to the catechism, he was rigid in his examination of parents and children. He knew nothing but Christ and him crucified, bringing the stores of a well-disciplined mind, the gold, frankincense and myrrh, to the feet of his Master. Feeble health drove him to this country, and when here, with enlarged views and a warm heart, he conceived a scheme of Christian Union upon the basis of the Bible and the Bible alone. Of course this was distasteful to his presbytery and ended in a separation. Three very remarkable papers emanated from his pen about this time, two of them in A.D. 1809. These were *A Declaration, an Address and a Prospectus of a Religious Reformation.* The burden of these papers was, the inefficiency of denominational organizations for the enlightenment and salvation of the world, and the necessity of a radical change of base in future assaults upon the kingdom of darkness. For the furtherance of these objects a society was formed in Washington County, Pa., to give expression and force to these sentiments, and not a great while thereafter two Churches were organized upon these principles. I am thus particular, Brethren, in this recital, because it was the initial movement which had much to do in shaping the current of events, issuing in what has been called the Reformation of the 19th century. In these movements in the Presbyterian Church headed by Thomas Campbell in Western Pennsylvania and Western Virginia, and movements in the same Church in Kentucky and Tennessee, under the lead of Stone, Marshall, Thompson, Dunlevy, etc., which latter were attended with great enthusiasm and irregularities, we find the expression of the then great want of the times, greater conformity to the scriptures and a higher life. By these independent popular movements, without any definite idea of primitive Christianity, a latent force was excited which has taken the body and form of what is now known as the Christian Church, sometimes called the "Disciples."

ALEXANDER CAMPBELL was born near Thane Castle, County Anthrim, North of Ireland, in September, 1788, and he was consequently seventy-seven and a half years old when he died. His education, literary and religious, was the labor of his father's life. As Hamilcar swore the boy Hannibal to a lifelong enmity to Rome, and made his God Baal a part of his son's name, so Thomas Campbell trained ALEXANDER to a perpetual war against the papal and all other corruptions and sins. He completed the education of his son in the halls of his *Alma Mater,* Glasgow University, leaving him in that institution in 1807, when he departed to America. The next year ALEXANDER, now a Presbyterian preacher, followed with the mother and other children, and being cast away on the Island of Ila, their voyage across the Atlantic was delayed till 1809. The son found his father reading the proof-sheets of his *Declaration and Address,* and then predicted that the leaven of those, would work a greater change than the author dreamed of, affirming, "in the *Bible alone* you will never find infant baptism and some other things practised by us. The restoration of primitive Christianity will work a mighty revolution." But the elder Campbell had counted the cost and launched his bark, trusting the voyage to the guiding-star of truth. The son entered heartily into his father's plans, not then dreaming that his more active nature and impressible force, would in a few years place him in the lead; and never did one great mind fall into the shadow of a greater with equal and truer delight. There was no falling back of the elder, but Providence gradually bore the younger, with firmer tread and more agility, far in the advance. Which was the leader mind, was soon determined by the acclaim of thousands. The father rejoiced more in the son than in himself—for had he not labored for this very end?

In 1812 ALEXANDER CAMPBELL, whose constant habit of reading the Greek New Testament made him an independent thinker on its contents, declared to the family that he had never been baptized. The subject was fully discussed, and on June 2d seven persons, including most of the Campbell family, were immersed by an obscure Baptist preacher by the name of Matthias Luse, into the name of the Father, Son and Holy Spirit. Weekly communion had been established; and immersion followed in the Churches heretofore named—composed of pious persons from all quarters of the theological heavens. After a year or two, by request, they united with the Red Stone Baptist Association, but an irrepressible conflict arising, these Churches joined the Mahoning Association of Ohio, known to be more liberal in feeling. This body gradually resolved itself into an annual meeting for Christian acquaintance, the gathering of statistics and the conversion of sinners. MR. CAMPBELL now announced the following propositions as fundamental in all efforts to keep the unity of the spirit in the bonds of peace, viz:

"Nothing ought to be received into the faith or worship of the church, or be made a term of communion among Christians, that is not as old as the New Testament. Nor ought anything be admitted as of Divine obligation in the church constitution or management, save what is enjoined by the authority of our Lord Jesus Christ and his Apostles upon the New Testament Church, either in express terms or by approved precedent."

The subjoined extract followed as a legitimate corollary from the foregoing:

"*Christian Union can result from nothing short of the destruction of creeds and confessions of faith, inasmuch as human creeds and confessions have destroyed Christian Union.*" That "*whenever the setting aside of creeds and confessions shall be attempted, Christians will give to the world and to angels, and to themselves, proof that they do believe the word of God.*"

On these self-evident propositions, he planted his feet, and reasoned and labored, as few have done, for the union of all God's children on the foundation of the Apostles and Prophets, Jesus Christ himself being the chief cornerstone. Both father and son, having assumed their independent position, found it convenient to devote much of their time to teaching classical literature. The son opened an academy at his residence, and the father, after spending some time in Ohio, Kentucky, and Indiana, came to reside with him permanently, and there departed his useful life at the age of ninety-one.

During the existence of his academy, MR. CAMPBELL became acquainted with brother Walter Scott, who was also teaching in Pittsburgh—an acquaintance which, ripening into intimacy, lasted till the demise of the latter in 1861. They were true yokefellows, each in his sphere contributing greatly to the scriptural knowledge and spiritual development of the other.

In his frequent tours, MR. CAMPBELL attracted great crowds, by the novelty of his teaching and the remarkable ability with which he discoursed on the stirring themes of both Testaments. His calm dignity, the profundity of his conceptions, and his extraordinary power of generalization, riveted every eye, and charmed, as well as instructed, thousands. His advocacy of immersion instead of aspersion, stirred the pedo-baptist heart, and led to a discussion, in the year 1820, at Mt. Pleasant, Ohio, with Rev. John Walker, a Presbyterian minister, on the action and subjects of baptism. This added to his celebrity, and increased the desire to hear the objects of his mission discussed. These events determined him to write, as well as preach, and in 1823 he began his career of publishing. August 3rd, he issued *The Christian Baptist*, and continued it seven years, liberally inviting into its pages those who differed with him. This being esteemed the best of his publications, the seven volumes were partially expurgated and condensed into one permanent volume by another hand. With transcendent excellencies, it yet has serious faults. No work on the Christian religion has, in our country, created so widespread a sensation. Opponents crowded into the arena of its pages like the Philistines upon Sampson, and with a similar result.

This publication, having finished its course of seven years, was superceded by the *Millennial Harbinger* which is still in existence, and has entered its thirty-seventh year, under the editorial charge of his son-in-law, our excellent brother, W. K. Pendleton. The public interest in these periodicals was mainly owing to the great amount of editorial matter, and the originality of their views. During forty years, he also published six voluminous reports of oral debates, a translation of the New Testament, and three or four other volumes, making about fifty books. His debates with Rev. Wm. L. McCalla, and the celebrated sceptic communist, Robert Owen, the one in 1823 and the other in 1829, had more to do in widening his influence, perhaps, than any of his other discussions.

In the winter of '29 and '30, he was an active member of the convention which sat in Richmond, Va., to amend the State Constitution. There has never been such a gathering in Virginia as in that convention, and it is probable there never will be again. The venerables James Madison and Chief Justice Marshall, and the eccentric John Randolph, of Roanoke, were stars of the first magnitude. I believe brother CAMPBELL established himself in the esteem of all his compeers, except Randolph. It is thought that his hopes have been realized in the independent existence of West Virginia. Though this convention was not the place for him, his preachings in Richmond, at that time, were among the happiest of his life, and their influence upon Virginia is felt to this day.

In 1840 he founded Bethany College, having the year before communicated to the speaker his intention, as an act of courtesy, as he was then in connection with Bacon College. The institution was needed, but I foresaw the burden, in connection with other labors, already too onerous, would overtax his powers. In this, as he afterwards confessed to me, I was correct. But the institution has done a large amount of good in furnishing teachers and in preparing ministers for their work. In the latter capacity its usefulness was cramped by an imperfect charter, the best that then could be obtained from the Legislature of Virginia. I believe this defect has since been remedied.

The College furnished a fair field for the President's extensive knowledge of the Holy Writings, and his lectures on the Pentateuch, the New Testament Biographies and Acts of Apostles, were such as few other men could deliver.

In 1847 he visited Europe, having received an invitation from the Churches there, to spend one season with them. Your humble speaker was honored by being named in the joint invitation, but circumstances prevented his acceptance. The labors and events of this trip, added to the burden of the College, seemed to have materially affected his mind and general health; but the deadliest portion mingled in his cup of baleful care and sorrow, was the sad news which awaited his touching the shores of his adopted country—the son of his old age—the child of his prayers and hopes, was no more! Wyckliffe Campbell had been drowned at his father's mill! I am told by those who were near him, that ALEXANDER CAMPBELL never was equal to himself after this stroke; but it was a long time before the admiring world perceived any change.

His debates with the Catholic Archbishop Purcell in Cincinnati, 1836, and Dr. N. L. Rice, 1843, in Lexington, Ky., are before the public as recognized textbooks, and speak for themselves. Having given a hasty résumé of some of the events of his life, such as our straitened time would permit, I now invite your attention, Beloved Hearers, to the second division.

II. Brother CAMPBELL'S character as a man in public and private relations.

In person, God set the stamp of a man of power upon him. In height he was five feet eleven inches and when in health and in his prime, muscular without fleshiness; his brain vigorous rather than massive, his nose aquiline; and if I used the word etymologically, his eye also, for *aquila,* is an eagle. His very dark grey eye had an eagle's fire. His voice was clear, and somewhat sonorous, but without much compass. When he was in his prime he could effectively address a very large audience in the open air with but little apparent effort. His countenance told of power, but was genial and capable of varied expression, a kindly humor often twinkling under his eyebrows. He impressed himself upon every one as a benevolent but discriminating power.

His *colloquial powers* were of an unusually high order. In every circle, he seemed to be the centre of attraction and radiance; his social discoursings reminding one of the nine-mile sweeps of the Mississippi. If I compare him with Webster, Chalmers, Calhoun or old Dr. Beecher, as a conversationalist, he is their superior. I must look further for his peers and find them in Luther, Macauley and Coleridge. In private, as in public debate, he was more the sage than the controversialist, and compelled a rare respect and deference. The universe was his library; his conversation a living study.

As a *writer,* his power was acknowledged far and wide. A scholarly gentleman of another Church once said to me "he is certainly orthodox in letters, whatever may be said of his theology." When quite young he had read Scott's Commentary through; he had committed the gems of the better English Poets to memory; the Proverbs and Psalms he had at his fingers' ends, all which seemed to be at command always. Up to a certain period, his composition was terse, lucid and sufficiently ornate, leading his readers with the gentleness of song, but the power was as resistless as the tide. To my taste, his writings have for some years declined in power. Diffuseness is weakness, and amplification inconsistent with his former vigor. Few of his speeches and fewer of his writings of late years fairly represent ALEXANDER CAMPBELL. At no period did he take much time to dress his thoughts. When his mind was on draught, he gave what flowed, and as it flowed, a characteristic of great cultured minds. His fine taste seldom left him at fault. He adorned every subject on which he wrote.

As a *speaker*, I never knew him equalled in his peculiar sphere. He was not what the world calls an orator, and could not be compared with J. N. Maffit, nor with the greater Whitefield. He had not Whitefield's voice—his action, nor his emotions, nor had Whitefield his mind. Nor had he Wesley's enthusiasm and directness. He had feeble exhortatory power and he was seldom tender. The pathos of Kirwen he could not approach. But he drew crowds equal to either of the orators.

He was clear. He was generally understood by the masses, always by the cultivated. His entire mastery of the Bible captivated every one; all felt his power there. In action and in mind, he was Webster rather than Clay. Grand and sublime was he, but it was the sublimity of his theme. He never seemed to make an effort, while he charmed by his exegesis—his severe logic or his loftiest rhetoric. He was like no speaker I ever heard—always gentle, courteous, commanding. But I am speaking of him as he was twenty years ago. Some years since, he first lost his local memory and forgot names, places and many faces; then his logical memory followed—he lost consecutiveness in reason, except at intervals; but his sentimental and devotional memory were retained. His proverbs, his maxims, his poetry, his aphorisms were ever at his tongue's end, and his love of nature survived the general breakdown.

Perhaps the most important and the most difficult task is to speak of him as a *leader*. He belongs to that class of men who will lead under any circumstances, whether they desire it or not. I am not certain whether MR. CAMPBELL desired to lead in the early part of his career; and I am sure that when Providence put him forward, he did not dream of the results which have followed.

Nature, education and circumstances made him a luminous radiating centre, but his position also made him equally a focal point, where were concentrated the rays emitted by a thousand minds—his correspondents on both continents. The suggestions and queries of every mail were invaluable. No man ever more scorned the idea of imposing his name upon a party than he did. He felt humbled when one would put *ite* to the syllables which designated him from among other men. In the newspapers which have lately alluded to him, he is generally spoken of as the talented *founder* of the Christian Church. Neither he, nor those who have been stigmatized as his followers, have felt flattered by that word "founder." He founded nothing that he called, or we call, religion. He was often at special pains to show, not only that the things which he taught were in the Bible, but that they had been severally recognized by leading authors, at different periods in the history of the Church. Our hymnbooks and periodicals rejoice in the name of *Christian.* We claim this name as heaven given, and it should be accorded to us, as I find it is now generally in this city, as in many other places. If others prefer to give their denominational names to their hymnbooks, periodicals and Church standards, let them suit their tastes. We have not so learned Christ, whose we are and whom we serve. MR. CAMPBELL and all his brethren, a half million strong, have as the Christian Church, belonged to no sect; but have labored for the abolition of all sects, by the restoration of the New Testament as the Constitution of the Kingdom of God, the true home of all Christians, who are the one body of Christ animated by the one Holy Spirit —its life.

Early in this century many independent minds, unknown to each other, were quickened by the prophesying of the two Apocalyptic witnesses. Thomas Campbell, Barton W. Stone and associates, Walter Scott and others, made great advances. In 1824, then a boy at college, though an offshoot of the Presbyterian Church, your speaker demanded immersion of a Baptist Church upon the confession of his faith in Christ and receiving it, forthwith preached what he first read in Romans x. Though the finely educated elder Campbell, and the genius Walter Scott,[2] equal to any man in analytic power and poetic fire, were his companions, the subject of this memorial had to be the leader. God willed it. Though Mr. CAMPBELL was not a proselyter he baptized many of our prominent men and convinced more.

His amiable disposition made him a native gentleman. With such a father it could not well be otherwise. The kindly terms in which they addressed each other and spoke of one another, was lovely to contemplate. Though conscious of his power, he was not self-asserting, but deferential and devout! His personal Christianity was a deep-seated principle.

Though the manager of vast interests in his family, religion was a daily business. Reading the Scriptures, expounding them, talking of the great themes of the Bible, singing God's praises, were as regular as morning and evening. Before God he was humble and devout. His home was visited by great numbers of all creeds, but especially by his brethren, to enjoy his religious conversation. Your speaker has been with him abroad and he often was my guest, once for weeks; he was always the same—a devout worshipper of God. I never saw one of any creed, whose mind dwelt as much upon the glories of Christ, or who rejoiced more in his divinity.

His friendships were strong, but they seldom outran his estimate of purity of life or his faithfulness.

But I suspend this imperfect portraiture for the consideration of

III. The closing scenes of his career.

Our dear friend's hair was a little frosted at the age of thirty-seven. For ten years past the snow that never melts, had buried his noble head in white. For near that period his beard has been permitted to flow like a glittering glacier from his chin, the whole an Alpine scene bathed in perpetual sunshine. It was an embodiment of wisdom, purity and love. As his overworked faculties gradually decayed, the sunshine of love and joy grew brighter. Jesus was ever with him, a perennial source

---

[2] Walter Scott arranged the gospel under six heads, three of duty and three of privilege. A younger hand tabulated the whole, under nine, prefixing it with the three items of the matter of the gospel.

of peace. He believed in the Spirit's presence and power in the heart, and therefore he enjoyed it rapturously.

Three weeks before his death he had taken a bad cold and nearly lost his voice, but for a week longer kept about. One of his nephews writes thus of the scenes up to Saturday, the day before he died:

"I am sitting up to-night with our dear uncle. We fully thought this would be his last night on earth. But he has survived the turn of the night and may possibly wear through another day. His strength is wonderful. All this night I have thought as I watched him of a giant grappling with a desperate foe, or of some noble animal struggling to be disentangled from the enemy's toils, chafed and fretted within its narrow boundaries. Death has no power to dim this great mind—his senses are as acute and clear as ever, and his beautiful nature shows the same in all things. His gentleness and patience mid his suffering, break all our hearts. Such sweetness and submission to the slightest wish of others around him—such kind consideration for every one who comes into his presence—his little expressions of greeting, and his inquiry after the welfare of those who come to see him, and such putting away of personal complaint or suffering, move every beholder to tears. All this could never be seen in a character less great and grand than his. He is himself, noble and good and great, as nature made him, to the very last. The commanding and fascinating elements of his character are intact in the midst of the wreck of matter. Such passages of Scripture as he has recited even in his wanderings, and such grand sentences as have fallen from his lips—such beautiful soliloquies upon the 'fleetness of time' and upon 'doing good while we can,' &c.—are wonderful, very wonderful to all of us."

I select from other letters before me, including one from Dr. Barclay, speaking of the constant raptures of the departed, the two following, one from his son-in-law, J. J. Barclay, written before his demise; the other from a niece, who was with him day and night, during his last illness, up to the time of his departure.

"On last Lord's Day I thought his Spirit would burst through the fetters of mortality, and enter upon the enjoyment of that eternal Lord's Day of which he has already so sweet and assuring a foretaste. His room is truly to him no other than the house of God, and the gate of Heaven. He said that he had rather be a door keeper in the house of the Lord than to dwell in the tabernacles of ungodliness. His mind is altogether absorbed in the contemplation of his glorious inheritance. His Spirit has already entered the vestibule of his God. He is as patient and gentle as a lamb, and talks only on religious subjects. The Lord grant that our last end may be like his.

"Yesterday three weeks ago he was at the church for the last time and spoke a few words at the Lord's Supper. I will never forget how that hoarse whisper, striving to rise with the great thoughts which carried his mind far above his physical weakness, sounded in my ears, for I knew I should never hear it again, in that place. Oh, it overcomes me entirely to recall all the events of the past week, all the suffering which he underwent before the spirit left its noble earthly tenement, though once, when we were watching him, in his suffering, he called it 'this poor house of clay.' Oh, it was so sad and so heartbreaking to see his extreme gentleness, his never-failing patience and consideration for others. And such beautiful sentiments I never heard from mortal lips. He was emphatically *himself*, through all, even when his mind wandered. The old, rare smile and the courteous gesture, were never wanting, and all those ways which distinguished him from every other person. He talked continually and repeated the grandest and most beautiful passages of Scripture, verses of his favorite hymns and from his favorite poets, so aptly and beautifully. Those grand and rapturous thoughts with which his mind has especially been filled in the last few years were on his lips continually.

"I wish you were here now, to see him lying in the parlor, more grand and noble in death even than he was in his life. Death has had no power over him to take away that look of greatness. He is the most majestic form I ever saw in the repose of death, a sweet smile lingers about his mouth. There is a crown of peace and serenity and that same unconscious nobility there was in life."

IV. This affords a suitable occasion for a few reflections.

What a fearful contrast between such a death—the sleep in Jesus—and the departure of a godless soul to its final account!

A life of pleasure, a life of sin, a foreboding. "Let me die the death of the righteous and let my last end be like his."

A long while since, David said, 'Mark the perfect man and behold the upright, for the end of that man is peace.'[3] "Precious in the sight of the Lord is the death of his saints."[4]

> So fades a summer cloud away;
> So sinks the gale when storms are o'er;
> So gently shuts the eye of day;
> So dies a wave along the shore.

"I heard a voice from Heaven saying unto me, write, blessed are the dead who die in the Lord, from henceforth: Yea, saith the Spirit, that they may rest from their labors; and their works do follow them." Our Brother was emphatically for more than sixty-five years a laborer; he was heavy laden; he needed rest. He literally wore out in the service. How sweet the angel tones of our text, and the Spirit's message to his weary spirit, now.

A good and great minister is a gift of God. Pastors and teachers are enumerated among the gifts of the Messiah, a largess from the Conqueror when fresh from the field of conflict and renown.[5] We recognize our departed brother, not as the *regium donum* to a single Church, but as a gift to this age. God, however, claims the right to resume his gifts. "The Lord gave and the Lord hath taken away."[6] Shall we not, Beloved, respond in the spirit of a humble submission and Christian resignation, "Blessed be the name of the Lord."

> "Death loves a shining mark, a signal blow;
> A blow which, while it executes, alarms,
> And startles thousands with a single fall."

But startled, we should be none the less resigned, though it is a severe test, for often "Like the evening sun, comes the memory of former times on my soul," with a sad subduing radiance.

---

[3]Ps. xxxvii: 37.
[4]Ps. cxvi: 15.
[5]Ps. lxvii: 17, 18. Eph. iv: 10, 11.
[6]Job i: 21.

I cannot moralize now. My spirit is too sad. A gloom settled upon me when on the 5th I read the dispatch: "ALEXANDER CAMPBELL died at his residence, March 4th, at 11.45 P.M.," and I cannot break the spell. My advices led me to expect it shortly, but we are never entirely prepared to part with those whom we love. I thought I should be composed, but I was not—I am not. Had I been present, when he went up, I might have exclaimed like Elisha, "My Father! My Father! the chariot of Israel and the horsemen thereof!"[7] But however much I might need it, I could not ask a *double* portion of his spirit to rest upon me.

The *Harbinger* is in good hands, exhibiting new life; the College is also in good hands, and has girded on its armor since quiet has been restored; but the venerable form now cold in the grave, shall be seen no more till, Beloved, we meet by the light of the world's funeral pyre, and see each other in the glare of the general conflagration. When He comes, whose right it is to reign, all whom we love shall also come. The burdens of our departed friend have some time since been divided among younger brethren, but his name is now only in history. His memory will be cherished while there are those who believe that the New Testament has a distinctive religion, which must sooner or later be adopted by those who are now divided into sects, and that the day is coming when there shall be one fold and one Shepherd!

God comfort the bereaved widow and care for the sorrowing children—the four survivors of the twelve!—and the brother, the sister and the thousands of sorrowing Israel. The Lord enable them to sing

> "O sweet is the season of rest
> When life's weary journey is done!
> The blush that spreads over its West,
> The last lingering ray of its Sun."

THE END.

---

[7] 2 Kings ii: 12.

Appendix V

A SYNOPSIS OF DIVINE REVELATION[1]

Dispensations

PATRIARCHAL (Adam)   JEWISH (Moses)   CHRISTIAN (Messiah)

Each of these "Dispensations" had its gospel, ordinances, laws, priesthood, &c. The gospel proclaimed by God to Adam is found, Genesis iii: 15, the gospel proclaimed by Moses to the Israelites, Exodus iii. chap., and the gospel of Jesus the Messiah, preached by the Apostles to the world, Acts. ii. chap.

Christianity contains a Gospel—Ordinances—Laws.

SCHEME OF THE GOSPEL OF JESUS CHRIST OUR LORD TO THE WORLD.

The Gospel Divisible into			
1st. News. Jesus is the Messiah, the Son of God	Involving three facts to be believed	1. Fact.—Death of Jesus for our sins according to the Jewish scriptures. 2. His burial in our earth. 3. His resurrection for our justification, according to the Jewish scriptures.	
2d. Commands, Believe and obey him	Involving three duties to be performed	1. Duty.—Belief of God's testimony concerning his Son. 2. Repentance unto life. 3. Immersion in water into the name of the Father, Son and Holy Spirit.	
3d. Promises. And you shall be saved	Involving three blessings to be enjoyed	1. Blessing.—Remission of all past sins. 2. The Holy Spirit the gift of God. 3. The hope of eternal life, to be attained by perseverance.	

[1] Burnet, "Christian Baptism," *Christian Preacher*, III pp. 195f. Cf. *Christian Baptist* (1835), preface. Also Forney, op. cit., pp. 36, 37.

Appendix VI

CONSTITUTION
AMERICAN CHRISTIAN BIBLE SOCIETY[1]
PREAMBLE

WHEREAS, The Sacred Scriptures, the Hebrew of the Old Testament, and the Greek of the New, are the only authoritative divine standard, containing the only revelation of God to the human race extant; and

WHEREAS, It is the duty of Christians, who are called "the light of the world," to acquaint the human family with those revelations, by faithfully and thoroughly translating and circulating them, we, whose names are undersigned, resolve to unite our labors under the following

CONSTITUTION

ARTICLE I. The name of this Association shall be the AMERICAN CHRISTIAN BIBLE SOCIETY.

ART. II. It shall be the object of this Society to aid in the distribution of the Sacred Scriptures, without note or comment, among all nations.

ART. III. Each contributor of one dollar annually, shall be a member.

ART. IV. Each contributor of twenty-five dollars at one time, shall be a life member.

ART. V. Each contributor of one hundred dollars shall be a life director.

ART. VI. All Churches, Bible co-operations, or Societies, agreeing to place their surplus funds in the treasury of this Society, shall be auxiliaries, and shall have the right to appoint one director; and, for every fifty members, they shall be entitled to another director. The Parent Society, located in Cincinnati, shall be entitled to one director, and another director for every twenty-five members; all which directors shall assemble at the time and place of the annual meeting.

---

[1] *Annual Proceedings*, 1849, pp. 49, 50.

ART. VII. A Board, consisting of a President, nine Vice-Presidents, Corresponding and Recording Secretaries, and Treasurer, together with twenty-five Managers, shall be appointed annually, to conduct the business of the Society. The President, two Vice-Presidents, Secretaries, Treasurer, and sixteen of the Managers, shall reside in Cincinnati, or the vicinity. The members of the Board shall continue in office until superseded by a new election, and shall have power to fill such vacancies as may occur in their number.

ART. VIII. The Board of Managers, and their officers, shall meet monthly, or oftener, if necessary, at such time and place as they shall adjourn to; seven of whom shall be a quorum.

ART. IX. The Board of Managers shall have power to appoint such persons as may have rendered essential services to the Society, members for life, or life directors.

ART. X. At the meetings of the Society, and of the Boards of Managers and Directors, the President, or in his absence, the Vice-President first upon the list then present, and in the absence of all the Vice-Presidents, the Treasurer, and in his absence, such member as shall be chosen for that purpose, shall preside.

ART. XI. The annual meetings of the Society, and Directors, shall be held in Cincinnati, on the Tuesday after the third Lord's Day in October, in each year, or at any other time, at the option of the Society when accounts shall be presented, and a President, Vice-Presidents, Secretaries, Treasurer, and such other officers as they may deem necessary, together with a Board of Managers, shall be chosen for the ensuing year, by the Directors entitled to vote on the Treasurer's books, at the beginning of the said month.

ART. XII. The President shall, at the written request of six members of the Board, call a special meeting of the Board of Managers, causing at least three days' notice of such meeting to be given.

ART. XIII. The whole of the Minutes of every meeting, shall be signed by the Chairman and Secretary.

ART. XIV. No alteration shall be made in this Constitution, except by the vote of two-thirds of the members of the Society and Directors present at an annual meeting.

Appendix VII

NOTES FROM SERMONS AND ADDRESSES OF D. S. BURNET

THE GOOD CONFESSION.[1]

"Jesus Christ witnessed a good confession."
—1 Tim. vi:13.

The Good Confession, more than any other peculiarity, distinguishes the people who choose to be called Christians or Disciples of Christ. What the text calls the Good Confession is exacted of every candidate for baptism, and upon it, rather than any other consideration apart from his hearty faith in it, the party is admitted to that holy institution.

. . . .

As far as this address can answer the demand, it is my purpose to show that the Primitive Church had no other doctrinal foundation; that the convert had no other claim upon baptism; and that the recent recovery from the apostolic ages of this formula has justified the terms, "Reformation of the Nineteenth Century."

. . . .

I. That the Good Confession is the historical and logical aspect of the Gospel.

. . . .

To a careful reader, nothing will be more apparent than that the whole purpose of the apostolic ministry was to argue and enforce the claims of Jesus upon the faith, reverence, and heartfelt obedience of a lost race. They drove this one point to the conviction and submission of all but the incorrigible.

. . . .

II. The Good Confession, that Jesus is the Christ, the Son of God, is the creed and foundation of the Primitive Church.

. . . .

[1]Moore, *Living Pulpit*, pp. 47-68.

The church was not yet in existence, but it was to be erected upon this foundation when built. . . . Until some one shall arise —no one has yet done so—and show that God ever authorized a religious society, Jewish or Christian, to be founded upon an uninspired document, it will be taken for granted, that Jesus meant what he said in these utterances, and that the Good Confession, as defined in the conversation between Jesus and his disciples, is the doctrinal foundation of the Church, as it is of the individual faith of each of its members. It may be objected that the whole New Testament is considered the rock of the Church. Truly, it is the Divine directory of the Church. The Ten Commandments were the constitution of the Jews, or the old covenant, the bulwark of the unity of God against Polytheism. The Good Confession sustains the same relation to the Christian Church. It is the new covenant and the development of divine society in God—the Father, Son and Spirit.

. . . .

III. The Good Confession is Divine. . . . It is claimed for this Confession that God made it (Matt. xvi:17). . . It is difficult to exaggerate the importance of this third proposition. If the Good Confession is the marrow and fatness of the Gospel, if it is the rock chosen on which to found the Church, no one could object to its being called divine. But the word divine receives a new power in this connection, where the act of the Spirit and the word of the Father are proved to constitute the Confession itself. The Church of Christ is pre-eminently a divine institution, and is degraded by the thought of an uninspired basis. The convert is not called upon to emasculate his reason and humble his manhood by bowing to a humanism in the vestibule of the temple of truth.

IV. The Good Confession is the most liberal confession of faith on record. . . . This may be inferred from its simplicity. There is nothing intricate in it. It involves the great fact of the Bible, the central truth of the whole revelation. Jesus is the Alpha and Omega of all sacred literature. It is truly a confession of faith, and not of opinions. In this respect it is unlike any symbol of any denomination.

. . . .

V. Christ made the Good Confession before the Jewish high-priest and Sanhedrin, during the administration of Pontius Pilate, and died for the making of it.... When they were baffled at every point, the presiding Hierarch, coming to the aid of the prosecutors, cried out, "I adjure you by the living God." (I put you upon your oath), "tell us whether thou be the Christ the Son of God. Jesus said unto him, Thou hast said." It is here we find the ground of his condemnation. He died for the Good Confession!

. . . .

VI. The Confession by which Jesus died is appointed for our life.... What mercy! Jesus died by our sin, and for it, and we live by his righteousness. He died for acknowledging himself to be our Messiah and God's Son—the God-Man Savior. We live by him. He died confessing, that we might live confessing! It is a brazen serpent cures the serpent's bite!

. . . .

VII. The import and value of this formula entitles it to the designation Good or Beautiful Confession.... The reception of thousands upon the simple confession of faith and obedience has caused some nervousness among those who require a recital of inward struggles, and delineations of the various shades of darkness and light, doubt and confidence, which may have marked the progress of the soul to final submission. Who has produced one precedent or precept for the admission of persons to baptism upon any other basis than the Confession? Echo asks, Who? and asks in vain! It must, however, be admitted that, like every other good thing, the noble Confession is liable to abuse by both administrator and subject. The preacher is warned against carelessness in building upon this foundation wood, hay, or stubble. His work shall pass the ordeal of fire. Let him look well, then, to the materials of his spiritual edifice. As a wise man, he will ascertain whether the candidate understands the Confession. He has Philip for his authority.

. . . .

VIII. All men will be compelled to confess Christ at the close of this dispensation.... Is it better, friendly alien, to receive an irrevocable sentence on the knees and confess the power of justice after a life's resistance, or to compound your difficulties in accepting the offered grace of the inevitable conqueror, by an expressive confession of his well-established claims, and a union of your interests and efforts with his rising cause?

. . . .

THE PASTORATE
(A Discourse)

* * *

DEDICATION
TO THE FOLLOWERS OF CHRIST

Who were represented in the State Meeting held in Hopkinsville, Kentucky, in October, 1855, where this Address, ordered by the prior Annual Meeting, was requested for publication, by that body; and to all Christians, who are desirous of seeing the cause of their Master efficiently sustained by permanent Churches, this Discourse is

Affectionately and Respectfully inscribed

By the
AUTHOR.

"And he gave some, apostles; and some, prophets; and some, evangelists; and some, pastors and teachers."
—Eph. iv:11.

Christ is a shepherd, a pastor, the pastor, the chief pastor, because he has the care of God's flock. But "Chief shepherd" implies under shepherds or sheep-herds, just as God's great flock embraces many minor flocks, whom their respective shepherds are required to feed, taking the oversight, not by constraint but willingly.

. . . .

Pastor and flock are correlative terms, and in God's government the flock has always required the pastor.

. . . .

The pastorate, then (in the light of Jeremiah iii. 15), is an office in the Church of God, and essential to the completion of the prophecies and promises that have gone before, concerning the glory which should follow. . . .

. . . .

The Bishop or overseer of the primitive Church was required to possess all the social virtues and the intellectual culture, demanded in a spiritual pastor of the flock; irreproachable, gentle, vigilant, amiable, a spiritual teacher, apt at his business.

. . . .

Necessity may be pleaded for the employment of men of secular avocations and inferior qualifications, to take charge of the Church of God, but certainly an effort—a series of efforts—should be made to furnish every city Church, and as many of the rural ones as possible, the labors of a competent Pastor, who shall rule well and *"labor* in the word and teaching," surrounded and sustained by such assisting fellow-workers as the community may furnish.

In the selection, the basis should be a good mind and an affectionate heart. Culture is much, but it is not everything. It is nothing, in the absence of something to be cultivated. . . .

. . . .

But the question is, shall the Churches be so content with their present attainments and moral influence, as to make no systematic efforts to furnish themselves Christian instruction and oversight, adequate to the present demands of society and the present elevation of the intellectual and spiritual standard.

. . . .

The Pastorate is not merely a scriptural office—an office which our present condition loudly demands; but it is a *work*, a labor. It is no sinecure, in which the incumbent may lounge through life. The office is like the love which should inspire the possessor of it, active, ever active.

. . . .

No man that desires not the good that it may be possible for him to do, "is fit for the kingdom of God," much less qualified to be a pastor in it. With me, a desire for the Christian ministry, is an indispensable qualification for the office, and it should never be forgotten in the employment of any one. No cold calculation or languid indifference, can enter *his* views and feelings, who sympathizes with the good Shepherd who giveth his life for the sheep.

APPENDIX VII   249

IS THE CHRISTIAN CHURCH
(SOMETIMES CALLED THE REFORMATION)
EVANGELICAL?[1]

. . . .

Our religion is the Christian religion, and Jesus is the soul of it—first, middle, and last. Therefore, the great value of the books of facts which the universal consent of two thousand years has placed first in the canon of the New Testament. These facts were gathered, grouped, and brought into effective array by the Spirit-inspired Apostles in their public addresses, and thus arranged, they were called the Gospel.

. . . .

The evangelical part of Christianity, the matter-of-fact portion, is the very portion, and the only portion, which is common ground, and which furnishes, in the present anomalous condition of Christendom, a firm and large footing for cooperation. The facts of the Gospel are the only parts of the system of truth which have secured a uniform acceptation among conflicting sects. Here they are one, they are evangelical. The boast of evangelical, when made to cover a fashionable religious faith, to the exclusion of any other form which fails only in the matter of popular acceptation, is, therefore, as empty as a blasted nut, and savors more of Phariseeism than Evangelism.

. . . .

While we, with all Protestants, disclaim the epithet Roman Catholic, we proclaim ourselves Catholic, in the true and usual sense of that word. *Roman* or *Greek* are *special*, and utterly inconsistent with the comprehensive and general term, Catholic. We are true Catholics, and are laboring to restore the true Catholic Church of God, by restoring the true and primitive grounds of faith and fellowship. *We hold no sentiment, adopt no formula, observe no ordinances, and practice no duties not sanctioned by all evangelical denominations, whether we employ the term evangelical in its ecclesiastical, or its etymological and true sense.* I repeat it, with all emphasis, that every form or expression of religion, held or uttered by us as a body, is voted

[1] *Is the Christian Church Truly Evangelical?* pp. 3-24.

in by the majority of the parties composing the Evangelical Association of Cincinnati, or the Evangelical Alliance, of London memory, with which the former originated.

. . . .

. . . It is a cardinal point in our practice to express our views of Scripture, as far as possible, in Scripture language. Our use of the Bible differs from the ordinary one. We do not *prove* our views *by* it; we *read them out of it*. The Bible is our religion written, and the basis of our religion felt and acted. As a proof book, a volume or spiritual logarithms, ready upon occasion for any comparison of ecclesiastical quantities, the Sacred Oracles have been made the Patriarchal head of everything called Christians, from the most mystical Sabellianism to the most material Socinianism, from the Hyperboreanism of Calvin to the moral indiscrimination of Winchester and Ballou. Leaving the system of Eclecticism, which selects a few favorite portions and arrays them against the remainder of God's Word, we have taken all God's Word as our word, and his will as our law.

. . . .

It has been customary for us, for many years past, to arrange the materials of the Gospel under three general heads, each one in turn divisible into three others, viz.:

Matters of Faith.
Matters of Duty.
Matters of Reward.

That is, the Gospel contains what is to be believed, what is to be done, and what is to be enjoyed, by sinners, in their reconciliation to God.

. . . .

What is to be believed? One of the most honored depositories of inspired wisdom thus states the matters of faith: I Cor. xv: 3, 4:

1. I declare unto you the Gospel, how that Christ died for our sins according to the Scriptures.
2. He was buried.
3. He arose the third day, according to the Scriptures.

Appendix VII

This is the Gospel, in its facts—in its history. It is the Gospel to be believed—the Gospel in which believers "stand," and "by which they are saved." No council, or other conclave, has said it. God has said it.

. . . .

What is to be done as matters of duty? . . . A careful analysis of the apostolic speeches, addressed to the unconverted of their day, will demonstrate that the elements of Gospel obligation were:

1. Faith, or belief of the Gospel.
2. Repentance of sin.
3. Baptism into the name of the Father, Son, and Holy Spirit.

Here again we have a catholic division and a catholic arrangement.

. . . .

The third element of the Gospel, as developed by a careful induction from the particulars of the apostolic speeches, is the experimental portion. It is the result of a sincere adoption of the cross as an all-sufficient and alone-sufficient sacrifice for human guilt, and the public acknowledgment of the obligations of gratitude to the Royal Sufferer and gracious Savior.

The subdivision, by universal consent, is:

1. Remission of sins.
2. The inhabitation of the Holy Spirit.
3. The hope of everlasting life.

. . . .

We have exalted faith into its true position, as the principle of Christian life, action, and enjoyment; and we have exalted baptism into the true expression and public recognition of faith on the part of a believing penitent, and the public guaranty of its blessings to him on the part of the Lord. This is always done by a reference to Divine rather than human authority, in the words of Scripture, with due regard to their contextual import. Baptism is of no more value than any other immersion in water, unless it is an act of faith; and not only so, it must be an act of faith in the blood of Christ as the procuring cause of the remission of sins, the appropriating baptism itself only "signing" and "sealing" what the blood of Christ procures.

There are no "future" sins. Sin is a transgression of law, and transgressions are matters of history. Therefore, it was necessary for Rome to invent indulgences, in order "to remit future sins." Repentance has reference to the future believer's baptism, for the remission of a sinner's sins, through the blood of Christ; but prayer and confession are the ordained means of remission to the saint.

. . . .

The spirit of Christianity is as important as the letter. Nay, more so. The Word was written that it might minister the Spirit by the hearing of faith, and that Spirit is the most exalted benevolence, as well as the warmest affection. All considerations of party interest melt before it, as polar snows before a tropical sun. The narrow conceptions of bigots and enthusiasts, and the bitter animosities of sectaries, must give place to views more consonant with the millennial glory, and better suited as a preparation for the coming of the adorable Majesty of Incarnate Love.

HIM, OF WHOM MOSES IN THE LAW, AND THE PROPHETS DID WRITE.[1]

Since Bacon established a new route to truth, and demonstrated that induction is the only way to certainty, philosophy has modestly restricted her inquiries to the ascertainment of what belongs to man in his earthly relations, physical, intellectual, and moral. Unaided by revelation it presumes no farther than the penetralia of our present condition.

. . . .

Now, there is no light irradiating the future but the Scriptures; There is no measure of duty to God, no pledge of blessing from him, but Christianity.

. . . .

Two important questions are here forced upon us: First, Who, of all born of women, is the Son of God—the Messiah? Second, of all the pretended communications from heaven, which is the veritable Gospel containing the only terms of pardon?

. . . .

[1] Burnet, "Him, Of Whom Moses in the Law, and the Prophets Did Write," *Christian Preacher*, II (Sept., Oct., 1837), 145-222.

Appendix VII

Those prophecies which are *biographical* are singularly happy in their descriptions, and minute without a parallel. The Messiah's personal history absorbs most of the prophetic biography. The following summary of prediction accomplished in the person, offices, and history of Jesus, is a sample of the light the Scriptures poured upon his pretensions several centuries before his birth. This is an abstract from Simpson with alterations and additions which the subject seemed to require.

. . . .

Jesus is the author of eternal salvation to those who obey him: happiness is the goal to which he leads us, by successive approaches; first by the law, the prophets, the Psalms and the New Testament evidence, to *faith:* by faith to *repentance:* by repentance to *submission:* and lastly, through continued obedience, to *eternal life*.

THE POVERTY OF JESUS THE WEALTH OF THE SAINTS.[1]

"For ye know the grace of our Lord Jesus Christ, that though he was rich, yet for your sakes he became poor, that ye through his poverty might be rich."

II Cor. viii:9.

Here . . . we find the salient point of the discourse, the poverty—the pauperism of the world.

. . . .

The true condition of faith in a sinner is to know this poverty and be prepared to receive the kingdom of heaven upon the principle of the first beatitude, "Blessed are the poor in spirit, for theirs is the kingdom of heaven." Thus much, is implied in the text.

. . . .

Ah, friends, we are paupers all, if Christ has not enriched us with pardon and peace.

. . . .

[1] J. M. Mathes, *The Western Preacher* (Oskaloosa, Iowa: Central Book Concern, 1877), pp. 7-23.

"Jesus was rich." When? If every auditor should analyze his conceptions of Jesus, he will find that he never thought that the hero of the four gospels was rich; he always felt him to be poor.

. . . .

Thenceforth (after his baptism) he is officially God's and the world may not claim his physical labors. He never thereafter earned a penny. He ransomed a world! . . . From his baptism his life was one of privation . . . Such voluntary poverty must have a purpose commensurate with the greatness of the sacrifice.

. . . .

The first step toward our enriching is the feeling acknowledgment of our poverty, and full confidence in the ability and willingness of the Saviour, who has tasted at every fountain of our sorrows and overcome our foe, to bestow the pardon which he has purchased by the imolation of himself.

. . . .

The salvation is of grace and not of works. You get a pardon, not make a purchase.

Appendix VIII

FOURTH OF JULY ADDRESS BY ISAAC G. BURNET, CINCINNATI, 1808[1]

It is with diffidence, fellow citizens, that I appear before you on this auspicious day to commemorate the deeds of heroism achieved for our Independence; youth and inexperience may appear presumptuous in such a station, but when I reflect that I stand here in obedience to your call, I feel assured that my imperfections, however great, will be judged with liberality and that young and inexperienced, my opinions will be received with candor, they may not meet with universal approbation. I could wish that no expression might escape me that could offend one of my respectable audience, but is it possible, that in so numerous an assembly of Freemen, celebrating the birthday of their liberties, there could be perfect coincidence of sentiment on questions of national policy? The range of human thoughts and the diversity of human opinion cannot be restrained by despotic power. The mind expanded by a liberal education is "free as air." Bigotry and superstition are the only tyrants of the human intellect; before the invigorating sunbeams of education, they will disappear as the gloomy phantoms of visions. The mind is an active principle and it is essential to its existence that it should be kept in perpetual exercise, the film of prejudice may overshadow it and weaken its energies, it may be depressed by misfortune, and overawed by the lawless violence of Power, it may be seduced by pleasure, and corrupted by licentiousness; but external force cannot limit the range of human thought, nor reduce to uniformity the opinions of men. The Wise Author of existence made us each susceptible of different impressions; what to one appears fit and proper, in the estimation of another is the highest absurdity. Although truth is immutable, we do not all view it through the same medium, some are hurried on to an unqualified approbation of things, through a blind zeal, enthusiasm usurps the empire of reason,

---

[1]Isabella Neff Burnet, *Dr. William Burnet*, pp. 68-73.

the understanding is led captive to a fanciful theory, would you argue with such, they will effect to disbelieve the most palpable truths, if opposed to the dogmatical opinions of their sect or the extravagant measures of their favorite party. Others through the medium of prejudice view everything with a jaundiced eye. Happy are they whose mental vision is clear, either from the mist of prejudices or the blindness of enthusiastic zeal.

It will be readily perceived that such a state of anarchy could not long subsist, without an utter extermination of the human species. The atrocious crimes of the French Revolution prove the savage disposition of men with power equal to his passions. Let those deluded mortals who dwell with apparent delight on the fanciful theme of man's perfectability and his capacity for self-government turn their eyes to those scenes of enormity and violence, exhibited in the various stages of that series of popular delusion. Let them behold the People in their majesty desolating the fairest portion of creation with lawless violence, with the feelings of nature extinguished, fathers and brothers in hostile array, pillaging the cities of their nativity, slaughtering their kindest friends and to complete the savage triumph, marching in exulting pride, with new-born infants at the point of their bayonette. If they can turn from those scenes of horror with feelings of complacency to the ruthless multitude who have thus outraged humanity, and say that man is capable of self-government, I must impeach the correctness of their judgment and the purity of their hearts. At the present eventful crisis, when one man by his extraordinary talents and more extraordinary good fortune, wields in a manner the sceptre of the world and by his fiat decides the fates of kingdoms, no government can be well administered, so as to secure its own Independence and the liberties and happiness of its people, without possessing an energy that can down domestic rebellion and with an avenging arm, resent the proud contumely of foreign nations. Not only is it necessary for the perpetuation of the human species, through preservation or order and the happiness of mankind, that man should be restrained of some of his natural liberties but in order to protect him in the enjoyment of his most valuable rights and dearest privileges those destructive dogmas which have demolished part of Europe and propagated by the refuse of European jails, have made such rapid progress in America, should be rooted from society. Transported for their crimes or escaped from the merited vengeance of the law; these outcasts just landed on our shores proclaim themselves American Patriots and set about the benevolent purpose of reforming our Government and teaching liberty to the only people who rightly understand and properly enjoy it. Such are some of our newspaper editors, who under the pleasing garb of Republicanism, a name which they dishonor, convey their poisonous principles to the very heart of their readers. Let my countrymen spurn such wretches, who revile their best patriots and pollute the morals of their best citizens.

It is not the energy of their government that America should dread in the exercise of its legitimate powers, it wears no terrible features; let them rather dread the rage of innovation to weaken its energies, let them dread the imbecility of its administration, which has brought our once happy and flourishing country to the very precipice of destruction, let them dread the little petty resentments and the deadly hatred that is demonstrated towards the only nation that dares to raise its voice against the universal dominion of the Gallic Conqueror, and is fighting, without allies and unfriended, the battles of the world. Let them dread the undissembled partiality and the obliging condescension that are discovered for another nation, whose crimes exceed the powers of description and whose ambition is bound only by the limits of the Universe.

France and England at the present eventful day hold in some respects the same station that Rome and Carthage did of old, Roman courage and perseverance at last triumphed and Carthage fell. Her rival fallen, Rome soon became the mistress of the world, the Republic gave way to the Empire, and the Romans soon carried the terror of conquest to the remotest regions of the Earth. The uncultivated regions of Parthia and the barren mountains of the North equally unknown and inaccessible, alone escaped in the wreck of the nations. The Republican virtues of ancient Rome were extinguished in the glare of Imperial pomp; their moral virtues were depraved by the influence of Imperial corruption. Literature was despised and honest men were persecuted. It was in this dismal stage of society, when the very name of Liberty was extinct and the last effort of virtue was expiring, that the savage conquerors of the

North sallied forth and with the fierceness of barbarian courage seized the Roman Provinces incapable of resistance. Rome in her turn must now fall: a new era commences. The world was whelmed in clouds of darkness, but virtue had resumed her dominion. The vices and luxury of Rome were buried in the ruins of the Empire: and in a long train of events the world had emerged from the might of Gothic barbarism and monastic superstition, which succeeded the mighty revolution that had been accomplished by rude and illiterate chieftains who despised the arts. As if infected with Roman corruption and in progressive order the nations of the earth have assumed their present aspect; an aspect more terrible to liberty than at the subjugation of Greece or the fall of Carthage. Virtue was then respected, it was indeed the passport to fame; but the demoralizing system of politics practiced by the Cabinet of St. Cloud is calculated not only to destroy the faith of nations, but to extirpate from the human breast all sense of moral obligation. In France despoticism is reduced to a science, the acts of intrigue, cruelty, violence and pillage appear to be the chief studies of the Ministers of State, and to exalt to the highest dignities the most expert in this school of Politics, is the first care of the French Emperor. They are the fittest minions of illegitimate Power; the firmest supporters of government founded in crimes and usurption, honest men would shudder at the atrocities of French Despotism, none but those who have been trained in the horrid deeds of the Revolution could view them with complacency; or take a part in their transaction.

Governments were instituted for the benefit of the people, and not to oppress them; to protect their rights and secure their happiness; not to satiate the avarice or delight the ambition of tyrants. It was to restrain the licentious passions of the human mind and to invigorate its virtuous propensities; to protect age and imbecility from the insults and aggressions of brutal strength; not for the wanton purpose of letting every man do as he pleases, but by mild, just and equal laws to fix the boundaries of right and wrong, by suitable penalties to enforce an observance of the laws of nature; to further virtue and punish vice. This can be done without infringing the proper liberties of man; no act should be prohibited that is not injurious to the public good; all unnecessary restraints are infringements upon the rights of the people and by being tolerated will imperceptibly induce oppressions.

To continue a system of Government where man will be free under restraint, founded on the nice distinctions between freedom and licentiousness, is a task arduous and important, one that has given more employment to minds of Philosophers than the studies of politicians or statesmen. To continue such a system was the object of the American Patriots who framed our excellent Constitution. They had pledged their lives, their fortunes and their sacred honor in the cause of independence; they had struggled with intrepid courage and persevering fortitude through the calamities and distresses of a seven-year war; they had seen the banners of slavery and oppression unfurled to subjugate them; they had heard their virtuous efforts stygmatized with the vilest epithets, rebellion was the ministerial outcry; in privations and suffering they had drained the cup of wretchedness; untutored in military tactics they had fought and conquered; they had witnessed the triumphs of liberty and in the arduous contest they acquired immortal honors. Such were the heroes of the Revolution.

After the peace of 1783, the American Republic resembled the shattered fragments of a vessel just escaped from the overwhelming violence of the tempest, without rudder or compass. The Articles of Confederation were feeble ties, to connect the opposite interests of thirteen independent states, jealous of each other and jealous of the power they delegated to Congress. They had toiled for Independence and obtained it, but it was the "baseless fabric of a vision." To institute a Government, accommodate the jarring interests of such a confederacy, required all the influence and all the talents of the heroes of the Revolution. They saw the necessity of a radical change; they saw their country just escaped from the jaws of the Lion, ready to devour itself by intestine commotions. They grieved at the sight. This was not the high prize for which they had suffered and bled. It was their ardent wish to see the temple of Liberty erected on a firmer basis, on a foundation that might defy the omnipotence of time. With such sentiments they met in convention and produced to an admiring world the elegant and harmonious structure of the American Constitution, one of the sublimest efforts of human wisdom. Around this let us rally as the Ark of our political safety. Let not the unhallowed hand of innovation invade this Sanctuary of our Liberties. Let us expel from our councils those political montebanks who commence their senatorial career by impious attempts to subvert the bulwark of our rights, the Independency of the Judiciary. I blush for our state that she has elected a Senator who would build his fame on the ruins of his country, who had scarcely taken an oath to support the Constitution, than he would that it should be a perjury, and with daring effrontery laid violent hands upon one of its main pillars. Let us preserve our Constitution unimpaired as the surest Palladium of our civil rights and transmit to posterity as their most invaluable birthright. May each succeeding anniversary of our Independence find us more happy and more free and while the nations of Europe are wasting their energies in fruitless contest may we under our own vine and fig tree enjoy the sweets of Liberty and Repose.

Isaac Gouverneur Burnet

July 4, 1808

Index

A

Abolitionist, 78, 160
Across a Century, 52
Acting president, 104
"Active benevolence," 126
Acts of the Apostles, 120, 144, 175
Address to the Churches, 97, 100, 220-225
Administration, 24
Africa, 150
Agents, 109, 130, 153, 154, 156, 163, 170, 171
Akron, O., 147
Alabama, 19
Allen, Bro., 114
American and Foreign Bible Society, 74, 93, 127
American Bible Union, 117, 175, 192
American Christian Bible Society, 8, 61, 64, 65, 70, 71, 73, 75, 80, 82, 83, 85-90, 92-95, 98-107, 109-112, 114, 116, 117, 120, 121, 127, 128, 131, 132, 138, 145, 152, 192, 194, 196, 197, 242, 243
American Christian Missionary Society, 8, 61, 92, 95, 98-100, 103, 105, 106, 110-116, 117, 123, 127-129, 131, 133, 139, 146, 150, 152-154, 156-160, 163, 164, 169-172, 192-194, 196
American Christian Publication Society, 8, 84, 92, 97, 103, 111, 115, 120, 121, 124-130, 136-139, 143, 152, 192-194
American Christian Review, 9, 175, 176
American Christian Tract Society, 8, 61, 71, 77, 82, 86, 99, 105, 113, 115, 116, 138, 192, 194
Amendment, 147
Ancient Gospel, The, 51, 52

Ancient Order of Things, The, 51, 71
Anderson, H. T., 172
Anniversaries, 7, 77, 103
Annual meeting, 103, 123, 149, 150, 158, 193, 171
Annual Proceedings, 8, 70, 74, 85-98, 100, 106, 109-111, 118, 120-124, 129, 130, 138, 146, 150, 153, 154, 156-161, 163, 164, 168-173, 176, 242
Apostolic, 27
Arkansas, 107
Arny, W. F. M., 78, 80, 81
Articles of Faith, 33
Associations, 72
Augsburg Confession, 9
Austin, G., 53
Auxiliary, 86, 92
"A. W. C." (*See* Archibald W. Campbell), 127
Ayers, S., 96

B

Bacon College, 57-62, 76, 107, 172, 173, 192, 193
Bacon, Francis, 58
Baird, Samuel J., 44, 45
Baltimore address, 174, 226-240
Baltimore, Md., 51-53, 150, 165-168, 170, 171, 176-179, 181, 182, 183, 187
Baptism, 19, 27, 30, 33, 34, 45, 52, 65, 85, 178, 179, 190; administrator of, 28; purpose of, 28; ritual of indiction, 28, 31
Baptist, 26-28, 31, 33, 34-36, 38, 40, 42, 47, 48, 50, 56, 58, 72, 75, 76, 87, 93, 95, 121, 140, 190, 192; associations, 48; polity, 48, 49; preachers, 32

Baptist Bible Union (see American Bible Union, and Bible Union)
Baptist Missionary Society, 74
Barclay, Dr. James T., 96, 99, 105, 125, 131-134, 136
Barclay, Mrs. Julia A., 125, 132, 135, 193
Barclay, Sarah, 125
Barker, Eugene C., 21
Bedford, O., 145, 147
Beecher, Henry Ward, 45
Beecher, Lyman, 17, 18, 40, 44, 45
Belief, 28, 29, 87, 108, 116, 123
Believers, 52
Bell, Ann, 166
Bell, Hugh, 166
Benedict, J. D., 166
Benevolence, 7, 76, 88, 89, 91, 99, 101, 122, 126, 134, 140, 149, 153, 159, 191, 198
Benevolent society, 84
Bernhardt, William H., 11
Bethany address, 174
Bethany College, 60, 62, 67, 68, 74, 76, 78-81, 84, 99, 105, 111, 113-115, 175, 197
Bethany enterprises, 105, 138
Bethany Press, The, 114
Bethany, W. Va., 90, 101, 120, 126-128, 138, 139, 145, 148, 174
Bible, 7, 28, 34, 35, 51, 64, 70, 73, 74, 82, 83, 87, 92, 94, 95, 100, 101, 104, 109, 110, 118, 119, 122, 128, 131, 135, 192, 193, 200
Bible Union (*see* American Bible Union, and Baptist Bible Union), 110, 117, 120, 121
Biblical titles, 148
Bingham, Mrs., 98
Birney, James G., 43
Bishop, 80, 147
Bishops (*see* Elders)
Bishop, R., 95
Blakemore, W. B., 11
Board, 101, 130, 147
Board of Church Extension, 193 (see, Church, Extension)

Board of Managers, 9, 99, 120, 132, 148, 153, 156, 158-160, 170, 171, 186
Boles, H. Leo, 17-19, 24, 26, 31, 33, 50, 62, 86, 87, 102, 152, 155, 179
Books, 51, 129, 132, 136, 139, 173, 187, 193
Book Concern, 131
Book Union, 125
Boston, Mass., 123
Bosworth, H. S., 171
Boyd, John, 30, 31
Boy Preacher, The, 17, 26-35
Brite, Mrs. L. C., 12
Broaddus, Andrew, 48
Brotherhood, 85, 93, 94, 97, 100, 102, 105, 106, 109, 114, 121, 122, 126, 128, 130, 132, 136, 139, 146, 148, 150, 160, 161, 166-168, 173, 175, 177, 190, 192, 197, 198, 200
Brotherhood publishing house, 126
Brown, John, 157
Brown, John Henry, 21
Buckeye Disciples, 145
Burnet, Daniel, 212
Burnet, Uncle David G., 21, 22, 31, 69, 154, 191, 198
Burnet, Miss Edith, 158
Burnet Fund, 190
Burnet, Gilbert, 17, 191, 209
Burnet House, 107, 158
Burnet, Ichabod, 213
Burnet, Isaac G. (father of D. S.), 17, 19, 22, 30, 31, 69, 192, 260
Burnet, Isabella Neff, 21, 23, 218, 219, 255
Burnet, Judge Jacob (uncle), 19-21, 30, 31, 36, 40, 41, 43, 45, 62, 63, 69, 107, 149, 191, 193, 198
Burnet, Jacob, Jr. (brother of D. S.), 89, 110, 156, 179
Burnet, Mrs. Mary (wife of D. S.), 62, 134, 136, 170, 179, 182, 186, 193
Burnet, S. B. (brother of D. S.), 156
Burnet, Thomas, 208

INDEX

Burnet, Dr. Thomas, 212
Burnet, Dr. Wm., Sr., 21, 213, 214-217
Burnet, Uncle William, Jr., 31, 69, 213
Burnet, William (Gilbert's son), 211
Burr, Nelson, 11
Butler University, 55

C

Calvinism, 32, 44, 69
Calvin, John, 73, 175, 188
Campbell, Alexander, 7, 18, 25, 27, 29, 30, 34, 36, 40, 46, 47, 51, 65, 69, 71, 72, 74-76, 78, 83, 87, 89, 90, 92, 94, 95, 98, 99, 101-105, 110-117, 120, 121, 123, 128, 138, 139, 144, 146, 148, 158, 159, 172-176, 187, 188, 190, 193, 196-199; age, 39; Bacon College, 59, 60; Bethany College, 62, 66, 67; break with Baptists, 38; change of attitude, 63, 64; letter to, 37; publisher, 42, 54; Rice debate, 65
Campbell, Archibald W., 126
Campbell, Geo., 89, 96
Campbell-Rice debate, 99
Campbell, Thomas, 18, 37, 100, 148, 198
Campbellites, 25, 35; a "Nameless party," 48
Campbell, Bro. T. F., 156
Canon law, 65
Carmen, Wm., 52-54, 166
Carr, John, 186
Carthage, O., 58
Cartwright, Lin D., 11
Cary, Alice, 107
Cary, Phoebe, 107
Catalogue of books, 97
Catholicism, 51
Catholics, 142, 144
Catholic Church of God, 143
Caucus, 48
Cause, 87, 94, 99, 104, 122, 124, 134
Centerville, Ind., 108

Central Christian Church, 33
Central Christian Herald, 141
Central Church of Christ, Dayton, O., 33
Centralism, 9, 105, 168
Challen, James, 35, 36, 38, 58, 73-75, 85, 86, 94, 96, 97, 100, 111, 112, 114, 133, 198
Chitwood, Jack, 11
Christian, The, 58, 59, 61
Christian Advocate, 44
Christian Age, The, 108, 117, 121, 124, 125, 130, 132, 144, 145, 175
Christian Baptist, The, 8, 25, 37, 38, 42, 55, 174, 192, 195, 196
Christian Board of Publication, 11, 38, 58, 64
Christian Chapel, 86, 157, 186
Christian Church, 36, 66, 103, 107, 117, 152
Christian Enquirer, The, 50
Christian enterprise, 122
Christian-Evangelist, The, 11
Christian Family Magazine, 68, 193
Christian Preacher, The, 8, 43, 50, 51, 54-62, 90, 192, 194
Christian Publication Society (see, A.C.P.S.)
Christian Review, The, 185
Christian Standard, 9, 173, 176, 182, 185, 191
Christian Sunday-School Library, The, 136, 137
Christian System, The, 46
Christian Tract and Sunday-School Society, 106
Chronology, 201-207
Church Extension, 158, 159
Church of Christ, 103
Church of England, 25
Christian unity, 35
Cincinnati College, 20
Cincinnati Methodist Church, 36
Cincinnati, O., 17-20, 22, 23, 26, 29, 30, 34, 40, 41, 43, 44, 50, 52, 58-60, 62, 63, 66-68, 74-77, 81-83; 86, 95, 96, 106, 117, 124-126, 130, 132, 135-140, 142, 148,

264 INDEX

149, 152-154, 156-159, 161, 163, 171, 174, 179, 181, 192, 193, 197, 255
Cincinnati Tract Society, 77, 85, 93, 97, 112
Circular, 145
Circulation, 106, 108, 122, 124
Civil Engineering, 58
Civil War, 22, 108, 153, 159, 161, 164, 165, 168
Clapp, M. S., 147
Clark, H. O., 98
Clark, S. S., 98
Clay, Henry, 65
Cleveland, O., 57, 173
Clinton Street Church, Cincinnati, O., 90
Coe Collection, 42
Coffin, Levi, 78
Cole, William R., 37
Colleges, 58, 60, 75, 82
Committee, 91, 96, 101, 109, 143, 171, 179
Committee of Seven, 92
Communion, 28, 37, 56, 190
Communism, 36
Conferences, 48
Confession of Faith (see, Good Confession), 18, 29, 45, 47, 52, 178, 192, 198
Congregation, 35, 45-47, 52, 66, 67, 81, 141, 143, 152, 165, 168, 179, 184, 186, 191
Congregationalists, 141
Connecticut, 42, 163
Connectional, 74, 105, 149
Constitution, 23, 24, 74, 95, 109, 110, 124, 147, 153, 242, 243
Controversy, 108
Convention, 7, 46, 82-116, 83-86, 88, 90-92, 94-98, 101-104, 110-112, 114, 115, 120, 138, 146, 156, 158, 160, 161, 168, 169, 176, 192, 196
Conversion, 56, 86, 93, 106
Cooperation, 9, 64, 65, 71-73, 76, 78, 81, 82-84, 86, 89, 90, 92-97, 99, 102-105, 109, 110, 112, 113, 120,
122, 132, 136, 138, 165, 176, 191, 194, 197-199
Corresponding secretary, 85, 100, 114, 123, 132, 136, 147, 148, 153, 154, 157-159, 168-170
Covington, Ky., 41
Cramblet, Wilbur H., 11
Crane, Thurston, 75
Creeds, 9, 28, 29, 33-35, 45, 46, 65, 188
Criticism, 118
Cross, Alexander, 149-151

D

Dancing, 85
Davenport, Bro., 96
Dayton Baptist Church, 38
Dayton Disciples Union, 33, 34
Dayton, O., 18, 23, 33, 34, 36, 42, 66, 192
Deacons, 166
Deaconesses, 166
Debates, 108, 146, 174
Declaration and Address, 100
Dedication, 5
DeGroot, A. T., 11, 38, 39, 50, 58, 62, 74, 76, 77, 104, 107, 108, 110, 120, 124, 138, 139, 158, 159, 162, 163, 172, 173, 175, 189
Delegate, 83, 89-91, 104, 110
Democratic, 47, 65
Democrat, 45, 140
Denomination, 35, 38, 46, 56, 59, 65, 68, 72, 77, 93, 121, 131, 140, 144, 155, 167
Dickens, Charles, 63
Directive, 96
Disciples, 106
Disciples of Christ, 7, 9, 25, 26, 34-40, 42, 46, 63, 65, 66, 69, 70, 71, 73, 74, 76, 77, 81, 82ff, 83, 85-88, 90, 93, 95, 96, 100-103, 105, 107-109, 113, 117, 120, 121, 123, 130-135, 140, 141, 144-150, 157, 160, 165, 168, 172-174, 176, 180, 186, 188, 190, 191, 193, 196-200
Discipline, 27, 157
Discourse (*see* Sermon)

INDEX 265

Dismemberment, 88, 89
Dissenting vote, 94
District Meetings, 96
Doctrine, 87, 122, 143, 157, 176, 183, 199
Doddridge, Prof., 89
Dover Association, 47-50
Dunkards, 166

E

Ecclesiasticism, 101, 134, 143, 146, 148, 157
Eclecticism, 143
Ecumenical, 95, 143
Edinburgh, Scotland, 166
Editor, 84, 102, 108, 111, 124, 128, 182
Education, 83, 86, 97, 102, 107, 149, 153, 191, 195, 198
Eighth and Walnut Streets, Cincinnati, O., 36, 38, 66, 67, 86, 125, 137, 152, 157, 172, 180, 186, 192
Elders, 63, 66, 67, 80, 166
Endowment, 61
England, 90
English Lutherans, 141
Enon Baptist Church, 29, 35
Enterprises, 94, 132, 135, 150
Epidemics, 43, 46
Episcopalians, 141
Erie and Kalamazoo Railroad, 43
Errett, Isaac, 8, 66, 145, 147, 148, 154, 156, 157, 159, 172, 173, 176, 182, 184, 186, 188, 190, 191, 194, 197, 198
Este, Hannah, 21, 22
Eureka, Ill., 107
Evangelical Enquirer, The, 42, 192
Evangelism, 46, 57, 72, 81, 123, 143, 144, 150, 154-156, 160, 165, 169, 170, 173, 184
Evangelical Alliance, 141
Evangelical Association, 140, 142, 144
Evangelical clergy, 141
Evangelical Society, 95
Evangelist, The, 58

Evangelists, 38, 46, 56, 66, 69
Executive Board, 156, 157
Expedient, 83, 91, 101, 104, 138

F

Faith, 24, 28, 32, 85, 101, 143, 199
Fall, P. S., 29, 114
Family of D. S. B., 219
Fanning, T., 157, 196
Farquharson, Charles, 166
Father (God), 119
Federal City, 161, 193, 200
Fellowship, 72, 89, 102, 176, 177, 192
Fillmore, Bro., 153
Finance, 154
Fire, 43
First Church, Cincinnati, 90
Floods, 43
Fogle, M. W., 12
Foreign missions, 105, 106, 122, 131, 132, 150
Forney, Frederic John, 55-57, 59-62
Fourth of July Address, I. G. B., 23, Appen. VIII, 255-260
Francisco de Miranda, 21
Franklin, Benj., 108, 124, 144, 152, 154, 163, 175, 176, 193, 198
Franklin College, 76
Freedom, 23, 27, 167
Free enterprise, 109
Free will, 45
Friends (*see* Quakers), 78
Frontier, 82, 172, 197

G

Gano, Maj. Gen. John S., 40, 41
Gano, Mrs. John S., 135
Gano, Mary G. (wife of D. S. B.; *see* Burnet, Mrs. D. S.), 40, 41
Garfield, James A., 147
Garrard, Israel, 98
Garrison, W. E., 12, 18, 38, 39, 46, 50, 51, 58, 62, 65, 72, 74-77, 83, 89, 99, 104, 107, 108, 110, 120, 124, 138, 139, 150, 158-160, 162, 163, 172, 173, 175, 189

Gatchell, H. P., 75
Gates, Errett, 173
Gaylord, Bro., 155
Genealogy, 24, 218
General agent, 130
General Convention, 18, 89, 93, 98, 99, 101-103
Georgetown, Ky., 57, 60-62
Gilbert, A. N., 179, 181, 186
Girls' school, 135
Goforth, Catherine, 41
Goforth, Mary, 40
Goforth, William, 41
Good Confession The, 28, 29, 35, 187, 188, 198, 244-247
Goodwin, Elijah, 90, 92, 96, 123, 129, 163
Gospel, 52, 55, 56, 70, 83, 106, 115, 134, 139, 141, 144, 169, 178, 241
Gospel Proclamation, 80
Goss, Charles Frederic, 21, 40, 43, 44, 63, 107, 158
Gottschall, Andrew W., 52, 165-167, 177, 179
Gould, C. H., 95, 98
Grace, 119
Green, Ashbel, 44
Green, Francis Marion, 115, 116, 136

H

Haldane School, 166
Hall, Alexander, 80, 95
Hall, Colby D., 12
Hamer, Janet, 12
Hand, George R., 75, 97
Harmon, Wilfred P., 12
Harper's Ferry, 157
Harrison, Wm. H., 20, 62
Harrodsburg, Ky., 62
Hatch, Wm., 61
Hayden, A. S., 63, 145, 160
Henshall, James G., 166
Heresy, 142
Heretic, 141
Hermeneutics, 118
Hiram College, 144, 172
Hiram, O., 107, 144

History of the North-Western Territory, 19, 20
Holy Spirit, 119, 168, 189
Home missions, 106, 122, 146
Hook, Alice P (Mrs), 12
Houston, Sam, 22
Howe, Henry, 77
Howels, B. B., 96
Human creeds (*see* Creeds)
Hygeia Female Atheneum, 62, 63, 66, 135
Hygeia, Mt. Healthy, O., 103
Hygeia, O., 133
Hymn Book, 138

I

Iliff School of Theology, 7, 11
Illinois, 107, 110, 129, 157, 183
Immersion, 18, 27, 30, 31, 41, 52, 54, 118, 178
Incarnation, 54
Independent, 87, 89, 91, 101-103, 168
Indiana, 36, 72, 88, 90, 93, 107, 108, 129, 163, 157
Indianapolis, Ind., 107
Industry, 24
Inexpedient, 138
Instrumental music, 190
Invitation, 52
Iowa, 107, 129, 183
Irvin, S. W., 129
Irwin, Dr. Wm., 97
Is the Christian Church Evangelical? 249-252

J

Jackson, Jethro, 124, 125, 130
Jameson, L. H., 129
Jenkins, G. S., 98
Jerusalem, 99, 100, 105, 131, 134, 190, 193
Jerusalem mission, 55, 125, 127, 130-136, 193, 195
Jews, 100
Johnson, B. W., 169
Johnson, Francis White, 21, 61, 62, 75

INDEX 267

Johnson, John T., 58, 59, 86, 90-94, 96, 109, 112, 114, 152, 198
Jones, John T., 110
Jones, Willis R., 12
Journal, 46, 50, 54, 58, 59, 68, 124, 144, 173, 193
Judicial, 24

K

Kansas, 30, 155, 158, 183
Keith, Beulah Irene (Mrs.), 12
Keith, Marvin, 12
Kendrick, C., 94, 96, 97
Kentucky, 19, 20, 29, 34, 41, 61, 72, 90, 109, 129, 149, 156, 160, 163
Kentucky University, 172, 187; (see Bacon College, and Transylvania University)
Kershner, Frederick D., 15
King James Version, 29, 83
Kingdom of God, 29, 55, 64
Kossuth, Louis, 139-142

L

Lamar, Mirabeau B., 22
Lancastrian Academy, 20
Lane Seminary, 44
Last Will and Testament of the Springfield Presbytery, 100
Law, 24, 29, 32, 37, 69, 83, 119, 252, 253
Lawson, B. S., 74, 85
Lawyer, 27
Leavenworth City, Kan., 159, 193
Legalism, 29, 65
Legislative, 24
Lexington, Ky., 46
Liberal, 166, 167, 194, 200
Liberal education, 23, 58
Liberia, Africa, 149, 150, 193
Liberty, 200
Library of Congress, 9
Lincoln, Abraham, 171
Literature, 60
Little Miami, 41
Little Miami Railway, 64
Lee, Robert E., 171
Legalism, 83

Legislate, 104
Leonard, Mrs. S. W., 95
Leslie, A. M., 98
Leslie, James, 98
Lexington, Ky., 181
Life Directors, 89, 95, 96, 98, 124
Life Members, 89, 95, 124
Life of Barton W. Stone, 138
Lillie, William, 147
Living Oracles, The, 89, 111, 117, 119, 121
Living Pulpit, The, 187
London, England, 133
Longworth, Nicholas, 18
Lord, Lee, 147
Lord's Day, 52, 178
Lord's Supper (see Communion), 45, 53, 56
Louisiana, 19, 21, 168
Loyalty Resolution, 168
Luce, Baptist Preacher, 18, 177, 181
Luther, Martin, 175, 188

M

Maffit, John Newland, 180
Mahoning Association, 34, 38, 72
Man, 51
Managers (see Board of Managers), 94, 129, 147
Marshall, Dr. N. T., 95, 98
Maryland, 30, 51, 129, 163, 165, 171
Masons, 78 (see Moral societies)
Mass meeting, 84, 104, 110
Mathes, J. M., 191, 253
McCammon, J. W., 97
McCartney, H. E., 12
McGarvey, J. W., 164
McKnight, Prof., 89
Means, 123
Medical College of Ohio, 20
Meetinghouse, 167
Melish, T. J., 94, 108, 112, 124, 193
Melita, 133
Membership, 28, 31, 95, 109, 110, 123, 177, 199, 200
Memoirs of Alexander Campbell, 30
Memorial address (Baltimore), 174, (see Appen. IV)

Memorial to A. C., 226-240
Memorial tribute (Bethany), 173
Messengers, 84
Messiah, 54, 55, 168
Meteors, 47
Methodist, 35, 76, 140
Methodist Book Concern, 117, 126
Methodology, 11
Miami Baptist Association, 33
Miami Canal, 40
Miami Territory, 19
Michigan, 43, 154
Midway, Ky., 107
Millennial Harbinger, 9, 30, 36, 38, 42, 47-49, 50, 52, 54, 57, 60, 63, 64, 72-76, 79, 80, 83, 84, 101, 104, 120, 121, 125-129, 138, 139, 145, 146, 155, 159, 166, 167, 169, 170, 174, 175, 177-185, 199
Millennium, 55
Milligan, Robert, 172
Milton, Ind., 108
Ministry, 58, 64, 66, 69, 88, 89, 111, 140, 141, 167, 178
Missionary, 7, 72, 83, 86, 87, 90, 94, 95, 99, 100, 104, 105, 123, 133, 134, 136, 145, 149-151, 153, 173
Missionary Chronicle, 55
Missionary enterprise, 186, 191
Missionary society, 91, 92, 94, 102, 135, 157, 190
Mission field, 134
Missions, 51, 64, 70, 76, 82, 89, 90, 100, 101, 105, 111, 122, 131, 132, 134, 144, 191, 198
Missouri, 45, 107, 129, 155, 157, 158
Mitchell, Bro., 80
Moderator, 49
Mohometans, 100
Monrovia, 150
Moore, Allen R., 64, 83, 84, 102, 198
Moore, William Thomas, 17-19, 24, 26-28, 31-33, 36, 39, 41, 46, 47, 50, 62, 67, 108, 136, 148, 152, 154, 155, 157, 158, 164, 172, 177-180, 186-188, 195-197
Monroe Doctrine, 24

Montague, William, 34
Moral societies, 78, 79
Morling, George W., 181
Morton, William, 96, 98, 99
Moslem (*see* Mohometans), 135
Moss, J. J., 73, 74, 80, 95, 97
Mothershead, Bertie (Mrs.), 12
Mt. Healthy, O., 103
Mount Pleasant, O., 78
Mt. Vernon, O., 147
Munnell, Thomas, 152

N

National City Christian Church, 161, (*see* Federal City, and Washington, D. C.)
Negro, 47, 149
Nelson, Robert, 149
New Hampshire, 45
New Harmony, Ind., 36
New Lisbon, O., 66
New Jersey, 19-21
"New Light," 19, 38, 40, 44, 45
New Orleans, La., 161
New Testament, 28, 70, 106, 111, 190, 242
New York, 129, 154, 163, 187
New York City, 40, 41, 78, 107, 117, 152
Ninth Street Baptist Church, 36
Nineteenth Century Reformation, 8 (*see* Reformation)
Nondenominational, 131
Nonimmersionist, 118
Norfolk, Va., 47
North Street Church, Baltimore, 52, 165, 166
"No soulism," 166
North Eaton, O., 160

O

Offices, 85, 90, 130, 147, 148, 153
Ohio, 18, 20, 30, 34, 36, 38-41, 43, 46, 57, 58, 63, 66, 72, 77-79, 81, 97, 103, 107, 125, 126, 129, 130, 131, 144-148, 156, 161, 171, 172
Ohio Christian Missionary Society, 8, 57, 145, 147, 148, 189, 193

INDEX 269

Ohio Disciples of Christ, 145
Ohio Evangelical Association, 139
Ohio in Africa, 149, 193
Ohio Life Insurance and Trust Co., 43
O'Kane, John, 75, 86, 93, 94, 96
"Old Light," 19, 40, 44, 45
Old Testament, 106, 242
Old World, 90
Oracles of God, 157
Order, 143
Ordinance, 56, 101
Ordination, 28, 29
Organization, 24, 45, 47, 64, 65, 70, 71-73, 76, 87, 88, 94, 100, 101, 102, 104, 105, 110, 112, 115, 128, 144, 145, 147, 173, 175, 191, 196, 197, 199
Organ of the Societies, 124
Original Sunday School Library, 125
Orthodoxy, 34, 143
Oskaloosa, Iowa, 107
Owen, Robert, 36

P

Paca Street Christian Church, 165, 166, 167, 169, 179, 181
Pagan idolators, 100
Palmer, H. D., 93, 96
Paris, Mo., 155
Parmly, Eleazer, 75
Partisan, 84
Party bias, 59
Pastor, 85, 90, 95, 152, 158, 172
Pastorate, 34, 66-69, 86, 157, 165, 176, 177, 247-249
Patterson, John, 186
Pelagian Controversy, 44
Pendleton, W. K., 75, 80, 94, 96, 97, 103, 113-115, 120, 127, 128, 138, 144
Pennsylvania, 18, 129, 163
Periodicals, 102, 139
Permanent fund, 189
Philadelphia, 165
Philadelphia Confession, 9
Philanthropist, The, 44

Pierson, Roscoe M., 12
Pinkerton, Dr. L. L., 93, 138, 181, 186
Pioneers, 88
Power, Frederick D., 17, 18, 23, 28, 31, 33, 50, 90, 136, 173, 178
Plan of Salvation, 83, 171; "Synopsis," 241
Platte City, Mo., 155
Pledges, 129
Polity, 146, 149
Powell, John T., 93
Prayer, 29
Preaching, 46, 51, 56, 66, 68, 69, 71, 95, 102, 106, 122, 129, 139, 141, 154, 155, 160, 167, 169, 171, 179, 186, 193, 194
Presbyterian, 18, 19, 25, 26, 28, 29, 44, 69, 76, 140, 141
Presbyterian, First Church, Cincinnati, O., 21
Presbyterian Sunday School, 27
President, 90, 100, 103, 107, 112, 115, 139, 147, 148, 157, 168, 172, 176, 186, 192, 193
Presiding elder, 147
Press, 101, 109, 111, 124, 128, 136
Preston, Wheeler, 21
Primitive Christianity, 27
Primitive Gospel, 46, 70
Prince of Wales, 157
Princeton, 19
Private enterprise, 84
Proclamation of Emancipation, 168
Proof texts, 143, 190
Protestant, 39, 93, 142-144
Protestant Evangelical Association of Ministers, The, 141 (*see* Evangelical Association)
Protestant Unionist, 108, 145
Protracted meeting, 155
Providence, 114, 142, 150
Publication, 75
Publicity, 61, 132
Publishing, 58, 82, 84, 86, 99, 101, 102, 106, 108, 111, 113, 117, 123, 124, 126, 136, 138, 139, 142-144, 146, 187, 193
Publishing house, 105

Q

Quaker, 78

R

Raines, Aylett, 37, 75
Ramsey, Dr., 95
Ray, Dr. Joseph, 143, 152
Ray's Arithmetic, 143, 152
Recommendation, 96
Recording secretary, 86, 171
Red Stone Association, 18
Reformation, 29, 30, 39, 40, 57, 70, 73, 83, 91, 113, 197
Reformation, 36, 45, 49, 71, 76, 82
Reformation of the Nineteenth Century, 187, 188
Reformer, 108
Register, 80
Religious tracts, 101
Repentance, 85
Reporter, 154
Republic of Texas (*see* Texas)
Resolution, 91, 92, 94, 96, 168, 185, 186
Restoration, 35, 39, 55, 92
Resurrection, 54
Revelation, 55, 241
Revised Version, 120
Revision, 89, 97, 115, 117, 192
Rice, G. W., 68, 121
Rice, Luther, 48, 65
Richardson, Robert, 29, 30, 78
Richmond, Va., 47
Rights, 23
Riots, 43, 63
Rist, Martin, 11
Robison, Dr. J. P., 153, 161, 176
Rogers, John, 59, 114, 129, 160, 186
Rogers, W. C., 91
Romanism, 118, 119
Romans X, 28, 30, 189
Roman Catholic, 143
Rowe, John R., 68, 121

S

Sacraments, 28
Sadler, M. E., 12
St. Paul's River, 150
Salvation, 29, 34, 99, 100, 103
Sands, Brother and Sister, 53
Sands, Sarah, 166
San Felipe de Austin, 22
San Jacinto River, 22
Santa Anna, 22
Science, 60
Scott, Walter, 8, 34, 39, 40, 58, 61, 74, 86, 93-98, 108, 114, 124, 148, 150, 171, 188, 197, 198
Scottsville, Va., 99
Scripture, 18, 27, 28, 32, 53, 54, 64, 66, 73, 89, 91, 103, 117, 143, 144, 160, 181, 188, 189, 192, 242
Secondary schools, 58
Second Advent (*see* Millennium)
Second Presbyterian Church, Cincinnati, 21, 40, 90, 94
Secretary, 160, 171
Sectarianism, 35, 37, 59, 101, 134, 136, 140, 157, 167
Sects, 39
Sectionalism, 107
Selected Sunday School Library, 125
Sermon, 142, 144, 155, 173, 174, 177, 179, 184, 187, 197, 244-254
Service, 28
Shaw, Henry K., 11, 15, 57, 58, 66, 74, 75, 79, 80, 138, 139, 145, 146, 160, 163, 172, 189, 190
Shelton, O. L., 12
Sincerity Seeking the Way of Heaven, 108
Skepticism, 51
Slavery, 17, 43, 44, 63, 78, 82, 107, 146, 149, 150, 159, 160, 168, 190
Slave trade, 149
Sloan, R. R., 145
Smith and Nixon's Hall, 140, 141
Smith, Benjamin L., 114, 115
Smith, Ephraim A., 75
Smith, Gen. Kirby, 163
Smith, Stanley B. (Mrs.), 12
Societies, 85, 86, 88, 90-100, 102, 104, 109, 113, 116, 122, 128, 138, 148, 153, 168, 175, 186, 199
Society system, 9, 64, 70, 81, 104, 175, 176, 191

INDEX

Solicitor, 61, 156, 159
Son (Jesus), 119
South America, 25
Spencer, Claude E., 11, 15
Spirit (*see* Holy Spirit), 116, 165
Spring Grove Cemetery, 184
Standard Publishing Co., 59, 66
State meetings, 96
State societies, 124
States' Rights, 46
Stevenson, Dwight E., 114
Stewardship, 56, 65, 72, 74, 76, 87, 89, 90, 94, 95, 99, 102, 103, 106, 109, 132, 154, 156, 177, 196 199, 200
Stone, Barton W., 40, 46, 148, 188, 198
Stowe, Calvin E., 44
Stowe, Harriet Beecher, 149
Stowe, Ohio, 63
Stratton, W. P., 97
Strickle, A. E., 129
Subscriptions, 95, 124
Sunday Schools, 26, 77, 163, 197
Sunday School Hymnbook, 138
Sunday School Journal, 125, 130
Sunday School Library, 96, 97, 106, 130, 136-138, 154, 193
Sweeney, Edward, 166
Sweeney, Martha, 166
Sycamore Street Church, Cincinnati, 34, 35, 66
Synods, 48
Synopsis of Divine Revelation, 55, 144, Appen. V, 241
Syracuse, N. Y., 179

T

Taylor, Alastair M., 171
Teaching, 57, 63, 167, 171
Tennessee, 19, 156, 157
Terry, William, 181, 186
Testaments, 100
Texas, 21, 22, 76, 123, 154, 155, 187, 192
Texas Christian University, 8
Theology, 121, 142, 199
Thomas, John Jr., 53, 166

Todd's Fork Association, 37
Toledo, O., 43
Trabne, James, 181
Tract, 108, 124
Translation, 89, 101, 109-111, 118, 120, 121
Transylvania University (*see* Bacon College, and Kentucky College), 35, 172, 187
Traveling agents, 61, 109
Traveling secretary, 157
Tridentine Confession, 9
Trinity, 27
Trust fund, 194
Tucker, Chloe (Mrs.), 160

U

Uncle Tom's Cabin, 44, 149
"Underground railway," 160
Union, 46, 71, 76, 78, 97, 103, 106, 116, 159, 161, 199
Unitarians, 48
United Christian Missionary Society, 85
Unity, 32, 71, 166, 177
Universalists, 48
University, 60

V

Van Sickle, H. Gordon, 12
Vardeman, Jeremiah, 41
Venezuela, 21
Version, 117-119, 121
Vice-president, 86, 104, 157, 158, 172
Virginia, 18, 20, 30, 46, 72, 94, 99, 126, 129, 156, 163, 168
Voluntary, 102, 103, 168, 191, 198

W

Walker, Williston, 18
Wallace, Rebecca, 20
Wallbank, T. Walter, 171
Walnut Street congregation, Louisville, Ky., 142, 185
War of 1812, 17

Ware, C. C., 11, 15
Warren, Ohio, 148
Washington, D. C., 161, 193 (see Federal City, and National City)
Wasson, Joseph, 186
Wesley, John, 73, 188
Western Reserve, 18, 20, 63
Westminster Confession, 9, 45
West Point, 31
West, The, 43, 67
West Virginia, 131, 144
Western Preacher, The, 191, 253
Western Reserve Eclectic Institute (see Hiram College), 144, 172
Weston, Mo., 156
Wharton, John A., 154
Wheeling, W. Va., 46, 47
Whig, 140
White, Alene Lowe (Mrs.), 12
Wilcox, Alanson, 66, 163
William of Orange, 17
Williamsburg, Va., 47
Winn, Kittie, 17
Women, 129, 135, 136, 193
Woolery, L. C., 114
Wooster, Ohio, 144-147, 163
Word of God (see Bible), 73, 82, 83, 87, 88, 111, 118
World Council of Churches, 199
Worship, 28, 56, 72, 101, 135, 190
Wiclif, 200

Y

Yale University, 42
Yearly meetings, 145
Year Book, 80, 100
Young, J., 96

Z

Zionist, 55
Zwingli, 175

www.ingramcontent.com/pod-product-compliance
Lightning Source LLC
Chambersburg PA
CBHW062006220426
43662CB00010B/1252